DOGS IN THE LEISURE EXPERIENCE

DOGS IN THE LEISURE EXPERIENCE

Neil Carr

University of Otago

www.cabi.org

CABI is a trading name of CAB International

CABI
Nosworthy Way
Wallingford
Oxfordshire OX10 8DE
UK

CABI
38 Chauncy Street
Suite 1002
Boston, MA 02111
USA

Tel: +44 (0)1491 832111
Fax: +44 (0)1491 833508
E-mail: info@cabi.org
Website: www.cabi.org

Tel: +1 800 552 3083 (toll free)
E-mail: cabi-nao@cabi.org

A catalogue record for this book is available from the British Library, London, UK.

Library of Congress Cataloging-in-Publication Data

Carr, Neil, 1972-
  Dogs in the leisure experience / Neil Carr, University of Otago.
     pages cm
  Includes bibliographical references and index.
  ISBN 978-1-78064-318-2 (alk. paper)
  1. Dogs--Social aspects. 2. Dogs. 3. Working dogs. 4. Dog owners.
5. Human-animal relationships. 6. Leisure. I. Title.

  SF426.C35 2014
  636.7'0886--dc23

                              2014011159

ISBN-13: 978 1 78064 318 2

Commissioning editor: Claire Parfitt
Editorial assistant: Alexandra Lainsbury
Production editor: James Bishop

Typeset by SPi, Pondicherry, India.
Printed and bound CPI Group (UK) Ltd, Croydon, CR0 4YY.

Contents

List of Tables

List of Figures

Acknowledgements

This book and all my work on dogs would never have existed without Snuffie and so a great debt of thanks is due to her. To Gypsy, who has striven so wilfully to fill the space left in my life by the death of Snuffie, an equally large 'thank you' is in order. Between them, these two dogs continue to help guide my research and impressions of the non-human world. My long-suffering wife (Sarah) and children (Ben, Tat and Gus) also deserve thanks for always being there for me and putting up with the fact that my brain rarely seems to be able to leave its work alone and as a result has subjected them to some weird and obscure holiday and leisure experiences. While I recognize this problematizes definitions of leisure and tourism, my own debate on this issue will have to wait for another day.

A wide variety of people have helped to make this book possible by giving their time freely to provide me with a vast array of information. I would love to name them all personally yet I am also keenly aware that doing so may be, despite my best intentions, a disservice. So instead I offer thanks to the folk at Guide Dogs for the Blind, UK; the Dogs Trust, UK; a range of hotels and other organizations in Whistler, Canada; and the Greyhound Board of Great Britain. In particular, I would like to thank the staff at the New South Wales State Library for coping with me and aiding me as much as possible. Similarly, I owe a debt of thanks to a range of people at the Kennel Club in the UK but special mention must go to the librarians at the Club who offered me so much help and never complained about my reluctance to leave the library. I would also like to give thanks to the anonymous reviewers of this book; your comments made me look again at my conceptual foundations and dig a little further down. As with virtually all review comments it was not a painless process to react to them, but it was a beneficial one (for me personally and hopefully also for the book) and for that I am very grateful. For everyone else who has helped to make this book possible you know who you are and I offer you my heartfelt thanks. If I have missed you from my list of thanks I am of course only human (as opposed to canine) and can only offer my apologies and still reassure you that I do fully value your help. Finally, as ever, as the author I take full responsibility for any mistakes or errors.

Neil Carr

1 Introduction

Why a Book on Dogs in Leisure?

The dog, *Canis familiaris*, has played and continues to play an integral role in the lives of many individual humans and societies throughout the world. This has been an evolving relationship since at least the Neolithic era (Herzog, 2010; Bradshaw, 2011; Power, 2012), with dogs being defined as the first domesticated animal (King *et al.*, 2009; Holmberg, 2013). These first dogs are actually more accurately defined as wolves. While debate continues about the exact time of the split between the wolves and dogs, according to Bensky *et al.* (2013) it began approximately 100,000 years ago. Today, there is a huge array of types of dogs yet they all have one thing in common: their relation with humans. The willingness of the wolf to share its space and time with early humans has been identified as a central reason for the evolution of the dog and this willingness is clear today in virtually all dogs, be they pets or working animals. It is the closeness between dogs and humans in general, and particularly between me and my dogs, that is the driving force behind this book.

Despite the apparent closeness between humans and dogs, it is clear that this relationship and indeed the dogs themselves have existed at best at the margins of academic interest and research (Budiansky, 2000; Coppinger and Coppinger, 2001; Wise, 2002; Csanyi, 2005). This view is supported by Westgarth *et al.* (2010: 38) who stated: 'It is surprising how little we know about the domestic dog'. More generally, as Herzog (2010: 16) pointed out: 'the study of our interactions with other species has, until recently, been neglected by scientists'. This does not mean we have not studied animals as objects, far from it, but that we have not focused significant attention, especially traditionally, on researching them from a perspective that sees them as sentient beings. The sentience of dogs is an issue that will be explored in detail in this chapter and referred to again elsewhere in the book.

As changes have occurred in academia and we have witnessed the development of understandings of animals as more than mere objects, there has arguably been a focus, as so often in research, on the exotic. Academics by and large seem to have, just like the general populace, an obsessive interest in the exotic, whereas interest in the everyday, the mundane, tends to be limited. It is into this latter category that the most popular pets, including the dog, fit. Indeed, McConnell (2005: xxvi) has stated that dogs have: 'been proof for decades of the saying "Familiarity breeds contempt". Scientists could study right whales or Serengeti lions or scissor-tailed flycatchers, but heaven forbid you tried to make your name as a researcher studying dogs.' Yet, as McConnell (2005) noted, this situation is changing. Indeed, Hare and Woods (2013: 125) have noted that: 'From being thought of as an unremarkable animal made stupid by domestication, all of a sudden dogs have become one of the most popular species for animal researchers to study.'

The field of leisure studies, as broadly defined, has similarly tended to ignore pets in general (Norris et al., 1999) and dogs in particular, focusing instead on the more exotic, wild animals in the tourism context (e.g. Coghlan and Prideaux, 2008; Markwell and Cushing, 2009; Duffy, 2014). Limited number of studies that have examined dogs in leisure have tended to focus on dog sports such as flyball and agility (Gillespie et al., 1996), as discussed in Chapter 3. Yet, while they are focused on a dog-related activity, the attention in most of these works has been on humans (e.g. Kemp, 1999; Baldwin and Norris, 1999; Gillespie et al., 2002; Hultsman, 2013). In contrast, the limited work undertaken in the veterinary sciences field on dogs in sport has focused exclusively on the mechanics of the animal (Pfau et al., 2011; Payne, 2013a, b; Birch and Leśniak, 2013), ignoring in the process the role of humans and the social construction of these dogs and the sport in which they are involved. This view is supported by Atkinson and Young (2005), who identified a lack of research by sociologists into blood sports in general and the sport of greyhound racing in particular. As will be discussed throughout the book other works, though small in number, have looked at dogs in a variety of settings but have generally failed to do so through a leisure studies lens, despite the activities the dogs and their owners are engaged in being clearly identifiable as leisure. More often than not they have focused on humans rather than the dogs. Even where attempts have been made to look at the dog and human as subjects, the data have tended to stem exclusively from the latter group (e.g. Kuhl, 2011), in the process arguably devaluing the voice of the dog.

History of the Dog and its Relationship with Humanity

Dogs have had and continue to have a complex variety of relations with humans. At one extreme there are people who harbour a deep-seated dislike, fear and even hatred of dogs; at the other extreme we see a strong bond of love and affection between people and dogs. Any examination of the nature of the position and experiences of dogs in the leisure environment needs to recognize the conflicting emotions that dogs can generate within the human population.

The relation between humans and dogs is complex and constantly evolving; it is also one that is specific to a given place and culture. Despite this, it is important to recognize that today dogs are more accepted as a 'member of the family' than at any time in history (Reichmann, 2000; Katz, 2003; Power, 2008). Or, as Rudy (2011: 29) said: 'we have never in history been closer to our pets than we are today'. Indeed, Sanders (1999: 9) pointed out that most people who own a dog today identify it as a person or something with 'person status'. Consequently, he stated that: 'Studies show that somewhere between 70 and 99 percent of pet caretakers define their animals as members of the family, and from 30 to 83 percent consider the pet to be a "special" or "close" friend' (p. 10). Indeed, reporting on a study in Australia, Power (2013) noted that 90% of Australians recognize their dogs as members of the family. Although not quite reaching the levels reported by Sanders, it is still important to note Herzog's (2010: 9) claim that 'Over half of dog owners think of their pets as family members.' The result is that as Racher (2005: 11) stated: 'dogs have become a major element of many families'. This view was echoed in an interview undertaken with one of the management team at the Hilton Hotel in Whistler in 2008 when he stated: 'Time and time again you see families come up [to Whistler] and the pets [dogs] are their children.' Such is the closeness between many people and their dogs that owners are said to form intimate and emotionally close and strong relations (not just bonds) with their animals and to even engage in conversations with them (Sanders, 1999). Indeed, it is not uncommon now to see it being claimed that owners place as much, or even more, value on their dogs and rely on them more for emotional support than they do on human members of their family (Sanders, 1999; Katz, 2003).

The move towards the positioning of the dog in the centre of the human family has arguably been an ongoing one throughout the history of the relationship between humans and dogs, but has become prevalent since the Industrial Revolution and the urbanization of formerly rural populations, and even more so in the last 100 years. Yet this trend can be traced back even further in its origin to the Renaissance era in Europe when the urbanized middle and upper classes began to keep pets; prime among which was the dog (Kalof, 2007). Indeed, Borsay (2006: 142) has stated: 'what underpinned the increasingly sentimental attitude towards the animal kingdom was industrialization and urbanization, which drew more and more people away from direct contact with agriculture and the associated rearing, deployment, and killing of animals'. While there is clearly a long history associated with the pet dog in Europe it is important to note that Hare and Woods (2013) have identified that the pet dog existed in China in as early as the 1st century BC. As the quotation from Borsay suggests it is not just that humans have been positioning dogs as an ever more central component of the family, but that the meaning behind the dog has also been changing; shifting from an animal to be used by humans in the process of their work and even survival (a tool or object) to a pet. Indeed, Serpell and Paul (1994) noted the adoption of first the word 'pet' and more recently the term 'companion animal' as signs to show the changing nature of how we view animals such as the dog. These terms shift the emphasis away from the economic value of the domesticated animal and its overt use as a tool of work towards a recognition of the social and emotional value of the animal, and by the highlighting of these values draw such labelled animals closer to the human family. Yet these values have not always been recognized, leading to the suggestion by Serpell (in Herzog, 2010), among others, that the pet has no function and therefore is without value. This consigns the pet dog to the bottom of the heap where it is not only a mundane animal, but a valueless mundane animal.

Just becoming a pet does not, of course, mean that a dog ceases to be an object or tool. Indeed, as will be discussed in Chapter 4, many dogs have been and still are owned as pets, if not solely then certainly partially, for the displaying of the owners' wealth and status. This trend, Power (2012) suggested, emerged with the growth of the middle class in western Europe in the 1800s and the growth in dog ownership among this population. The Council for Science and Society (1988: 4) saw this situation having continued into the contemporary era where: 'Unusual and expensive breeds of dog or cat, for example, may be owned as much for reasons of prestige as for anything else.' They further pointed out that: 'Animals kept solely as status symbols are often admired and well looked after, but only as long as the image they project corresponds to the owner's expectations.' The construction of pet dogs as symbols of the status and wealth of their owners is something that ensures the continued positioning of the dog by humans as an object or tool. The Council for Science and Society also raised the issue of the pet dog as a play toy, hobby or recreational tool, identifying an emphasis on the dog as object in these instances. However, as part of bringing dogs into the house and out of the traditional working environment they have, thanks to humans, assumed more human characteristics (in a process that identifies all that can be wrong with anthropomorphism) and through this potentially negative minefield have emerged, at least partially, as a creature with rights: a sentient being.

The result, as Rice (1968: 210) noted, was that even by the 1960s in the USA and elsewhere, 'many pets [especially dogs] are part of the family. Their status may be that of an amusing child, a pleasant companion, an understanding friend, or a loving soul-mate. They receive the attention and affection customarily given to people.' Such a view was also noted by Mann (1975) and is supported by Joseph (2010) who saw animals functioning increasingly as companions, able to alleviate loneliness, make humans feel loved and loving, and provide a conduit through which social bonds between people may be established. In this way the companion dog, it is possible to suggest, is perceived not as an object, but as a subject (Council for Science and Society, 1988) – a sentient animal. Consequently, there is a 'relationship' between a companion dog and human owner, which contrasts with the dog as object, with whom a relationship cannot exist.

While acceptance of the dog as a member of the human family has its origins in North America and north-western Europe, there is evidence to suggest that it is becoming a global trend, with dogs being more commonly seen as family members in such diverse places as Australia and New Zealand, India, China and South-east Asia. This trend and its implications will be discussed throughout the book but particularly in Chapter 7, which is concerned with the dog as human cuisine.

The nature of the relation between dogs and people both influences and is influenced by how the sentience of dogs and hence their 'rights' are perceived. Questions of sentience and animal rights will be discussed later in this chapter as they colour the entirety of this book, how it is written and how it will doubtless be perceived by the reader. As we see dogs becoming ever more accepted as members of the human family we have witnessed an increasing discussion of the intimate, platonic bonds that can and do develop between dogs and their human family. These relationships are perceived and displayed as ones where 'The warmth and depth of the affection a dog can display towards its owners and all members of the family, especially to children, is legendary' (Reichmann, 2000: 353–354).

Why have we witnessed a growth in the number of dogs living as a member of a human family, often sleeping inside, on or near the humans' bed; travelling in the family car; and going on holiday with the family? One of the most commonly cited reasons is the supposed affection that dogs display to their family members (Reichmann, 2000). This affection is claimed to be unconditional and honest in a way that is incomparable to that available from most human–human relationships (Reichmann, 2000). It is further suggested that in our post-modern society where people increasingly lead isolated lives, separated from their kin and alienated from their neighbours, dogs offer a source of by affection that is not available elsewhere (Katz, 2003). Such a view is supported by the New Zealand Companion Animal Council (2011), which stated that 53% of New Zealanders acquire a dog primarily for companionship.

Based on the recognition of the dog as a source of companionship and affection it has begun to be viewed as a means of increasing the mental health and well-being of people in general (Miklósi, 2007; Wood et al., 2007; Zilcha-Mano et al., 2012), and elderly (Norris et al., 1999) single people in particular. With specific reference to children, dogs have been identified as an aid to their healthy physical and psychological development (Endenburg and van Lith, 2011). The dog also offers the opportunity and drive to enhance the fitness of the owner through its need for exercise (Brown and Rhodes, 2006; Cutt et al., 2008; Yabroff et al., 2008; Oka and Shibata, 2009; Reeves et al., 2011). The benefits of dog ownership do not, according to Wood et al. (2007) and Messent (1983), accrue only to the pet owner. Rather, dogs have the potential to facilitate positive social interaction between owners and non-dog owners that benefits the wider society through the development of a sense of community. Such a claim is well known to most dog owners whose animals often act as social lubricants and initiators of conversations with other owners. Such benefits assume that all social interactions between dogs and their owners and others are positive, which, unfortunately, is not the case. Despite this, as long as the positive encounters outweigh the negative ones, then the presence of dogs in society can be argued to be positive for social cohesion. Furthermore, the dog may offer security (which is often more imaginary than real with pet dogs who are as likely to invite a stranger into the house as bark threateningly at one), which can be very important for those living by themselves (Gillespie et al., 1996). Overall, as Rogerson (1991) and Herzog (2010: 68) noted, we: 'bring animals [and particularly dogs] into our lives because they make us feel happier, healthier, and more loved'. The reasons why we bring dogs as pets into our lives undermines the argument that a pet is without function or value; rather they are beyond economic valuing and are certainly not valueless to research either in their own right or in the context of their relations with humans. The result of all these reasons for bringing dogs into our lives is an increasingly close bond between dogs and humans that blurs the distinction between animals and humans and ensures dogs are seen ever more as a member of the family.

The idea that dogs help to ensure the mental and physical well-being of humans, while prominent today, is something that appears to have been in existence since at least the medieval era in Europe; then, royalty often kept dogs for the emotional outlet they offered when the humans were faced with the reality of the isolation with which their positions presented them (Kalof, 2007). This just goes to show how ideas, like fashion, come and go and that the current position of the dog is not necessarily the one it will be situated within in the future.

The term 'pet' has developed negative connotations of ownership in recent years, suggesting the animal is owned as an object for the benefit of the human and consequently its rights are not necessarily taken into consideration. As a result, we have seen the emergence of terms such as 'companion animal' and 'pet guardian'. The notion that an animal can be the companion of a human suggests that both actors are in a relationship where if there is not equality there is at least recognition of the rights of both and as such both are empowered. In this sense the relation between dog and human may, in Goffman's words, be seen as a 'with' (Sanders, 1999): a coming together of two sentient beings in a way that in its ideal is mutually beneficial. The problem, as Herzog (2010: 74) saw it is that many pets are not true companions and that really 'The terms *companion animal* and *pet guardian* are linguistic illusions that enable us to pretend we do not own the animals we live with.'

That not all dogs are treated or viewed in the same way is as apparent today as it has been historically. The medieval royals of Europe who were keeping dogs as emotional confidantes were also keeping dogs for hunting and baiting. Today, we see farmers who keep dogs as tools of work and at the same time have a pet dog who is treated in much the same manner as a huge number of the urban dogs of North America and Western Europe. This inconsistency and how it is justified or explained away will be discussed later in the book.

Current and Historic Scale of the Dog Population

While we may consider the mass ownership of dogs for non-work specific reasons as a relatively modern phenomenon this is not actually the case. Indeed, it has been estimated that by the late 1700s in England approximately 1 million dogs were being kept for reasons other than work (Kalof, 2007). More recent figures regarding dog ownership in the UK are noted in Fig. 1.1, which demonstrates a significant rise in the dog population over the last 50 years to 8.5 million in 2013. The figures for the UK indicate that in 2009 the dog population was spread across 23% of the nation's households (Australian Companion Animal Council, 2010). There is difficulty in attempting to closely

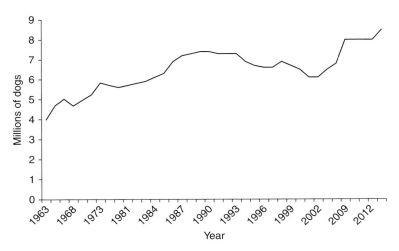

Fig. 1.1. Number of dogs in the UK. (From: Godwin, 1975 (for 1963); Carding, 1975 (for 1966–1973); Pet Food Manufacturers Association, 2010a (for 1965 and 1975–2004); Pet Food Manufacturers Association, 2010b (for 2009–2012) and Pet Food Manufacturers Association, 2010c (for 2013).)

analyse trends in the number of dogs in the UK and elsewhere over time, as the methods employed to estimate the population size have altered. However, it is fair to say that we have witnessed a large increase in the dog population throughout the second half of the 20th century and into the 21st century.

In 2009, 36% of Australian households were estimated to own at least one dog, with 3.41 million dogs living in the country. It is worth noting, however, that this number has been declining in recent years from a peak of 4 million in 1998. In comparison, in the USA an estimated 40% of households owned one or more dogs in 2009 and there were 77.5 million dogs in the country. These figures were reported to have declined slightly by 2011 when it was estimated that 36.5% of American households owned at least one dog and the total population in the country was approximately 70 million (American Veterinary Medical Association, 2012). Whether these differences represent a decline in dog ownership or are due to differences in the methods used to estimate them is, unfortunately, impossible to say. North of the border in Canada, there are an estimated 84 million dogs; they are now more common than children in Canadian households (Anonymous, 2013b). The number of dogs living in New Zealand is also significant, standing at 700,000 in 2011 and spread across 29% of the nation's households (New Zealand Companion Animal Council, 2011).

Dogs as Sentient, Self-aware Beings and Their 'Rights'

'Sentience' is a term that is inherently biased and as a consequence somewhat limiting when attempts are made to apply it to non-human animals. The reason for this is simply that the term has been constructed by humans and from a human perspective where humans are always at the top of the tree: the hegemonic power. It refers to the ability of animals (human and non-human) to think and undertake reasoned action, and their level of self-awareness. With these concepts comes the view that if something has them then it also must have agency; an ability to self-determine. Implicit to the notion of sentience is that creatures that have it are more than automatons that exist at the behest of biological processes. This suggests there is more to a sentient being than an agglomeration of atoms and chemical reactions. This has been referred to as a consciousness but can, in decidedly non-scientific language, also be referred to as a 'soul' (for want of a better word, and not implying any religious affiliation, of which I have none). The debate about whether non-human animals can be considered to be sentient is a highly emotive one where science, religion, politics and law, and personal belief collide. The balance of this debate is prone to change over time and is a culturally and therefore spatially specific issue.

How we, as individuals and societies, view the sentience of dogs has a profound impact on how we use and treat them and is, as a result, crucial to understanding the position and utilization of dogs in the leisure experience. From a scientific perspective the dominant position of the 20th century was that dogs, like most animals, are not capable of conscious thought and, therefore, are not sentient beings (Masson, 1997; Thomas, 2000). It is within this context that Griffin (2001: 29) has stated that: 'Behavioralists have been insisting for decades that the only appropriate scientific view of animal behavior is one that treats the animals as nearly as possible like mindless robots.' This view is supported by Boakes (1992 in McConnell, 2005: 271), who has said that: 'Attributing conscious thought to animals should be strenuously avoided in any serious attempt to understand their behavior, since it is untestable, empty, obstructionist and based on a false dichotomy.' Boakes' view of animals is underlain by the notion that unless it can be proved that they are sentient beings then we should continue to view them as lacking sentience. Thio (1983: 18) identified this view as a modernist one, whose proponents claim: 'there is a world of difference between humans (as active subjects) and nonhuman beings and things (as passive objects). Humans can feel and reflect, but animals, plants, things and forces in nature cannot. Furthermore, humans have sacred worth and dignity, but the others do not.' Consequently, while humans are self-defined as being sentient and therefore deserving of inherent rights concerning their freedom and welfare that encapsulate both their physical and mental wellness, it is clear, as MacFarland and Hediger (2009: 1) claimed that: 'Many have contended that other animals deserve no such opportunities because they lack the abilities, particularly the cognitive abilities, to make use of them.' Yet even something as apparently concrete as this perspective needs to be set against the realization that leading scientists such as Charles Darwin thought that animals, including dogs, were sentient beings (Morell, 2008). Indeed, Darwin is quoted as saying that: 'dogs possess something very like a conscience. They certainly possess some power of self-command' (Knoll, 1997: 15).

A shift has been occurring in scientific thought in recent years away from the previously dominant behaviourist paradigm (Duncan, 2006) and towards the realization that many animals, including dogs, experience a range of emotions.

There are those who, as Griffin (2001) noted, suggest animals have at least simple thoughts (compared to humans), though these are probably different from those experienced by humans. This position is exemplified by Kiley-Worthington (1990: 95), who has stated: 'That mammals at least feel something like pleasure or joy cannot be denied by any person who is prepared to admit that animals feel pain.' Others, such as Bradshaw (2011: 210), are happy to state that: 'dogs share our capacity to feel joy, love, anger, fear and anxiety. They also experience pain, hunger, thirst and sexual attraction.' That this shift is an emerging one explains why as McConnell (2005: xxvii) noted:

> In contrast to the beliefs of most dog lovers, current beliefs among scientists and philosophers about the emotional life of dogs are all over the map. Some argue that only humans can experience emotions, while others argue that non-human animals experience primitive emotions like fear and anger, but not more complicated ones like love and pride. At the other end of the continuum, some say it is good science to believe that many mammals come with the whole package, being capable of experiencing emotions in ways comparable to the way we experience them.

While the recognition that dogs experience emotions hints at a change in the position of scientific thinking regarding the sentience of dogs, it is important to note that discussions about how animals experience emotions is often set within the traditional scientific bulwarks of chemical reactions and evolution. This arguably relates to the traditional view that: 'a phenomenon that is not publicly observable and confirmable is not the stuff of science' (Horowitz, 2009a: 3). Consequently, the only way science can look at emotions, in animals or humans, is by distilling them down to the biological and chemical and away from the fuzzy reality in which emotions are experienced. Such a view of the emotions experienced by dogs and other animals allows them to be seen as biological processes necessary to the survival of the species. In this way an animal that experiences emotions can still be viewed as an object, an automaton reacting subconsciously to chemical inducements rather than a self-aware, sentient being. This view is echoed by McConnell (2005: 271), who identified that: 'Some people assert that while animals may "have" emotions, they aren't actually conscious of them.' It is from this perspective that it may be argued that most scientists today are willing to attribute sentience to animals; but I would suggest this is a poor imitation of what sentience really is, something more than the merely subconscious, automated reading of emotions as chemically induced events in the body. Bradshaw (2011: 211) goes a little further than many scientists when stating: 'dogs do possess some degree of consciousness. In other words, they are probably aware of their emotions, but to a lesser extent than humans are,' while at the same time recognizing that there is little agreement across the scientific community on this point. Consequently, it may be argued that, while agreement on animals possessing a range of emotions may have been reached, there is an ongoing debate raging as to whether this equates to animals being self-aware, sentient beings capable of individual agency.

It is against the backdrop of the traditionally dominant view of animals as lacking sentience that laws, rights, and welfare issues and standards relating to dogs – indeed, to all animals – need to be viewed. In virtually all cases it is clear that animals are viewed as objects, or property (Sanders, 1999; Bekoff, 2007; Rudy, 2011); not all that different in cold legal language from inanimate possessions. The implications of being an object as opposed to a sentient being are clear. An object has no rights and needs no rights; its welfare is of no concern as it is clear that an object has no feelings or emotions. Even where we see the advancement of the idea that animals have rights and are sentient, as argued below, Francione (2004: 120) has stated that: 'The status of animals as property renders meaningless our claim that we reject the status of animals as things. We treat animals as the moral equivalent of inanimate objects with no morally significant interests.' This highlights how existing laws based on one view of animals may be poorly equipped to handle significant shifts in the notion of what the non-human animal is and is capable of.

Against the view of dogs and other animals as objects lacking sentience or only possessing a poor form of sentience that consists of experiencing emotions as nothing more than chemical reactions in the body is a voracious voice that demands that dogs are sentient, self-aware beings capable of feelings (Siegal, 1994; McConnell, 2005; Bekoff, 2007). This is a viewpoint that is being increasingly voiced in relation to animals in general (Bostock, 1993; Lehman, 1997; MacFarland and Hediger, 2009). Jane Goodall (2007: xii) goes as far as to state: 'There was increasingly compelling evidence that we are not alone in the universe, not the only creatures with minds capable of solving problems, capable of love and hate, joy and sorrow, fear and despair.' *The Cambridge Declaration on Consciousness*, written by Philip Low (2012) and ratified by some of the world's contemporary leading thinkers, is written in a much drier and less emotional academic prose. It stated: 'the weight of evidence indicates that humans are not unique in possessing the neurological substrates that generate consciousness. Non-human animals, including all mammals and birds, and many other creatures, including octopuses, also possess these neurological substrates', and clearly recognizes the potential sentience of the non-human animal through its possession of a consciousness. Bringing the focus back to dogs Steiner (2005: 243) has indicated that they: 'exhibit behaviour that strongly suggests rich emotional lives and complex ways of negotiating their environments'. Similarly, the rich consciousness of dogs and their potential to have a soul is illustrated by Horowitz (2009a: 139) who wrote:

> Look a dog in the eyes and you get the definite feeling that he is looking back. Dogs return our gaze. Their look is more than just setting eyes on us; they are looking at us in the same way that we look at them. The importance of the dog's gaze, when it is directed at our faces, is that gaze implies a frame of mind.
> It implies attention. A gazer is both paying attention to you and, possibly, paying attention to your own attention.

Following on from the views of people such as Goodall and Steiner, Bekoff (2007: 18), among others, has suggested that: 'ethical values tell us that animals should not be viewed as property, as resources, or as disposable machines that exist for human consumption, treated like bicycles or backpacks'. This turns the matter of the rights and welfare of animals away from something that is simply related to the sentience of animals and therefore within their power (such as it is) and into a human construct where our ethical values have a bearing on the animal. In this way, as normal, the human is the one in the position of power, dispensing animal rights and welfare according to human ethical standards.

The leading proponents of the notion that dogs have sentience are the owners of dogs, in particular pet dogs (Sanders, 1999). Ask almost any person who has a pet dog and they are likely to tell you that their dog understands and empathizes with them: two clear indicators of sentience. Are these people right or are they delusional, interpreting animal behaviour through rose-tinted human eyes and as a result guilty of anthropomorphism, of imposing human traits on objects or non-human animals – dogs in this case? Certainly tradition-ally such dog owners have been viewed as eccentric for voicing such opinions (Rudy, 2011), but arguably such an opinion is beginning to change, though the more extreme views espoused by some owners are still ridiculed, as society em-braces these views in a manner that is at least partially driven by the widening ownership of pet dogs and the changing views of the scientific community.

The question of sentience is crucial because it forms the basis of arguments surrounding the 'rights' of dogs. If they are mere objects, devoid of any sign of sentience, then we can all too easily dismiss the notion that dogs have any rights at all. Rather, as simple objects they are owned by individuals who may do as they wish with said objects with impunity. On the other hand, if dogs have a level of sentience akin to that of humans then by default they should also have the rights that have been enshrined for humans in a variety of uni-versal laws thanks to the United Nations, among other bodies.

With the argument about the sentience of dogs still unresolved it is difficult to determine what the rights of dogs should be. Therefore, rather than relying on science to provide the answer, societies and individuals must continue to decide for themselves on the question of sentience and the related issue of rights. To me, it is clear that dogs do have a kind of sentience; that they are capable of independent thought and of understanding and interacting with dif-ferent species (most notably, though certainly not exclusively, humans). Is this sentience the same as humans possess? No, I would suggest that it is not, while at the same time suggesting that just because it is not does not mean it is of lesser importance.

So where does this leave the debate about the rights of dogs? If we assume they are sentient beings then we must accept they have rights; rights that relate to their physical and mental well-being. Yet since the dog cannot speak the same language as humans there remains the potential for misinterpretation, wilful or not, with good intentions or otherwise, concerning the needs of dogs and hence the requirements for their welfare and by extension the defining of their rights. At one extreme Rudy (2011) has stated that those proposing the strongest animal rights have suggested we should stop breeding domesticated animals; that we should not cuddle or walk them or use them in our leisure. For me personally this is several steps too far and is also a human-oriented view rather than one that truly takes the animals' views into consideration. Domesticated animals exist because of humans and would cease to exist without our active involvement. While we can argue that the initial involvement was misguided, abandoning such animals now will lead to their extinction, something that is more appalling, at least to me, than the original domestication of animals. With specific reference to the dog, it is clearly an animal that through its heritage and human-influenced breeding is strongly bonded to humans. To deprive it of such contact is to take a moral high ground that ignores the mental well-being of a species and the associated right of the dog to be with humans if it so wishes.

Consequently, rather than suggesting a blanket ban on dogs to fit well with an idealized standpoint on animal rights that ignores the reality of human–animal interactions that can be beneficial for and desired by all participants, I adopt a more nuanced approach that has the welfare of the dog at the centre. In this way I have no argument with the five freedoms promoted by the Royal Society for the Prevention of Cruelty to Animals (RSPCA), among others (freedom from hunger and thirst; freedom from discomfort; freedom from pain, injury and disease; freedom to express normal behaviour; and freedom from fear and distress (Royal Society for the Prevention of Cruelty to Animals, 2012)) but I would position them in a framework that is constructed around the recognition of the sentience of animals and therefore sees them as social actors rather than passive objects.

Within my perspective the focus is on ensuring the physical and mental well-being of the dog and recognizing that the interaction between dogs and humans can be central to both the achievement and destruction of this well-being. In this manner I would fit under Rudy's (2011) definition of an 'animal welfarist'. In this way I recognize that the lives and welfare of dogs (like all domesticated animals but more than most) and humans are closely intertwined and to speak only of or to one is to miss this crucial point. To me, this means that it is necessary to reject Rudy's (2011: 9) assertion that animal welfare means 'humans still hold all the power'. Yes, one may have more of one type of power than the other but this is not the same as saying dogs have no power of any kind. Even if humans do hold more power, from a welfarist standpoint the important point to note is that with this power (indeed power of any kind) comes the responsibility to wield this power appropriately; not for the benefit of those in power but rather for all (human and non-human). The core issue then is not power but responsibility and the responsible use of power. In this way I would suggest that Kiley-Worthington's (1990) assertion that animal welfare is ultimately a matter of moral judgement is not entirely accurate. We may as humans be in a position of power where we can impose our moral values on animals, but welfare is about more than this, it is about being able and willing to listen to the animals and their needs, and bend our morality to meet their position rather than simply impose it on them. Looked at in one way, such a position suggests a lack of equality between humans and dogs but this is based on the idea that there is no difference between dogs and humans. There are differences and to ignore them is disrespectful to both species. I agree with Singer's (2004) view that the concept of equality extends beyond treating different animals in exactly the same way or giving all the same rights. The important point is not equal treatment, but equal consideration, which can lead to different rights for different animals. 'Consideration' becomes the key word here: of truly listening to and considering the 'other', human or otherwise.

Cultural Constructions of 'Dog' and the Human Owner/Companion

As Bekoff (2007: 156) noted: 'How animal images and live animals are represented in advertisements, on television, in movies, in cartoons, and in other forms of entertainment influence what people come to believe about them.' In this way the media may be seen as the constructor of the sociocultural view of the 'dog'. Yet this is an oversimplification of a more complex reality that is at the heart of the never-ending debate surrounding the relation between human agency and structure. The media as the representation of culture certainly builds a picture of what a dog is and how it relates to humans and should be treated, but the media is itself influenced by the images held by the individual. In effect it is a never-ending feedback loop with no beginning and no end. To try and find which originally caused the other is a fruitless endeavour when the reality is that they are both intimately related to one another. The situation is even more complicated when it is recognized that we are dealing with not just the view of humans but the dogs' perspective as well. This leads to the question of whether the sentience of the dog is simply a product of human cultural constructs or a reality now being integrated into human culture. The answer is that one feeds off the other. Dog sentience is real but its specific nature is coloured in the eyes of humans by human culture, which in turn is influenced by the media.

There are instances where fictional dogs have morphed into physical tourist attractions, as shown in Fig. 1.2 where Gromit, of Wallace and Gromit fame, has become a larger-than-life and very colourful tourist attraction in parts of the UK; the representation in Fig. 1.2 was spotted outside the entrance to Bristol Zoo. Statues such as the Gromit one are popular tourist attractions because of how they depict the character seen on television and at the movies. They are a physical embodiment of the anthropomorphic fictional character and as such they help to reinforce the message that Gromit purveys: that dogs are sentient beings capable of multiple complex feelings and feats. In this way Gromit provides an excellent example of how society perceives and constructs the dog. Yet these perceptions and constructions can also be influenced by the reality of dogs and their own inherent characteristics. The list of other dogs who have been portrayed in human culture and in doing so helped to shape how we view dogs is without end. It includes, among others, my own favourite; Dog, a cartoon character created by Murray Ball and a wonderful representation of both the Collie and the quintessential New Zealand farm. A detailed examination of the role of dogs in fictional media is beyond the scope of the present work, but will be examined in a chapter of a book I am editing about domesticated animals (Carr, forthcoming a).

Just as the dog is a cultural construct in the eyes of humans, so is the dog owner or human companion. Society depicts acceptable images of dog owners and human companions, helping in the process to mould the behaviour of these people and how they wish to be perceived by society. At the same time, the behaviour of these people influences media representations of the 'good'

Fig. 1.2. Gromit at Bristol Zoo, UK (2013).

dog owner. These images are depicted both in factual and fictional media: the latter including everything from Wallace (the 'owner' of Gromit) to Wal Footrot (the owner of Dog) and George (the Famous Five owner of Timmy).

Culturally and Temporally Specific Nature of Dogs and Human–Dog Relations

Given that the nature of the dog (as viewed by humans) and the dog owner is a cultural construct of humans and that culture is both temporally and spatially specific (Massey and Jess, 1995; Gullotta *et al.*, 2000), it is not surprising that how dogs are viewed and the relations between them and humans are specific to time and place. In this way definitions of the 'good' dog and the 'good' dog owner are also specific to place and time. While there is plenty of observable evidence to support these claims, and many of this will be highlighted throughout this book, it is worth noting that to date: 'Cross-cultural comparisons of dog behaviour and dog-keeping practices are limited' (Wan *et al.*, 2009: 206).

The place and time specific cultural definitions of dogs and their relations with humans colour the rules and regulations relating to the governing of dogs' behaviour and where they are allowed to go. Consequently, as we will see in this book, laws, rules and regulations governing dogs alter temporally and spatially. This reality also applies to the unwritten social rules about dogs and their owners. Everything from the exercising of dogs, sports associated with dogs and whether dogs are allowed inside the family home and on the furniture, to the eating of dog meat and the provision of cuisine and holidays for dogs are influenced by and specific to culture. When talking about temporal specificity it is important to remember that this refers not only to linear time but also to differences between human generations.

The result, as will be seen throughout the book, is that the experiences and position of dogs in leisure are constantly changing and contested, with conflicts often occurring between different groups. The nature of these conflicts and the philosophical issues they often throw up will be discussed throughout the book with an attempt to provide potential roadmaps that may contribute to conflict resolution. Such paths often entail compromise, as will be seen, but they need to recognize the sentience of dogs so they become actors in the process rather than merely objects that can be positioned at the whim of humanity.

Author's Own Standpoint

Writing anything for public consumption always requires authors to place their ideas and beliefs on display because only by doing this can the written word be contextualized and believed or fairly rejected. As such, this public display is both unnerving and empowering (for both the reader and the author). Often, such displays are either hidden in between the written words or behind a public mask that is all too often constructed around the beliefs of others, commonly famous philosophers from history (Foucault being very popular in certain fields, for example).

This entire book and everything dog related within it is a consequence of the fact that I am a dog owner so it seems appropriate to begin explaining my standpoint by giving a brief background about how I have reached this point in my life and the implications of it. My first dog, Snuffie, entered my life as an 8-week-old Border Collie mongrel in February 2001, from the Queensland RSPCA in Brisbane. She was ostensibly to be a dog for my 2-year-old son, with the two of them able to grow up together. By this point in my life I was 29 years old and had never had anything other than a goldfish as a pet. As a child, dogs had never really entered my life and my only brief encounters with them had been rather scary. I was not, it is fair to say, a dog person, a dog lover, in any respect. This was all to change and I could and perhaps should write an entire book about the journey but this is not that book so I will skip over all but the barest bones. Simply put, in the 9 years prior to her untimely death (I sat with her after much soul searching while our family friend and vet administered a lethal injection to put her to sleep and out of the misery that was a slow-spreading but inoperable cancer in her spinal column), Snuffie became my dog first and foremost and a family pet a distant second. Barely a day went by in all that time when we did not spend time walking together (as all Border Collie owners will doubtless attest, such dogs and owners can easily walk forever, or so it seems) or engaging in the simple play of throw and fetch. The result: I am now a confirmed dog lover and in particular a lover of mongrels. It seems I am forever destined to have black and white mutts in my household who have a passing relation to the purebred Border Collie, and Gypsy is my current canine companion.

Rudy (2011: 36), when talking of his own relationship with his dogs, stated: 'As my dogs and I work hard to learn a common language and share a life together, we are all becoming something new, something part human, part dog, a part of one another.' I have talked previously of the notion of the 'dumanog', a human–dog hybrid that fits well with Rudy's description (Carr, 2006). Similarly, using Goffman's concept, Sanders (1999) saw the dog and owner as a 'with'; where they are perceived to be a group whose members are together. This togetherness is demonstrated and reinforced not just by the leash that links them in public but the looks and physical contact they each give one another in a show of ongoing reassurance.

While I remain wedded to the existence of the dumanog in the moment it is important not to oversimplify a more complex reality. While my dog and I can at specific moments be a dumanog, at others we are separate, clearly a human and a dog. This description of the relationship a human can have with a dog is reflected in the views of Wedde (2007: 284) who stated that: 'I know that the dog and I are utterly different in ways that neither of us will understand; and yet we inflect each other's behavior, and we inhabit a shared world that is simultaneously comprehensible and mysterious.' The important point to remember is not the nature of the relationship with their dogs that, like me, Rudy and Wedde think they have, but that not all dog–human relations are like this or necessarily even need to be for the benefit of all participants. The idea of the relation between a dog and human being specific to the moment allows me to position myself as both owner and companion to my dogs, who can themselves be pets, companions and simply 'dogs'. In this way, we can each of us be many things at different times and in different circumstances.

Outline of Book Content

Following on from this introductory chapter the book looks, in Chapter 2, at the working dogs who exist within the leisure environment. Some of these animals are directly employed by the leisure industry, while others have been utilized by the industry in marketing leisure experiences and destinations. The focus of Chapter 3 is on dogs and sport, looking first at sports that are based on dogs before examining those that have been developed to cater to dogs. The link between the working and sports dog is seen to be a close one, with many sports involving dogs having grown out of the work for which various breeds of dog have been developed. Chapter 4 then examines the notion of the leisured dog and the dog as an object of human leisure. The former necessitates a discussion of whether dogs actually have leisure, while the latter is grounded in the discussion surrounding the idea of the dog as a sentient being.

From looking at the types of dogs and their experiences in leisure, Chapter 5 examines the ways in which the leisure experiences of dogs are provided for. A central facet of this chapter is an analysis of whether such provisions are really for dogs or for their owners. Chapter 6 then focuses more specifically on the provision of kennels, dog day care and other services that are ostensibly provided for dogs but in reality are strongly oriented towards dog owners' perceptions of their animals' needs.

In the initial book proposal, Chapters 7 and 8, which look at dogs as cuisine, and cuisine for dogs, respectively, were one chapter. The logic of this was to bring together what I saw as being two sides of the same coin. The credit for splitting this into the two chapters in the final version of the book rests with the publisher. On balance, I think I prefer the final version as it gives space for the two issues to be addressed separately, without one dominating the other. At the same time, I would urge the reader to see the linkages that exist between the two.

The final chapter attempts to bring together some of the main ideas raised in the book, but more importantly it seeks to suggest a future for research on dogs in the leisure experience.

2 Working Dogs

Introduction: Dogs as Tools

It is not the intention of this chapter to examine working dogs per se, though such a focus is not without value. Rather, this chapter focuses on working dogs where they intersect with the leisure environment. Consequently, one of the foci of this chapter will be examining how the presence of working dogs in an environment has been utilized to construct idealized images of leisure and tourism landscapes. This discussion will cover both contemporary uses of representations of working dogs in landscapes to promote places as tourist or leisure environments, and how such use has evolved over time, and how the representation and positioning of the working dog may have altered. Another focus of this chapter will be a discussion of the extent to which dogs are employed as workers in the tourism and leisure industry and the history of this use. This chapter will also encompass a discussion of the changing role of working dogs in the face of the changing nature of experiences sought by tourists and leisured people. The discussions within this chapter will be grounded in the issue of animal rights and will discuss changing patterns in the use of working dogs in leisure and tourism experiences in line with altering social moral values, focusing on the construction of dogs as tools or objects to be used and/or owned by humans in the leisure and tourism environment.

Dogs at Work in Leisure, Tourism and Hospitality Experiences

There is a wide variety of tasks in which dogs are employed within the leisure environment. They are an interesting reflection of the diverse nature of dogs and the skill sets they have to offer. They include the sniffer dogs who patrol the airports of the world, searching for a diverse array of materials that include drugs, foodstuffs and explosives. Another arena in which dogs are employed is that of search and rescue, where they are tasked with finding lost and/or injured individuals out in the rural/wilderness landscape. Search and rescue operations in such areas have a long history and their growth is a reflection of the growing utilization of such spaces by people seeking outdoor hiking, climbing and skiing/snowboarding experiences. Consequently, the date of establishment and size of search and rescue dog associations is largely a reflection of the history and popularity of these types of tourism/recreation in the areas in which the associations are located. For example, in the UK the Search and Rescue Dog Association (SARDA) was formed in 1965 in the Scottish highlands (Locke, 1987), reflecting the wilderness of the region and its growing popularity with tourists. By 1971 SARDA had devolved into separate Scottish, English and Welsh associations, and today they exist under the wider umbrella of the National Search and Rescue Dog Association (SARDA England, 2014). In comparison, the American Rescue Dog Association was formed in 1972 after people in the Seattle area began training their dogs for avalanche work in the late 1960s (American Rescue Dog Association, 1991).

The most established image of the search and rescue dog is that of the St Bernard, which is not surprising as such animals are said to have been helping those lost in the Alps of Switzerland since the 17th century (Locke, 1987). Such has been the popularity of the image of the St Bernard rescuing the lost individual that it has entered the realm of fiction and fantasy. Indeed, Ash (1934) even suggests the notion of the St Bernard as a rescue dog in the Swiss Alps was a fabrication of the 19th century. Yet both the 'real' and more obviously fictional images of the St Bernard rescuing the unwary traveller are likely to be grounded, albeit often rather tenuously, in reality. It is just that the fictional and even apparently real descriptions are often not very accurate representations of what these dogs have done in the past or are capable of. Rather, these depictions are an example of how the dog in fiction and contemporary society in general has been anthropomorphized; of how it has been given human characteristics (or at least idealized human characteristics) and abilities that promote its loyalty to humanity and its role as carer and protector of humans. In doing so, such depictions draw dogs ever more into the 'family' as integral members but at the same time arguably distance them from what they really are (i.e. dogs), which can unfortunately set them up for failure.

The growth in the position of the rescue dog as a key component in ensuring the safety of those venturing into remote and wilderness areas during their leisure is exemplified by the number of call-outs that SARDA in the UK receive annually. Back in 1966, just after the formation of the organization, it received only four call-outs. In comparison Palmer (1983: 121) stated that: 'Taking at random one year during the last ten, rescue dogs were called out on 32 different occasions to take part in searches in the following areas – the Northwest, the Borders, Ben Nevis, Cairngorms, Glencoe and Central Scotland.' By 2009 SARDA Scotland was called out 81 times (SARDA Scotland, 2014).

A specific component of the work undertaken by the search and rescue dog community is locating people trapped in avalanches. This growing line of work reflects the expanding numbers of people skiing and snowboarding, and doing so in the back country, where the risk of avalanche is higher than on the groomed slopes. Consequently, it was in 1978 that the Canadian Avalanche Rescue Dog Association was established in Whistler, Canada, reflecting the strong growth of the resort as a skiing destination at that time. These dogs increase the potential of surviving an avalanche exponentially as they 'can search one hectare in 30 minutes. A line of human probers would take four hours to cover the same area' (Ogilvie, 2006: B9).

The working dogs employed by the police and various military units tend to cross over into the arena of sport and leisure. In this case, the dogs and their handlers have a long history of putting on demonstrations of their skills for the enjoyment of the public. These dogs are clearly working animals though the demonstrations are in many ways a spectacle, a staged event, rather than the real work for which they are trained. Yet while giving these demonstrations to a leisured audience the dogs and their handlers are still working. Rather than it being their 'job' per se it is an opportunity for them to demonstrate their importance and worth to the public, and an ideal means through which their parent organizations can engage with the wider community and champion their work and objectives. The crossover between work and leisure is further amplified in this case when the establishment of police dog trials as a competitive sport is recognized. The rationale for the establishment of these trials is similar to that of sheep and gun dog trials, which are discussed in detail later in the chapter.

Dogs have the potential to undertake a vital role in the development of children through play. The place of play in leisure has long been established, as has the notion that play can and does act as a significant learning tool/environment in which childhood development can occur. It is a widely held belief that children and dogs are natural bedfellows in many ways and that the presence of a dog in a family will aid the development of a child as it grows up and they spend time playing together. In addition, the term 'pet therapy' (which can also be referred to as animal-assisted therapy) was coined in 1964 by the child psychiatrist Boris Levinson when he realized that children who were struggling for one reason or another could potentially be aided by dogs, through play (Herzog, 2010). Here then we see the dog as a potential tool, employed either formally or informally to aid the development of the child through play; a significant driving force behind the decision my wife and I made to bring our first dog into the family.

A recent development in the roles adopted by working dogs in the leisure experience is that of 'canine ambassador' or 'meet and greet dogs' that are beginning to work in airports. One of these dogs works at Miami International Airport as a volunteer alongside her owner. Her role is to help soothe the nerves of the frazzled traveller by simply being there to receive a pat, cuddle or gentle stroke. In effect this Golden Retriever, Casey as she is known, is a therapy dog and as such is doing work similar to those that visit hospitals and retirement homes. The work may seem easy for a dog; after all, most love a stroke and a show of affection. Yet as Casey's handler points out, this is actually hard work for the dog. Being placed in an environment where there are huge numbers of people and being subjected to approaches from numerous strangers, not all of whom may approach her or touch her in a manner she is entirely comfortable with, can be extremely stressful for her (Hess, 2012). The canine ambassador programme is also operating at Los Angeles International Airport and Mineta San Jose International Airport in the USA (Kleven, 2013).

Changing Role of Working Dogs: From Work to Sport

One of the oldest forms of work for the dog has been on the farm, herding animals in general and sheep in particular. Such was the need for the sheepdog that its breeding and training became a specialized activity and the best dogs highly prized assets. Here arguably is the foundation on which modern sheepdog trials is based; as an avenue by which the quality of sheepdogs may be improved, tested and demonstrated (Moore, 1929; Halsall, 1982). Yet the underlying rationale for sheepdog trials may be more simply viewed as a competition between human owners to see whose dog is best (Halsall, 1982). In this way the sheepdog trials are arguably little different from any other sport and the dog is clearly an object within the context of the sport. The trials offer breeders and owners a chance to demonstrate the ability of their dogs and – arguably, more importantly – their own skills in breeding, raising and training their dogs. In this way any benefit to the development of the breed actually becomes of secondary importance to the competition and status to be gained by the humans from winning. While the UK was the home of the first sheepdog trial, the exact location has been a matter of some debate though Bala in North Wales is clearly the leading contender, hosting a trial in 1873 (Jones, 1892; Moore, 1929; Drabble, 1989).

While fine in theory, sheepdog trials are arguably limited in their ability to develop a working dog or prove the worth of a dog as a successful sheep herder. Indeed, Whyte (1927: 112) has stated that:

> A mere win at a dog trial does not necessarily provide absolute proof of a dog's usefulness, for he may have been kept for the purpose of trial work only and trained to concert pitch by an expert at the game with an undue sacrifice of time and labour. Great dogs perform their greatest feats not necessarily always on the trial field; but perhaps more often when mustering on the mountain ranges.

Whyte (1927: 115) further questioned the reliance on sheepdog trials as a means of ensuring the breeding of working sheepdogs by asking his readers to: 'Just imagine what would be the fate of those sheep if left to some of the highly strung, excitable dogs seen competing at dog-trials nowadays.' This needs setting within the context of New Zealand, which he was writing about, and the fact that at one time sheepdogs in that country were expected to stand guard on untended flocks overnight, or even retrieve lost sheep by themselves during the night.

The dogs Whyte spoke of are sports dogs rather than working dogs and he marks the transition of them and their owners from the arena of work to that of sport. Speaking about the early movement of sheepdogs into the dog show arena Whyte clearly predicted the continued movement of the sheepdog from working animal, through sporting beast and to leisure object when speaking of the creation of the sheepdog as a pedigree animal for show (the rise of dog shows will be discussed in detail in Chapter 3). He suggested that the pedigree sheepdog raised for the show arena and leisured lifestyle would become a poor imitation of its ancestors with all of the beautiful looks that are associated with the Border Collie of today and none of the brains that made it such a useful tool on the farm (Whyte, 1927). Similarly, Moore (1929: 25–26) stated that: 'show qualities in sporting dogs were practically valueless without satisfactory proof of working merits'. Whether this is the case or dogs have simply continued to change in response to the changing requirements of humans is an important question. The working sheepdog can still be found on farms throughout the world; its brains highly valued, its ability to undertake long, hard work un-questioned, its often mongrel appearance and pedigree of little concern. We may in an abstract sense see all sheepdogs as 'sheepdogs' with a common root but in reality today those bred for working, for sport and for show are all very different, and different characteristics are more highly valued across the three groups. The important point is that whether the sheepdogs are working in the fields, focused on trials or dedicated to the show arena, they have all been bred and trained by humans in a manner that contextualizes them as objects for work or leisure.

Whether limited or not in their ability to aid the breeding and training of effective sheepdogs for work on the farm, sheepdog trials have become a popular sport throughout the world. This includes countries such as the UK, Australia and New Zealand, as well as Canada and America (Moore, 1929), with the main focus being those nations with a history of sheep farming. Not surprisingly, trials generated an International Sheep Dog Society in 1907 that had organizing and promoting trials and improving the nature of the sheepdog as its twin founding principles (Palmer, 1983). Under the auspices of this organ-ization, betting on trials was banned (Halsall, 1982). Just as watching sheepdog trials is not related to financial gain, nor is participation monetarily driven, at least directly, with prizes of limited value the norm (Halsall, 1982). Though the potential to earn a profit from breeding a prize-winning sheepdog does need to be kept in mind, even this does not appear to be a leading reason for taking part in the sport. Rather, it seems to be for the joy of proving an ability to breed and train a dog and then to work with it.

By as early as 1877 the Bala trials were attracting over 2000 spectators (Moore, 1929), and from 1976 to 1999 the BBC produced the television series *One Man and his Dog*, which brought the sport of sheepdog trials to a mass, and mainly urban, audience. Such was the popularity of the show that at one time it attracted 7.8 million viewers (Palmer, 1983). From its demise as a regular series to 2013 the show continued as a series of annual specials before be-coming part of the BBC's *Countryfile* programme in 2013. A similar programme entitled *A Dog's Show* ran on New Zealand television from 1977 until 1992 (Jukes, 2003). Why did people watch these programmes? Was it to see the skills of man and dog or to admire the beauty of the idealized rural landscape? The answer is 'probably a bit of both' but the result was that in addition to giving urbanites a glimpse into an aspect of rural life the programme helped to place the sheepdog (also known as the Border Collie) as an iconic emblem of this life and the rural landscape.

The televising of sheepdog trials split opinion, with the purists suggesting that in constructing the trials to meet the requirements of television the integrity of the sport was lost as it became pure entertainment. In other words, they were concerned about the loss of the authenticity of the sport and its dislocation from its roots. While not necessarily disclaiming this, the other side of the debate saw it as a sacrifice worth making to bring an aspect of the rural way of life to an urban population and in the process to bridge the gap between rural and urban dwellers (Drabble, 1989). Today, the sport continues to be a popular one with a loyal fan base and a committed group of participants, though it is best described as a niche sport.

Irrespective of the merits of sheepdog trials it is worth noting the following quotation from Jones (1892: 76), who was writing not long after the creation of the first trials: 'the freedom from the infliction of distress or pain or death upon any of the animals engaged in the operations – a condition too seldom characteristic of the sports and pastimes in which people take pleasure'. When put into the context of blood sports (as discussed in Chapter 3), which were diverse in nature and still popular in 1800s Britain, Jones' statement about sheepdog trials can be seen as arguably a major step forward in terms of the rights and welfare of animals (particularly of dogs and sheep in this instance).

Today, the sheepdog is not only used in the herding of sheep for farming and sport but also as a tourist attraction. Across the rural landscape of the UK, where the use of sheepdogs has a long history, operators are now offering tourists the opportunity to see demonstrations of the abilities of these animals and their handlers. In this way not only the dogs but also the shepherds are being reinvented, transforming them from agricultural workers to tourism industry employees. For example, one farm in Inverness-shire, Scotland, offers sheepdog demonstrations with a 'true native highland shepherd', speaking of an authentic experience for the tourist. This operator, like the sled dog operators discussed later in this section, recognizes the potential to tap into the appeal of puppies by not only putting on demonstrations but offering the opportunity for visitors to meet 'friendly Collie pups'. In this way also the nature of the animal is being changed, turning it into an attraction and focal point for the affections of visitors and away from its role as an agrarian working animal. These pups for petting, an activity also offered in at least some of the farms in the UK that have opened their gates to tourists, are representative not of the traditional notions of the agrarian working dog but of the dog as part of the family, as a pet. Visitors to the countryside are now also enticed to learn how to become a sheepdog handler, as farms offer the opportunity to learn the skills that have been associated with shepherding. Such an example, known as the Lake District Sheepdog Experience, exists in the Lake District of the UK where the operator provides the dogs, and the experience is open to everyone, from pure novices upwards (Anonymous, 2013a).

Another company, called Shepherds Walks, offers – unsurprisingly – walking holidays, in rural Northumbria (UK). As shown in Fig. 2.1, the company plays on the notion of the shepherd as the knowledgeable country person, depicting the operator of the walks with the tools of the shepherd: his crook and his Border Collie, which by default must be a sheepdog, irrespective of the lack

Fig. 2.1. Shepherds Walks tourism promotional imagery (2008). (Photo courtesy of Shepherds Walks, UK.)

of sheep in the picture. The notion that tourists who undertake an experience with this company are gaining an authentic one is underlined on the company's website by the knowledge that when the company was set up by the owner in 1999 he was then 'a full time Hill Shepherd' (Shepherds Walks, 2013). In this instance neither the 'shepherd' nor the 'sheepdog' are really what they are depicted as being. They are not agrarian workers out of a romantic idyll; rather they are operators in the tourism industry, not herding sheep but herding tourists instead, while at the same time feeding off the imagery of both shepherd and dog as quintessentially rural and experts/masters of the rural landscape.

The movement from working dog to sports dog can also be seen in the emergence of field trials as a way of training and encouraging the breeding of gun dogs (Brown, 1934). The first of these took place in the UK in 1865, with the Kennel Club becoming involved from 1873 onwards (Moore, 1929). The logic behind such trials is obviously akin to that behind sheepdog trials and has been seen as beneficial to the quality of gun dogs by various proponents

(Scales, 2000). While largely agreeing with this view, Alington (1929) cautioned that, although the field trials enhanced some aspects of the gun dog, they, have at best done little for and at worst been detrimental to the dog's nose or game-finding ability. This, Alington argues, is due to the breeding of dogs for trial purposes that has emphasized not chasing animals, and hence means the dogs have little interest in sniffing or hunting out prey.

The popularity of field trials as a sport has increased markedly over the last 150 years. In the UK, for example, Kennel Club records indicate that in 1900 the number of trials held under the auspices of this organization was 11 and by 1950 had grown to 92. The number continued to expand, with 583 trials occurring in 2000–2001 and 655 in 2010–2011. How many of the participants are engaging in the trials purely for the sake of the trials as a sport and how many are participating in order to hone the skills of both dog and human for the hunting season is, unfortunately, unclear.

With the emergence of sled dog racing the sled dog has also witnessed a movement from working to sport dog. The first organized racing event is said to have occurred under the auspices of the Nome Kennel Club in Alaska in 1908 (Hood, 1996). The reasons for the origin of these races are arguably multiple and interwoven. One, in common with that associated with field and sheepdog trials, was the desire among enthusiasts and owners of sled dogs to ensure the quality of the breed (Garst, 1948). In addition, it may be suggested that the racing of sled dogs emerged from competition between different individuals working sled dog teams on the same routes. Finally, it is important to recognize that the desire to preserve a way of life as a part of the heritage of the early explorers of Alaska and the northern regions of Canada has, and continues, to play a significant role in the establishment and continuation of sled dog racing as a sport. Indeed, within the context of the Yukon Quest (discussed below) it is claimed that this event: 'embodies all of the qualities of the land that northerners love and those that set northerners apart' (Firth, 1998: vii). This is clearly the case for the Iditarod, a sled dog race that was created to commemorate the transporting of diphtheria serum in 1925 over approximately 1000 miles of largely wilderness to the community of Nome, Alaska (Hood, 1996). The whole mythology surrounding the race speaks of man (European settler) against nature at its harshest (in an Alaskan winter) and the nobility of the dogs involved. Yet the creation of the race owes much to the American political climate during the time of the first race in 1967 and the country's relation with the then USSR. As Hood (1996: 19) stated, the race was created: 'as part of the one-hundredth anniversary of the purchase of Alaska from Russia'. A further layer explaining the creation of the Iditarod was the desire to ensure the future of dog sledding and the survival of its history in the face of the advent of the snow skidoo (Hood, 1996). As Coppinger (1977) stated, the preservation of sledding in the face of automation contributed to the creation of an entire sport and not just one race. The desire to preserve the heritage of the sled dog is, however, clearly one that has been controlled and coloured by the white Anglo-Saxon settlers of North America. As such it has largely airbrushed over the reality that the breeding and running of sled dogs appears to have originated in what is now Siberia over 4000 years ago (Coppinger, 1977).

Whatever the origin of sled dog racing, today it is a diverse sport that encapsulates a variety of offshoots in terms of the nature of the dog teams, what they are required to pull and how far they are expected to run (Table 3.1). Yet within this mixed bag there are events that stand out as being iconic of the sport. This status is strongly linked to the heritage of the sport and of the earlier explorers of the frozen north of the North American continent. So the iconic events of dog sledding are firmly based within northern Canada and Alaska, despite the sport now being popular in almost every corner of the world (including New Zealand, with its annual Wanaka Sled Dog Festival, which began in 1996 (Ibbotson, 2012) and the Sled Dog Association of Scotland, which was inaugurated in 1991 (Sled Dog Association of Scotland, 2007a)). Furthermore, they are the long- and ultra-long-distance, multi-day events that test the endurance of dog and man (for these events have long been constructed as sites of hegemonic masculinity reflecting the exploration of northern Canada and Alaska by the rugged, outdoors male). That this ignores a strong, though minority, representation of women in these events for a significant period of time is something that would be very interesting to pursue within a gendered framework, but which lies outside the boundaries of this book. For a history of the involvement of women in these events readers are urged to go to the book by Hood (1996) on the Iditarod. What we see running through all of these iconic events is the construction of an image. It is one that is an example of the contested and constructed nature of authenticity, which means the events do not necessarily present an accurate picture but rather one that the organizers and many of the participants (both passive and active) wish to buy into. The Yukon Quest, which is a 1000-mile race that was first run in 1984 (Firth, 1998), fits the iconic image of the sport of dog sledding very nicely as does the Iditarod, which was first run in 1967 (Hood, 1996). As befits an iconic sporting event, both now attract major sponsors and are covered on global television. The result, Firth (1998: vi) suggested, is that many Europeans now refer to the Yukon Quest as 'winter's Tour de France', comparing it to another iconic sporting event in the process.

In an ironic feedback loop the success of events such as the Iditarod and Yukon Quest has morphed them from just sporting events with cultural roots and associated implications into a multi-billion dollar business (Hood, 1996) where once again the dogs and mushers are effectively working. The difference is that instead of transporting goods and people for 'work' the participants are now helping to sell dog food to a world market, testing and marketing new equipment to an increasing population of amateur racers and selling all the other brands associated with the events. Even the transporting of people is back on the agenda now for sled dogs, thanks to the success of events such as the Iditarod, as we see tourists paying to be transported along the route of the race in sleds behind the last competitors (Hood, 1996).

Sled dog rides as a tourist attraction are not only restricted to following the iconic races. Rather, they have expanded to become something that tourists can do for anything ranging from a short afternoon break from their skiing holiday in destinations such as Whistler, Canada, to multi-day tours that are often operated as a sideline by those professional mushers who race in events such as the Quest and Iditarod (Coppinger, 1977; Evans, 2008). Examples of dog mushing holidays abound on the Internet across the snowscapes of Canada, the USA and Europe. The dogs have also become a tourist attraction in their own right as some tours now offer people the chance to get up close with the pups in their enclosures as seen in Fig. 2.2. Such an activity, while undoubtedly attractive to the tourist, serves an important purpose for the development of the dog. Through the constant attention they are given by a continuous stream of visitors they become accustomed to the human contact that is an integral part of the sled dog tourism experience, as differentiated from the life of the working sled dog. While it may be argued that only sociable dogs make the grade in this form of sled dog work, it is true that the dogs who get to meet and greet the visitors thoroughly enjoy doing so and love the attention they receive in return.

Today, dog sledding is a popular sport in many parts of the world, with reports of a team even being run on the beaches of Hawaii in the 1970s (Coppinger, 1977), and has its own international organization, the International Sled Dog Racing Association, which was founded in 1966 (Palmer, 1983). In North America the sport features a mix of happy amateurs and a strong professional contingent whereas in places such as Europe it is almost entirely a pastime of the amateur (Firth, 1998). The nature of the races also differs outside of the sled dogging spiritual home, with events tending to be across much shorter distances. This may be a reflection of the amateur status of most participants, the lack of history of sledding as a means of transport, differences in the amount of appropriate available space and different land access regulations.

Fig. 2.2. Puppy petting as part of a sled dog tour.

Within the context of this section, the important distinction between sled dog racing in Alaska and northern Canada, and elsewhere in the world, is that in the former it is clearly something that has stemmed from the use of sled dogs for work whereas in the latter it has only ever been a sport. Yet today it is a popular global sport with many countries running their own national championships and the existence of a European Championships since 1984 (Firth, 1998). Interestingly though it has yet to become a sport of the Winter Olympics despite having been a demonstration sport at the 1932 Olympics at Lake Placid (Firth, 1998).

It is interesting to see that sledding today is firmly associated in the minds of many with the Husky. Yet as Coppinger (1977) noted, some of the earliest sled dogs are likely to have been the ancestors of the modern Samoyed, though how much they are comparable to the Samoyed of today is open to debate. More recently, the early outdoorsmen and explorers of Canada and the northern states of the USA utilized basically any dogs they could find that had stamina and strength, with mongrels the most common among them (Coppinger, 1977). Furthermore, it is clear that throughout the history of the sport of sled dog racing almost every type of dog has been utilized either as part of a team or as an entire one, including – according to Coppinger (1977) – Walker Coonhounds, Border Collies, Scotch Collies, Golden Retrievers, Labrador Retrievers, Pointers, Dalmatians, Airedales, German Shepherds, Belgian Shepherds, Doberman Pinschers and Weimaraners.

If you visit the dog sled operators of today you are unlikely to find many dogs who would meet the breed standards of a Husky, as defined by the Kennel Club, or any other northern breed. Indeed, my own experience of an operator in Austria in 2013 was that alongside Huskies he was running a couple of Husky/Collie crosses, arguing that the cross offered exemplar strength and endurance as well as being easier to train and more friendly towards guests of the business than pure Huskies. Similarly, the husband of a couple interviewed in Switzerland in 2013 who ran a sled dog tour operation had previously raced sled dogs with a team of collies at one stage and one mixed with 50% collies and 50% Huskies. The picture in Fig. 2.2 also clearly shows that sled dog operators do not always use Huskies though at the same time most advertise their businesses with pictures of this breed. It appears to have been the Europeans who most enthusiastically bought into the idealized image of the Husky as 'the' sled dog. For example, the Swiss Club for Northern Dogs, which was set up in 1959, restricted entry to its races to northern purebred dogs only, such as 'the Siberian Husky, the Alaskan Malamute, the Bearhound, the Finnish Spitz, the Norwegian Elkhound and the Akita' (Coppinger, 1977: 143).

Even though the search and rescue dogs are clearly working when out in search of lost people, there is a strong element of leisure in the whole experience of these dogs and their handlers, who tend to be volunteers (leaving aside for the moment the whole concept of whether the dog actually 'volunteers'). With volunteering undertaken during one's free time, for at least partially internally driven motivations and desires, it has been widely recognized as a form of leisure (Henderson, 1984; Stebbins, 1996). In this way, the meet and greet dogs at airports and their owners may be said to be engaging in leisure as much as work. This neatly exemplifies the problematic state of attempts to view leisure and work as a binary when the reality is clearly much more complex and dependent on the perception of the individual involved. However, in these instances it is not a case of the 'individual' involved, but of the individuals involved (i.e. the dog and its owner). Is the activity being engaged in by both felt as work, leisure or a mixture of both by both participants? This is a question that needs more detailed analysis to be able to answer but such work should be situated in the context of recognizing the 'with' nature of the relation between dogs and their owners and the social agency and of both.

In the blurring of the divide between work and leisure for dogs and arguably also for their owners (or handlers, given that dogs are not always owned by those who work with them daily) we see the potential for multiple meanings to be associated with dogs in any 'one' activity. For example, in the contemporary world of dog sledding the dog can be seen as object, tool, leisured creature (discussed in detail in Chapter 4) and leisure companion to humans. It has been suggested that work, or at least work in a quasi-form through sport, can be utilized as a means of giving dogs a value of self-worth. In an interview with Scotty Allan, one of the great early dog sled racers at the beginning of the 20th century, he stated: 'Maybe it [the publicity stemming from his races and wins] will bring about a world-wide change in regard to dogs; change useless pets all over the earth into worthwhile, self-respecting animals – give them useful work. Dogs are like humans in that they are better off and happier if they have responsibilities' (Garst, 1948: 4). This quotation is interesting in many ways for it shows Allan viewed dogs as sentient beings and sought ways to ensure their happiness. At the same time it shows the distain of this outdoorsman for anything so frivolous, in his view, as pets.

Overall, this chapter has aimed to show the diversity of the roles working dogs play in the leisure experience and how many of these roles have, over time, morphed into sport and leisure pursuits. In relation to the dogs, the dominant theme of the chapter has been of them as objects or tools that have been utilized by humans. In this way they fit the conceptualization of dogs as objects that was discussed in Chapter 1 with all the related implications relating to their rights and welfare. Whether these dogs really are only objects or are at least treated as such by their owners will be discussed in Chapter 3.

3 Sport Dogs

Introduction: Defining Sport Dogs

Within this chapter 'sport dogs' are defined as canines that are required to take part in a sporting activity at the behest of their human owners. These sport dogs are distinguished from the working dogs and leisured dogs who form the foci of Chapters 2 and 4 though the shifting boundaries between them are recognized. Sport dogs are animals used by humans in the leisure environment in a formal sporting event for recreational purposes and/or in search of a victory in an event. This chapter will look at the extent and nature of a variety of sporting activities where dogs play a prominent/dominant role and will look at changes in these sports across space and time. This analysis will be situated within discussions of changing social norms and values relating to the rights of animals in general and dogs in particular, including the use of representations of sport dogs as a means of constructing personal identity.

The range of sports in which dogs have taken and/or still take part is truly impressive and ranges from widely known sports to those that are best described as 'fringe' activities known by relatively few people beyond their active participants. In this way the range of dog sports is arguably very similar to that of sports in general. A list of sports in which dogs take part is provided in Table 3.1; while it may be desirable to say this is an exhaustive list such a claim is avoided due to the knowledge that new sports appear to be emerging frequently and that finding 'every' niche sport is difficult if not impossible. My publisher made a logical plea for ordering the material in Table 3.1, potentially differentiating between those sports that are still actively engaged in and those that have faded into history. The problem is that while the prominence of some of these sports may have changed and the nature of others has morphed over time it is very difficult to say with any certainty that any of the sports in Table 3.1 are confined to history. Consequently, beyond grouping the sports and providing brief details

© N. Carr 2014. *Dogs in the Leisure Experience* (N. Carr)

Table 3.1. Dog sports.

Sport	Brief description
Bull-baiting	A bull is positioned to enable several dogs to attack it with the bull ultimately being killed
Badger baiting	Entails placing dogs in a badger's burrow with the intention of seeing which is the first to kill the badger (Smith, 2011)
Other animals used in baiting with dogs include bears, otters, horses, mules, monkeys, wallabies, kangaroos, lions. Racoon and baboon baiting was also noted by Fox (1888)	References to these kinds of baiting can be found in Scott (1820), Strutt (1875), Fox (1888) and Ash (1934)
Ratting	Normally a case of seeing how many rats a dog can kill in a set time but, according to Fitz-Barnard (1975), there have been instances where dogs and humans have been pitted against one another to see which can kill more rats
Earthdog	'Terriers run through a narrow tunnel in the ground that has wooden sides and ceiling and a dirt floor. At the end of the tunnel are caged rats, which the terriers must "work." Working the prey may mean barking, growling or scratching at the cage' (Mehus-Roes, 2009: 22). Mehus-Roes also mentions an emergent version of the sport called 'strongdog', which is for larger breeds and entails them dragging a stuffed badger skin out of the ground. These are 'staged' versions of the work to catch and kill vermin that was traditionally undertaken by terriers
Dog fights	Discussed in detail later in this chapter
Dog and man fights	'a man fighting a bull-dog with his fists. Both combatants were attached to stakes by a chain' (Fitz-Barnard, 1975: 191)
Hare hunting	On horseback, with the use of hounds
Otter hunting	Was focused on freshwater otters and used Otter Hounds (bred specifically for the task). There were approximately 20 packs of hounds used for the sport in Great Britain in the early 1900s (Cameron, 1908)
Conger eel hunting	Reportedly occurred in Normandy, France (Jesse, 1866a)
The lesser chase, *la petite chasse*	The following have all been hunted using dogs 'the BADGER, MARTEN CAT, and SQUIRREL; the POLECAT and STOAT' as well as the wildcat (Scott, 1820: 445)
Fox hunting	Undertaken on horseback with a pack of Foxhounds
Fox hunting with fell hounds	Undertaken on foot due to the steepness and unevenness of the terrain in the wilder regions of the UK (Drabble, 1989)

Continued

Table 3.1. Continued.

Sport	Brief description
Beagling	The use of a pack of beagles to hunt for hares on foot (Longman, 1896)
Truffle hunting	Reference is made to truffle dogs in as early as 1866 by Jesse (1886a) and also by Stonehenge in 1875. Today, although a variety of breeds of dog appear to be used to sniff out this fungus, the Lagotto Romagnolo appears to be most closely associated with the activity
Private hare coursing	The chasing of hares by hounds for the private indulgence of the owner
Public hare coursing	The chasing of hares by hounds in a public setting in which betting is a central feature. It is a more recent form of coursing than the private version
Enclosed public hare coursing	Differentiated from public hare coursing in that the activity takes place in a fenced-in area. The popularity of the sport was short-lived in the late 1800s in the UK (Ash, 1935)
Coyote coursing	A sport undertaken with the people on horseback or in cars (Almirall, undated)
Other animals used in coursing include rabbits, deer, wallabies and kangaroos	In all coursing the hound, rather than its human owner, is the killer of the prey (Salmon, 1977)
Lure coursing	Like live coursing, lure coursing is undertaken outside of arenas such as those used for Greyhound racing but a lure is used as a replacement for a live animal (Mehus-Roes, 2009)
Greyhound racing	In Greyhound racing the live hare of coursing is replaced by a mechanical lure. The sport emerged out of America, where the first track was opened in 1921 (National Greyhound Racing Club and Genders, 1990)
Greyhound hurdling	Never as popular a sport as Greyhound racing but undertaken at the same venues
Whippet racing	The racing of Whippets is only undertaken on an amateur basis
Afghan racing	Differs from Greyhound racing in that it is an amateur sport without any formal betting industry involvement
Dog sledding	Involves the pulling of a sled by a number of dogs (the specific number varies across different races) guided by a 'musher'. Racing occurs over a range of distances including the ultra-long iconic events that are examined later in this chapter
Skijoring	'a driver on a pair of skis is pulled by a team of one, two, or three dogs' (Flanders, 1989: 96). It is in effect a combination of cross-country skiing and dog sledding (Mehus-Roes, 2009)

Continued

Table 3.1. Continued.

Sport	Brief description
Pulka racing	A low-profile sled (pulka) is pulled by a dog or dogs with musher skiing behind attached by a long bungee (Hood, 1996)
Lead-dog contests	A test of gee/haw skills used in dog sledding by requiring 'dogs to negotiate a set course successfully' (Hood, 1996: 384)
Stampede/scramble races	Dog mushers begin the race lying in a sleeping bag, must then pack sled, harness team, then go (Hood, 1996)
Weight pulling	Dogs pull sleds or carts on wheels or tracks onto which weights are incrementally placed. As with human weightlifting, dogs are categorized by size to allow all dogs to compete (Hood, 1996; Mehus-Roes, 2009)
Gig racing (also known as dryland mushing)	Three- or four-wheeled carts raced with sled dogs where there is a lack of snow (Hood, 1996; Sled Dog Association of Scotland, 2007b).
Scootering	One or more dogs pull a two-wheeled scooter with a musher on it (Sled Dog Association of Scotland, 2007b).
Bikejoring	One or more dogs pull the musher on a bike (Sled Dog Association of Scotland, 2007b).
Carting (drafting/driving)	Often undertaken as a non-competitive leisure activity but also undertaken as a sport (Mehus-Roes, 2009)
Canicross	Cross-country running while hitched to a single dog (Sled Dog Association of Scotland, 2007b; Steele, 2007).
Field trials/gun dog trials	Events that focus on the demonstration of the required traits for specific types of dogs depending on what role they have been traditionally bred to fulfil
Sheepdog trials/herding	The former is focused on the herding of sheep while the latter can include other animals such as cattle and ducks (Mehus-Roes, 2009)
Schutzhund	A form of dog trial to test protection dog traits (Mehus-Roes, 2009). It is basically the same as ring sport (Gillespie *et al.*, 2002)
Police dog trials	A spectator event
Water rescue	'Dogs are tested on their ability to save multiple victims, take a boat line from one boat to another, tow a drifting boat to shore, and rescue an unconscious victim from under a capsized boat' (Mehus-Roes, 2009: 27)
Tracking	Focuses on the following of a predetermined scent trail (Mehus-Roes, 2009). It is the basis of search and rescue dogs' work (American Kennel Club, 2012b)

Continued

Table 3.1. Continued.

Sport	Brief description
Dog agility	Dogs must run through an obstacle course as quickly and with as few faults as possible (Mehus-Roes, 2009)
Flyball	Involves a team of four dogs and handlers, with the dogs running a fixed length, catching a ball that they cause to pop out of a box and returning with it to their handler (Mehus-Roes, 2009)
Obedience	Is defined as: 'A natural extension of basic dog training' but one that goes well beyond the level of obedience training associated with the average pet dog (Mehus-Roes, 2009: 24)
Rally	'Dogs follow a course with a number of stations; at each one is an instruction to perform a specific [obedience] command' (Mehus-Roes, 2009: 25)
Canine freestyle/dog dancing/ heelwork to music	'Dogs and their handlers perform choreographed routines in time to music, sometimes with props and costumes' (Mehus-Roes, 2009: 19). There are an estimated 90 clubs in the UK offering dog dancing activities (Copping, 2012)
Disc dog	Involves the throwing of a disc by the handler and catching of it by a dog. The sport incorporates two events: distance and accuracy, and freestyle, with the former being self-explanatory and the latter involving choreographed movements set to music (Mehus-Roes, 2009)
Dock jumping	Focused on measuring the distance a dog can jump into water (Mehus-Roes, 2009)
Dog show	Discussed in detail later in this chapter

of those that are more obscure, I have resisted the temptation to structure the material in the table. Rather, examples of the difficulty associated with doing so are highlighted throughout this chapter.

While a case could be made for a detailed analysis of all the sports listed in Table 3.1 such an undertaking is beyond the limits of this book (it would represent at least one book in its own right and probably more). Rather, this chapter will be selective in the dog sports it discusses, seeking to use them as exemplars of how dogs are used in sport and viewed by their human owners and the spectators of the sports.

The nature of the sports in which dogs take part, just like any other sport, are subject to change over time in response to changing circumstances that lie outside of the control of these sports. Changes in the economic climate, societal views about the rights and welfare of animals, land ownership rules and regulations, and the development of new leisure experiences have arguably all played a role in changing the nature of sport dogs over time. Illustrations of this will be provided in the following sections, demonstrating how and why blood sports and dog shows have risen and fallen in popularity and changed both the sports and the dogs in the process.

Dog Shows

If asked to define 'dog shows' the first image likely to come into one's mind is that of Crufts, where purebred dogs are paraded around a judge and the 'best in show' is selected. However, dog shows encompass a far wider array of events that all have as their basis a desire to highlight particular characteristics of different breeds of dog, and in doing so encourage the development of these traits to raise the standard of desired behaviour and physique among specific breeds. The first dog show appears to have taken place in 1775 and was focused on presenting the quality of hounds (Wagstaff, 1995). As such, this show was created to highlight the values of a working dog rather than purely as a place for a demonstration of the prowess of dog breeders in a sporting or leisure context. The distinction between working dog shows and dog shows as we know them today as places primarily for the showing of the physical characteristics rather than the abilities of dogs is one that has evolved over time. The initial shows, as with the one noted by Wagstaff were, it seems, mainly focused on the working dog and within this context particularly the sporting dog (Jackson, 1990), which in the early days of the shows can be more accurately read as hunting dogs. Consequently, there is some disagreement about when the first dog show was held. Indeed, Pearce (1874) and Halsall (1982) suggested that the first dog show did not occur until 1859 and that it took place in Newcastle, UK. Even then we had to wait over 30 years more before the arrival of the iconic dog show, Crufts. It was in 1891 that Charles Cruft held the first Crufts, though it was not until the following year that the first show under Kennel Club rules and regulations was held (Wagstaff, 1995). While the Kennel Club may well be synonymous with Crufts, the organization was actually originally formed in 1873 to regulate the conduct of all dog trials and later shows (Crufts, undated).

The focus of those involved in breeding dogs for dog shows became, relatively quickly, the look of the dog rather than any qualities that it may previously have been bred for. These 'looks' are defined by the 'breed standard' for the dog, something that is set by a selective group of breeders under the auspices of breed societies; these are largely run by breeders and judges who are or were breeders themselves (Bradshaw, 2011). With the focus of those competing in dog shows being the creation of the perfect-looking dog (Bradshaw, 2011) the other characteristics of these dogs have arguably been ignored or at least forced into a poor second position. Consequently, as Ash (1935) noted with specific reference to Greyhounds, a good show Greyhound does not need to be a good courser or, more recently, runner. Such a view clearly mirrors the concerns with the evolution of the sheepdog into a show dog, as discussed in Chapter 2. Similarly, in commenting on breed standards, Herzog (2010: 123) noted that 'While breed standards pay lip service to a dog's temperament, in reality there is more emphasis on the color of the rims of its eyes and shape of its head than on traits that would make it fun to live with.'

While initially focused solely on the showing of breeds, highlighting their physical characteristics rather than any mental or physical abilities, Crufts has evolved in line with changing social trends relating to dogs in leisure and sport. Consequently, by the early 1950s dog obedience as a sport had gained a position in the Crufts calendar (Wagstaff, 1995). Today the dog show phenomenon is huge, with the American Kennel Club (AKC) sanctioning and licensing over 16,000 events each year (American Kennel Club, undated, a). Alongside this, in the USA in 2010 there were 185 breed-specific clubs (American Kennel Club, 2010). While these may well incorporate a number of individuals who breed and show dogs for a living, there will be a significant number of others for whom it is a leisure activity, albeit often a very serious one.

The scale of dog shows and their development can be seen by looking at the number of dogs entered at Crufts each year. Figure 3.1 shows there was a significant increase in the number of dogs being entered at Crufts between 1891 and 2012, with the largest number of entrants to date having been 23,000 in 2008. The number of human visitors to the event peaked at 160,000 in 2008 before declining to a low of 138,000 in 2011 then bouncing back to 145,000 in 2012 (personal communication with the Kennel Club, 2012). The decline in visitor numbers between 2008 and 2011 has arguably been a result of the negative publicity the Kennel Club and Crufts have been dealing with regarding the inbreeding of purebred dogs and associated health problems that stemmed from a BBC production aired in August 2008. Analysis of the reasons for the growth in visitor numbers in 2012 is beyond the scope of this book but such work would certainly be of value. The American equivalent of Crufts, the Westminster Kennel Club dog show, attracts an audience of 3 million people each year (Martin, 2013).

The economic implications of dog shows are also significant. In the case of America, it has been estimated that attending shows run under the auspices of the AKC generates US$330 million of consumer spending each year, with most of it being spent on items such as accommodation, food and transportation (American Kennel Club, undated, a). This clearly links these events to the wider hospitality and tourism industry. It is also clear that involvement in the sport can be a very expensive business. While there may still be room for the willing amateur to dabble, just as there is in all sports, there is a need for the investment of significant sums of money to play at the top. 'Show quality'

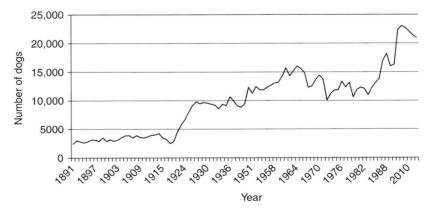

Fig. 3.1. Number of dogs entered at Crufts. (From: Jackson, 1990 (for 1891–1990); personal communication with the Kennel Club (for 2007–2012).)

dogs, as Herzog (2010) noted, will cost several thousand dollars, and many dog show contestants now feel the need to employ someone to parade their animal around the show arena. To put these costs into perspective, my current dog is from the Otago Society for the Prevention of Cruelty to Animals where adoption of a dog costs NZ$250, which includes neutering, vaccinations and microchipping.

Dog shows and the breeding processes that have become associated with them have proved to be highly controversial. Most recently there has been concern that the breeding practices undertaken by at least a segment of those involved with dog shows has led to genetic mutations that can cause significant discomfort/distress to dogs and threaten the long-term viability of some breeds (Rooney *et al.*, 2009; Herzog, 2010). As noted above, this came to a head with the airing of a documentary by the BBC in 2008 that resulted in the RSPCA, Dogs Trust and People's Dispensary for Sick Animals, and the pet food manufacturers Pedigree and Hills Pet Nutrition withdrawing their support of Crufts (Bateson, 2010). The BBC also made the decision not to provide coverage of the 2009 event (Jones, 2008). However, it is important to note that the concerns voiced by the BBC production had already begun to be aired in a variety of publications (Crispin, 2011), though not in a manner that was able to reach the general public in the same way as the BBC did. Crispin (2011) noted the earliest of these publications was in 1963 and was actually undertaken at the request of the Kennel Club, a point that confirms the comment made to me by members of the Kennel Club in 2012 (personal communication) that the BBC documentary was based largely on material gathered by or at the behest of the Kennel Club.

While public concern with the practices of at least some dog breeders may be a recent phenomenon the issue itself is nothing new. Indeed, writing in 1927, Whyte recognized that while: 'Pedigree itself is alright; it is the misuse of pedigree that is harmful' (p. 112). With specific reference to the Border Collie, Whyte suggested that the focus in the show arena on the physical appearance of the Collie had led to a dumbing down of the animal, as noted in Chapter 2.

Faced with public outcry and a resultant downturn in sponsorship and attendance, in 2012 Crufts instigated vet checks on all best of breed winners whose breed has been deemed as being most at risk of problems stemming from inbreeding. This encompassed 15 breeds in total (Kennel Club, 2012). The Kennel Club has also moved to ban the registering of pedigree dogs bred from the mating of first-degree relatives (Nicholas, 2011). Such steps are arguably only small ones, but it is true that organizations such as the Kennel Club need breeders and breed societies to follow any direction the Club gives; so rapid, drastic changes, however desirable, are arguably likely to be unproductive as breeders and societies could simply fail to accept them.

The breeding of dogs to 'show standard' speaks volumes about concerns with animal rights and welfare. While it may well be unfair to label all breeders and show competitors as 'uncaring', the rules and standards that drive the processes of dog shows objectify dogs. In the process they ignore the rights of dogs in preference of meeting an ideal imposed upon them for no other reason than fashion. The result, by 2008, was unfortunately largely what Whyte had predicted: a misuse of pedigree that failed to be of any benefit to the dog or take any note of its rights and dignity as a sentient being.

The breeding and preparation of dogs for the show arena with the aim of presenting the perfect specimen that meets all of the 'breed standards' identifies the animals of the dog show as objects for the leisure pursuit of the human owner. Participation in dog shows, as in other leisure experiences, can aid the construction of the identity of the human self, as well as fostering a sense of pride, prestige and social status. In addition, the show circuit offers people an opportunity to become part of a subculture and in the process gain social interaction with like-minded individuals (Sanders, 1999). In all these instances it is possible to see the dog as an object of human leisure or a tool for the attainment of leisure-related goals. In these cases the rights, welfare and dignity of the dog can take second place (if considered at all) to the desires of the human owners.

While it is clear that dog shows have been in existence for well over 100 years, it cannot be claimed, as Mehus-Roes (2009: 12) attempts to, that: 'Conformation, the judging of purebred dogs against a written breed standard, is the granddaddy of organized dog sports.' Rather, as will be demonstrated in the next section of this chapter, there are many sports involving dogs that are far older and to which many of the lines of dogs who are now seen at dog shows have strong ties.

Dogs and Blood Sports

'Blood sports' is an emotive term that brings together conflicting views surrounding the hunting of a variety of animals and the use of fighting animals. These sports are grouped together under this heading because the blood of dogs or other animals is likely, though arguably not a necessity of the sport, to be spilt during a sporting event. While they may today be viewed in many countries with public disdain/repugnance, they are among the oldest of sports and many have at various stages been extremely popular among the general populace and members of high society. There are far too many of these sports to study them all in this book and consequently one with the longest history has been deliberately left out. This is the sport of coursing and its modern day incarnation, Greyhound racing. A detailed look at Greyhounds in sport will be available in a book I am editing that focuses on domesticated animals (Carr, forthcoming).

Baiting

The history of bull-baiting, where dogs are deliberately set upon a captive bull, can be traced back to at least the 12th century (Griffin, 2005). Whether it was first developed as a sport or as a means of improving the quality of the meat prior to the butchering of the bull appears to be debatable. However, by the 16th century its popularity as a sport among the common people and royalty in countries such as the UK was beyond doubt (Jesse, 1866b). It is important to note that by this time the baiting of bulls prior to slaughter for human consumption had long since ceased to be a widely held legal requirement (Griffin, 2005).

It was not until the end of the 1700s that the UK witnessed the demise of widely held and publicized bull-baiting events as public opinion in the country began the swing towards a recognition of the rights and welfare of animals that is arguably still taking place today. Although bull-baiting in the UK was outlawed in 1835 (Semencic, 1984) this Act of Parliament really only rubber-stamped a change in social values that had already taken place. This change had shifted the definition of bull-baiting from one of mainstream sport/ entertainment, where fans included the British monarchs James I, Charles I and Elizabeth I (Gniadek, 1993), to abhorrent inhumane treatment of animals (Griffin, 2005). Consequently, by the time the ban was enacted the popularity of the sport had already declined such that its cessation had already largely occurred by 1835 (Reid, 1980). Does this mean that baiting has been consigned to the history books? No: Gniadek (1993) identified the continuation of such practices with differing animals baited in different countries, such as the badger in the UK.

By the 16th century it is clear that a variety of animals other than bulls were being used for baiting by dogs, as seen in Table 3.1 and depicted in Fig. 3.2. All were set around the central theme of a pack of dogs being set on another animal – be it bull, bear or virtually anything else it seems – in an enclosed space for the purpose of seeing the dogs attack the animal and it in turn attempt to defend itself. Yet just as in the case of bull-baiting, the baiting of other animals seems to have its origins outside of the arena of human entertainment. Indeed, the baiting of monkeys was used as a method of testing dogs' abilities to attack horsemen at a time when dogs were used as a weapon in war, and bear-baiting seems to have its origins in the training of dogs to attack humans threatening the owners' home (Kalof, 2007). It is only later that such activities morphed into leisure experiences to be watched and bet upon.

Although baiting in all its variety was a popular sport in the UK, it is important to note that it was by no means restricted to that country. Rather,

Fig. 3.2. Horse baiting. (From: Strutt, 1875.)

baiting occurred at the same time in most European countries and for similar reasons (Kalof, 2007). It is also worth noting that the reasons for the demise of baiting outside of the UK are similar to those discussed with specific reference to that state. However, it is important to recognize that baiting is not a sport that has been entirely consigned to history. For example, as noted by the World Society for the Protection of Animals (2011) bear-baiting still occurs in Pakistan.

Dog fighting

Another dog blood sport with a long history is that of dog fighting. Indeed, it can be traced back as far as ancient Egypt, Rome and Babylon. Like baiting, dog fighting as a sport seems to have emerged from the training of dogs as weapons to be used in battles between human armies (Kalof and Taylor, 2007). In this way there is a similarity between the transfer from working dog to sports dog between the fighting dogs discussed here and the sled dogs and sheepdogs noted in Chapter 2.

More recently, dog fighting is known to have a history of at least several hundred years in Japan and to have been undertaken by Elizabeth I and James I in England (Daly, 2001). Indeed, public dog fighting events were commonplace throughout the UK right into the early 1800s (Griffin, 2005). Yet in 1835 such events were deemed illegal thanks to the Cruelty to Animals Act. Despite this ban there are reports of organized dog fights still taking place in parts of London well into the 1840s, albeit out of public view (Moss, 1961). While the popularity of dog fighting may have declined since its peak it still exists today in those countries where it has been deemed illegal. For example, Mehus-Roes (2009: 100) stated that: 'Although today dogfighting is illegal throughout the United States (and a felony in 48 states), it continues seemingly unabated.'

In countries where dog fighting is illegal it is an underground activity, confined to the dark corners of leisure (Meeks, 1974; Reid, 1980; Semencic, 1984; Gniadek, 1993). Indeed, when writing in 1888 Fox stated that dog fighting: 'although contrary to law, is still extensively carried on in many countries' (p. 9). In a comment that speaks volumes for the social acceptance, or lack thereof, of the ban on dog fighting in the UK from 1835 onwards Fox (1888: 9) went on to say: 'it [dog fighting] will no doubt receive a large share of the attention of all lovers of genuine sport for ages to come'. As well as being a source of entertainment in its own right, dog fighting appears to have been, and still be, a site for another popular leisure activity: that of gambling. Speaking in the 1930s in relation to dog fighting in the USA, Johns (1939: 11) pointed out that: 'At one American [dog] fight the stake holder is reported to have held over thirty thousand dollars,' something that allowed him to contend that it was by no means a poor man's sport.

Even in countries where it is not an illegal sport, dog fighting today tends to take place away from the limelight in the face of international condemnation and increasingly vocal domestic concerns about animal rights and welfare. The problem with dark leisure is, of course, that in taking place away from the public gaze it is very difficult to assess its extent. While there have been those who have suggested the growing popularity and continuation of dog fighting as a sport in countries such as the USA, UK, India and Japan at various times (i.e. Semencic, 1984; Gniadek, 1993; K9Obedience.co.uk, 2009), there is a dearth of proof to either support or refute such claims. Indeed, when asked in 2012 about dog fighting, the British Columbia Society for the Prevention of Cruelty to Animals (BCSPCA) reported that despite believing such activity did occur in their region it lacked any solid evidence to support this suspicion. Similarly, though pointing to an increase in the number of complaints about dog fighting registered by the RSPCA in the UK and the number of 'dangerous dogs' seized by the police as evidence of 'a huge rise in the number of dog fights', Siddique (2008) was unable to identify any actual increase in dog fighting (i.e. criminal convictions or arrests for dog fighting). Daly (2001) pointed to arrest figures for dog fighting in the UK in the 1990s (108 convictions for allowing dogs to fight or being at a fighting event, with the RSPCA itself claiming to have provided evidence that led to 97 convictions between 2007 and 2012 (Anonymous, 2012a)) as proof of the small scale of the sport. Nevertheless, care needs to be taken, as these figures report only on those caught and not necessarily all those taking part in the sport. Daly is, however, likely to be correct in suggesting that the UK's 1992 Dangerous Dogs Act has helped to curb the possession and breeding of dogs who have traditionally been used for fighting. At the same time, since dog fighting had already been illegal for over 150 years in the UK this act in and of itself is unlikely to stop dog fighting. Indeed, attempts to eradicate the sport from the UK seem to be no more successful now than they have been since the 1835 Animal Cruelty Act, with a core of supporters still keeping the sport alive (Daly, 2001). The concern about the current practice of dog fighting, as identified by Barry Fryer, Chief Superintendent at the RSPCA, is that: 'It is sad to say too, but I think it is probably the truth that we [those seeking to uncover and stop dog fighting] are just reaching the tip of the iceberg' (Anonymous, 2012a). In comparison to the UK, Kalof and Taylor (2007: 324) claimed that at the time of writing their paper there were: 'more than 40,000 dog fighters in the urban centers of the United States'. When all the concerns about the extent of dog fighting are taken together it becomes valid to suggest that there is a significant multinational, if not global, issue that needs to be addressed and also that more work needs to be done to truly identify its scale.

The continuation of dog fighting in countries such as the UK appears to be marked by changes in its nature. While the fight is still the focus, the location of the event is changing. The traditional formalized fights within constructed rings may still exist, but less structured, informal fights are also now being organized. These are, of course, much more difficult to monitor and prevent. This new type of fighting has been referred to as 'chain fighting' or 'rolling'. Harking back to the earlier history of dog fighting this has seen dog fights reported in parks in inner-city London, UK. It has also seen, supposedly, owners taking advantage of technology to place two fighting dogs in the lifts of high-rise buildings and let them fight from the top to the bottom of the building (Anonymous, 2009). There is clearly a need for much more research to critically assess the validity of what are little more than claims about the nature of dog fighting in the 21st century. Such work is, of course, not without danger given the illegal nature of the sport. In addition, there is a need to determine why, despite occasional arrests and convictions, there appears to be a significant disjuncture between the number of reports to organizations such as the RSPCA and the number of cases going before the courts. Finally, on the subject of dog fighting, while it may not be surprising given the technological era we live in it is nonetheless depressing to find that you can now download to your mobile phone an app that allows you to 'play' a game called *Dog Wars* that is in effect virtual dog fighting (Huston, 2011). Not only does this game continue the objectification of the dog, it potentially makes it 'cool' to engage in dog fighting, be it real or simulated. The debate about the spillover of notions and concepts from virtual reality to the world of flesh and blood is a long and ongoing one that cannot be covered in this book. Suffice to say that while something like *Dog Wars* may not encourage real dog fighting and the objectification of dogs it does nothing to discourage either of these.

Hunting

The fox hunt emerged as the pre-eminent hunting activity of the elite of rural English society around the 17th century (Jobson-Scott, 1933), arguably in response to the loss of more desirable hunting adversaries from the landscape. However, the first recorded fox hunt with hounds in the UK was in 1534 (Jack, 2009). It has never been an animal hunted for food and though it was at one time hunted in order to reduce the population's impact on farm stock (Tantara, 1893) such days are long gone. Within this context it is a sport, like many others that have emerged since the Industrial Revolution, which has developed a set of regulations and a specific code of conduct/manners (Moss, 1961; Elias and Dunning, 2008). Within this context the actual killing of a fox becomes only a minor part of fox hunting. Instead, dressing appropriately, taking part in all the associated pre-, during and post-hunt activities, and breeding and caring for the necessary animals (i.e. horses and Foxhounds) are arguably the major components of the leisure experience of fox hunting even if the killing of the fox remains a crucial moment in the whole experience. The centrality of the hound to the experience of fox hunting was eloquently summed up by Cox (1697: 4) who stated: 'No Musick can be more ravishingly delightful than a Pack of Hounds in fully Cry, to such a Man whose Heart and Ears are so happy to be set to the tune of such charming Instruments.' This view of fox hunting has all the hallmarks of a leisure experience grounded in the fulfilment of personal desire through the feeling of pleasure.

The construction of a lifestyle around fox hunting can also be said to have developed around beagling. As one ardent supporter stated: 'Through hunting, I have been to more enjoyable functions and met more charming people than through anything else. This is only one of the many reasons that no amount of attempted brain washing by intellectual "anti's" will ever change my views on the sport' (Lloyd, 1971: 65). Lloyd also affirmed the central part of the breeding of the dogs to the leisure experience and the walk and exercise in the rural environment offered by the sport of beagling. Similarly, Scott (1820) has identified the healthy exercise afforded by sports such as beagling and fox hunting as one of the main benefits claimed by their adherents.

While it may not be seen or claimed as the main reason for partaking in many blood sports, the control of a specific animal population has been identified as a rationale for such pursuits (Scott, 1820). Alternatively, there have been persuasive arguments made by the hunting lobby that by managing the species to be hunted, those involved in such sports are actually ensuring the health and maintenance of populations that may otherwise have been threatened with extinction (Griffin, 2007) as a result of having been classified as vermin. Indeed, Salmon (1977: 114) has claimed that: 'Where coursing is practiced the hounds have served to control the population and strengthen and improve the quarry they hunt.'

By the 1870s it was estimated that there were approximately 120 packs of Foxhounds in England and Wales (Stonehenge, 1875). By this time fox hunting was not a sport reserved only for those in the UK; rather it had spread as the emigrants from that state had spread out across the globe. In Australia the Adelaide Hunt was the first to be formed, in 1842 (Cameron-Kennedy, 1991).

Yet the rise of the fox hunt as a leisure activity coincided in the UK with the rise of public concern about animal welfare. Arguably this is also tied to a period when the population was shifting from rural locations to urban centres and in the process losing its links to a rural reality of human–animal relations (Borsay, 2006). As a result, even in the 1800s the proponents of fox hunting had to defend their leisure pursuit. Calls upon the Christian Bible were made to point out that God had placed all animals on earth for the use of man, making fox hunting permissible by default. It was further claimed that the construction of the sport always gave the fox a 'sporting chance' of escape (missing the point that it was only a sport or game for the human participants and rather a matter of life or death for the fox). Finally, attempts were made to elevate the sport of fox hunting above the 'common' blood sports such as cockfighting and baiting; to give it legitimacy by appealing to its nobility (Scott, 1820), something that had been noted as a key feature of the sport by Cox as early as 1697. Indeed, Stonehenge (1875: 156) goes so far as to state that: 'The NOBLE SCIENCE, as fox-hunting is called by it votaries, is, by commen consent, allowed to be the perfection of hunting.' The 'nobility' of fox hunting and probably even more importantly of fox hunters was also noted in 1788 by Blane. Here we see a reinvention of a notion that had long been around in the sport hunting environment: that fox hunting can be differentiated from a simple case of hunting where the death of the prey is the focus of attention, to a sport for gentlemen. This is highlighted in Blane's (1788: 55–56) reading of the work on coursing by the Roman, Arrian, in which he stated:

> The true Sportsman does not take out his dogs to destroy the Hares, but for the sake of the course, and the contest between the dogs and the Hare, and is glad if the Hare escapes, and if she flies to some brake that is too thin to hide her, and tries to conceal herself, and seems to decline the contest, he will call off the dogs, especially if she has run well.

The fight to preserve or ban fox hunting in the UK would continue until it was finally banned in 2004. It would see opponents taking extreme measures to stop the hunts and proponents marching on London in 1998 in their hundreds of thousands to state the case for the continuation of the hunt (Griffin, 2007). While hunting with hounds (not just the hunting of foxes but the hunting of all animals with hounds) has now been banned in the UK and in Germany this is not a global phenomenon or even a European one. Indeed, as of the end of 2012 hunting with hounds was still legal in France where the anti-hunting lobby is relatively small and seems unlikely to oversee a ban in the foreseeable future (Astier, 2012).

Today in the UK, the debate continues to rage, with supporters of fox hunting continuing to hope for the overturning of the ban. In the meantime they are allowed to continue to 'hunt', though instead of chasing live foxes, a fake scent trail is used. Many hunt enthusiasts see this as an unsatisfactory situation, yet on the face of it these events still give humans the opportunity to explore the countryside as they did when chasing a live fox, to engage in the same intricacies associated with the sport and for the dogs to be exercised in a manner in keeping with the hunting of live foxes. If differences in the nature of the dog are required to follow a scent trail rather than a live animal then it can be argued that the highly skilled breeders of Foxhounds will be able to develop their packs to cope with the changing nature of the sport in a relatively short period of time. Indeed, the challenge of doing so could be seen as an inherent part of the leisure experience. The main concern with the current law in the UK that bans live fox hunting but allows packs of Foxhounds to continue to follow scent trails is what happens if in the course of the latter they disturb a fox and then chase it. Under the current law this is legal but it provides a huge grey area that is satisfactory to neither the fox hunting fraternity nor the anti-hunting lobby. The easiest answer of course is to ban even scent trails for Foxhound packs but that would surely be the death knell for all these animals. Mass destruction of these dogs would result, given that rehoming them as pets is not an option and their reason for existence as a tool of a sport would be removed. For those, including myself, who value the preservation of the fox and see its hunting as unsavoury we must recognize that banning hunting has equally unpleasant consequences for another animal: the dog.

As well as being a leisure experience, fox hunting and the trialling of hounds that is closely associated with it have been utilized by the tourism industry to promote destinations to potential visitors. The aim here would appear to have been to promote a destination in line with the social construction of the rural idyll. An analysis of the tourism brochures produced by the town of Keswick in the centre of the English Lake District between the early 1900s and 2008 demonstrates that up until 1981 pictures of hounds being used to hunt on foot (the hilly nature of much of the terrain preventing horse-mounted hunting) were a common feature of this promotional material. In comparison, the first time that hound trials were pictured in the brochures was 1981 and they have appeared sporadically since then until their most recent appearance in 2006. It may be suggested that not only do these pictures speak volumes about the construction of destinations to fit preconceived images of rural ideals that are held by urban visitors, but that the removal of pictures of hunting with hounds reflects the changing opinion in the UK regarding the acceptability of this form of sport. With the anti-hunting lobby dominated by an urban population, the same target population of the Keswick tourism industry, it is no surprise that as the calls for banning hunting began to grow in the 1980s the brochures sought to distance the destination from such activities while at least to an extent still trying to provide an image of traditional rurality in the form of a more acceptable hound trial rather than a hunt.

Going back to the earliest images of dogs in the Keswick brochures it is interesting to see the dog depicted in Fig. 3.3. Today, this image speaks of a socially unacceptable blood sport, that of otter hunting, and even one that by the time of its publication was outside the mainstream of blood sports. The trend in the Keswick brochures in terms of their depiction of the working dog and rural landscape has arguably seen a move away from the reality of rural life towards a more airbrushed version. In this, the authenticity is what the urban visitor wishes to believe and see rather than what may have happened, and indeed arguably would still happen, if urban politics did not dictate the rural lifestyle so strongly.

Fig. 3.3. Otter hunting depicted in Keswick tourism brochure (circa 1910s), UK. (Photo courtesy of Keswick Tourism Association, UK.)

Where does the dog fit in?

It may be argued that in blood sports the dog is nothing more than a tool to be utilized by humans in pursuit of their own pleasure. As such it is akin only to a fishing rod or a gun. Yet if this is the case then how does the claim by Cameron-Kennedy (1991: 2) that: 'The true foxhunter regards the knowledge and interest in hounds as infinitely more important than the ability to ride after them' fit in? Here we see a proponent of the fox hunt espousing the Foxhound as the focus of his leisure. Such a focus was restated in an interview with one of the UK's leading experts on Foxhound breeding for hunting in an interview in 2012. However, it is still the focus on a tool; a highly valued one to be sure, but a tool nonetheless. The focus is in its way no different from that applied by the trout fisherman to his lures. The same could be said of the puppy shows noted by Collier (1899) as being an integral part of the fox hunting experience where the year's pups are displayed and assessed for their potential as part of the pack. The devotion that goes on behind the scenes in the creation of the perfect pack – for the perfect hound is only perfect within the context of the pack in which it is situated – is exemplified by the following statement by Collier (1899: 40):

> The sire and dam of a foxhound are selected with the care and with the minute observation of special qualities which the English squire has so conspicuously displayed in the breeding of the wonderful animals that he, and he alone, it would appear, has set before the admiring gaze of the world.

Here we see the hallmarks of Stebbins' (2007) concept of serious leisure, where the work of breeding the perfect pack of Foxhounds requires skills and knowledge accrued over a lifetime. Yet still, for all the devotion lavished on the breeding of hounds they are still objects of human leisure (both in the breeding and the hunting of foxes).

It may be difficult within blood sports to see the dog as anything other than an object or tool, even if a highly prized one. This is because to do otherwise is to admit that the animal may have sentience, to be capable of feelings such as fear and pain. If these thoughts were allowed entry to the arena of those who use dogs in pursuit of blood sports then questions would have to be asked of the legitimacy of their own actions in placing their dogs in the arena of a blood sport. Such a blinkered state is not unique to blood sports proponents but is instead depressingly widespread.

It is interesting to note that at the time of the initial experiment in Greyhound racing in North London in 1876 (Ash, 1935; Belton, 2002) *The Times* (quoted in Croxton Smith, 1927: 3) commented:

> The new sport is undoubtedly an exciting and interesting one. It is, perhaps, entitled to the commendation bestowed upon it by the promoters. 'It is,' they say, 'well worthy of the attention of the opponents of sports involving cruelty to animals, as it will afford an innocent recreation to all, without the faintest shadow of the reproach of cruelty attaching to it'.

This speaks of a recognition of the growing public view against blood sports but misses the point that cruelty can come in a variety of guises and not just in the death of an animal at the mouth of a hound. It misses the point that Greyhound racing can be cruel for the hounds involved if their welfare is not considered. The construction of the racing Greyhound as an object is clearly still strong given the focus of the work undertaken by Payne (2013a) at the behest of the Greyhound Board of Great Britain (GBGB). This work focused on the spaying of bitches or the use of oestrus suppressants to prevent a drop in the performance levels of these animals during their dioestral period. Such work has nothing to do with the welfare of the animal and everything to do with the competitiveness of the dog as an object. While it may be argued that placing a dog on the pill or having it spayed does not 'hurt' the dog, this is to miss the point that it fails to take into consideration the rights of the dog as a sentient being. Instead, such rights are ignored in favour of the potential earnings to be gained by the dog owner and the rest of the Greyhound racing fraternity. It is interesting to note that Payne (2013a) found no racing benefits associated with spaying Greyhounds, though still argued that such an operation could have health benefits for dogs, and may be helpful when seeking to rehome them at the end of their racing career. I am no vet so will resist attempting to question the former claim but clearly evidence is needed before the latter can be seen as a valid point.

A question to ponder is how the dog is viewed when it is highly valuable, in a purely financial sense. Does it have the potential then to become an object, albeit it a very expensive one, or do its sentience and associated rights take precedence? A lack of research precludes an easy answer to this question but there are plenty of examples in dog sports that suggest a battle must be waged in the minds of owners between the financial value of the dog and its rights. For example, it has been suggested by Price (2012) that some of the sheep trial dogs in New Zealand are worth as much as NZ$10,000. Similarly, Coppinger and Coppinger (2001: 160) noted that: 'A superior [sled] dog took on great value and could be sold to would-be competitors for big money.'

So how does the objectification of dogs in blood sports compare to the case of non-blood sports involving dogs? It is interesting to study the writings of amateur sled dog racing enthusiasts to see how they talk about the sport and their dogs. There can be a tendency here to write about the dogs in a similar manner to that of describing a car or other vehicle. They are presented as an object; a useful one to be sure, that enables participation in and enjoyment of an activity, but an object nonetheless. For example, Flanders (1989: 2) has talked about how: 'It's a lot of fun getting together with a few other drivers [of dog sleds] and their families to go on an overnight camping trip.... During the day you can take different trails and explore areas you might otherwise never see' and how 'Winter is not the only time to enjoy your sled dogs' (p. 4). Similarly, when writing about dog shows Ash (1934) clearly saw the dog in this environment as an object (as distinct from a tool) for the human to show off for the benefit of the human. It is within this context that Ash stated: 'It is part of human nature to display one's goods' (p. 205).

Perhaps, though, it is an oversimplification to think of sports dogs as simply objects or tools. Rather, it may be necessary to think also about the quality of the care these animals receive and whether their owners see them as entities whose welfare and dignity is inherently important. In this way the dog can still be a tool of the sporting arena while at the same time being differentiated from an inanimate object. In this context we need to consider whether a dog is suffering by its participation in sport or, equally, would suffer if it were not allowed into the sporting arena. Consequently, it is important to bear in mind the joy that dogs such as Greyhounds, sled dogs and Foxhounds are said to find in the work they do. For example, in an interview with the GBGB in 2012 it was stated that: 'They [greyhounds] enjoy racing, they're bred to race. They thrive on their racing.' Similarly, in an interview with one of the UK's leading breeders of Foxhounds in 2012 he stated: 'all they [Foxhounds] want to do is go hunting'. In this way it is being argued that these dogs are happiest when engaging in these sports; they are genetically hardwired to enjoy themselves when doing this work.

If we accept that dogs very often enjoy the sports they are part of, and I see no reason to doubt it, then we have to recognize how owners have the potential to utilize this joy for their own purposes, objectifying the dog and dismissing its rights and dignity. On the other hand, owners may cater to this joy and in the process elevate the dog above the status of object by recognizing its inherent right to fulfilment of its desires. Consequently, while all dogs in sports may be used as tools or objects, it is important to consider the intention behind the use, the care of the animal and how the animal's own opinions are considered by the owner. Doing this allows us to judge accurately whether the use of a dog in sport is ethical. If it is, then the dog's engagement in a sport will not adversely impact upon its welfare; rather, it will benefit it.

The Emergence of Sports for Dogs

A variety of sports have emerged relatively recently that, while not necessarily considering only the needs and desires of dogs, have arguably a far greater focus on these than any of the traditional sports that involve dogs. These are listed in Table 3.1 and include agility and flyball. These sports, arguably like all dog sports, focus on the physical abilities of dogs and their associated desires. As such they have emerged out of the work-related reasons for which specific types of dogs were originally bred by humans (Mehus-Roes, 2009). However, these new sports differ from the traditional ones in that they have not emerged out of hunting for the survival of humans or as a method of training through which dogs have been processed for the benefit of humans. Rather, the sports have been developed to give an outlet for the physical desires of dogs and an opportunity for their owners to enjoy time and exercise (both physical and mental) with their dogs. In this way, these sports are more dog-oriented than are the traditional ones. They also reflect the changing social status of dogs and the growing view that they do have needs and rights regarding their physical and mental wellness. Finally, they reflect the growing recognition of the close relation between dogs and humans that, while not necessarily a meeting of equals, is something more than the use of an object by a human. These sports therefore recognize the relation between dogs and their owners as one of a meeting of two sentient beings. While this may be the idealized view of sports for dogs it is worth noting that the American Kennel Club (2012a) stated that agility was originally: 'designed to be halftime entertainment at the Crufts Dog Show' in 1978. This places the origin of the sport in a firmly human-centric setting even if it has evolved since then.

Since the introduction of sports for dogs such as agility and flyball they have become hugely popular (Pfau *et al.*, 2011; Birch and Leśniak, 2013). Among these activities, agility is viewed as the fastest-growing sport involving dogs (American Kennel Club, 2012a). Just how rapid this growth has been is illustrated by looking at the boom in trials and the associated number of entrants held under the auspices of the AKC. In 1994 this organization held its first agility trial and went on to hold a total of 23 trials that year catering to 2000 entrants. By 2008 there were over 2100 AKC-sanctioned trials generating nearly 840,000 entries (American Kennel Club, 2012a). The scale of involvement in sports for dogs is further illustrated by Hultsman (2013: 2), who stated that: 'agility is one of the fastest-growing sports in the dog world (hundreds of thousands participate in agility activities and events worldwide based on the registration numbers of the three major agility organizations)'. Sports for dogs competition is no longer just a local- and national-level phenomenon, with a World Championships for agility having existed since 2011.

The rationale for human involvement in sports for dogs is in many ways similar to that of people involved in other types of dog sports discussed earlier in this chapter. Issues of self-identity, social interaction and the acquiring of prestige and status are all potentially influential. What makes these sports distinct is that through participation in them, as Sanders (1999: 9) noted, there is also the potential to: 'enhance the positive relationship between the animal and his or her human companion'.

Like all other dog sports though there is still the issue of who is in power. The dog involved in agility may gain as much enjoyment from the activity as the dog involved in sledding or racing, but in all cases access to the sport and continuation in it is at the behest of the human. There may be a benefit for the dog but if the voice of this animal is not listened to by the owner then participation in the sport can rapidly become a chore for the animal where its love of the activity is lost. This highlights that just as in the case of human sport there can be many benefits to the participant but to be truly beneficial the individual must have the right to decide when to stop rather than being coerced into continuation. If a dog is 'forced' to participate in a sport, irrespective of the sport, then its position as an object is assured and its welfare subjugated or ignored. In this case the opportunity for enhancing the relationship between the dog and its owner, with both viewed as sentient beings, is lost.

Perhaps the most contentious of the new sports for dogs is dog dancing. The images of dogs and their human partners in fancy dress engaging in a dance routine can be viewed as the ultimate expression of the anthropomorphization of dogs. To detractors of the sport these dogs are seen to be engaging in unnatural and demeaning behaviour that pays little attention to their rights and may even potentially imperil their welfare. Such a view has gained support from an unlikely source in the form of the Kennel Club; unlikely in that this organization has long been blamed for all that is wrong with dog breeding. It may be cynically argued that in seeking to curb the worst excesses of dog dancing, the Kennel Club is simply trying to rebrand itself as a proponent of dog welfare, but having spoken to various members of the organization I would have to say that, while it may not be perfect, the Club is truly trying to engage in such processes not just for the benefit of public relations but for the benefit of dogs. Either way, with specific reference to dog dancing the Kennel Club has moved to ban the dressing of dogs in a manner that demeans them, and their participation in dance moves that are dangerous to their health, including among others dancing on their front paws (Copping, 2012). Yet while we can suggest some aspects of dog dancing are demeaning and potentially physically harmful it is important to look a little more closely at the sport to fully understand it and the position of dogs within it.

Dog dancing, or heelwork to music as it is also known, is clearly an extension of the desire of humans to instil in their dogs a level of obedience that allows them to function in an environment dominated by human rules and regulations. Just as in the case of basic obedience exercises, such as sitting and waiting, most dogs will happily engage in the exercises. While the human may be focused on their dog successfully obeying an order they are given, the dog is much more interested in the attention received and the opportunities such work gives for interaction with their owner. So, as in all forms of obedience work, we see in dog dancing the canine involvement being based on reward, be it in terms of treats or simply time and attention given by their owner. Hence, no matter how it is dressed or the tasks it is asked to undertake, if the owner is positive in their rewards the dog will show all the signs of happiness available to a dog: an upright wagging tail, a 'smiling' mouth, an alert posture. The dog does not really care what, if anything, it is wearing. They, lucky as they are, have no personal anxieties about their physical appearance unlike the neurotic human species. The predisposition of the dog to happiness and a lack of care about its own physical appearance are wonderful strengths but at the same time weaknesses that can be exploited. In this instance the Kennel Club is correct to point out that some acts and outfits are demeaning. Dogs may not think this, but we as humans know it to be true, and as the dominant partner in the human–dog relationship it is beholden to us to ensure that dogs are not demeaned. To do otherwise is to exploit them, irrespective of whether it affects their happiness or not.

Sport Dogs and Constructions of Humans' Personal Identity

The dogs who have been talked about in this chapter have been identified as objects and tools used for the enjoyment of their owners and spectators. However, another layer needs to be added to our understanding of the rationale for the use of these dogs. They are not only tools of leisure but also objects that identify the nature of the individual as they wish to be seen by their peers and the wider society. Such a use is not, as we will see in Chapter 4, unique to the sporting dog but certainly applies to it. For example, those who immerse themselves in the sport of dog sledding are not necessarily only taking part in the sport but seeking to associate themselves with the cultural imagery that pervades the sport (as noted in chapter 2). Similarly, those who have and still seek to engage in the sport of dog fighting, in addition to doing so for enjoyment or financial benefit are often doing so out of a desire to be associated with the masculine culture that is identified with the sport (Evans *et al.*, 1998; Kalof and Taylor, 2007; Lee *et al.*, 2010). While Kalof (2007) suggested that the fighting dog is considered a reflection of the nature and status of its owner, the same, in many ways, can be said to be true of all dogs and their owners. The difference with the fighting dog is that its ability to fight is what gives the owner his (for they are predominantly, though undoubtedly not solely, male) status and 'honour' (as the word is defined within dog fighting circles). The fox hunting fraternity also utilized the hunt (and even continue to do so today when it is banned in countries such as the UK) to show themselves to the world in the manner in which they wish to be seen. As such, Griffin (2007: 8) talks of the hunt as: 'an ostentatious demonstration of wealth, power and prestige'. In this way the dogs are as Sanders (1999: 6) put it: 'a decorative addition to the self'.

Given the level of investment in personal identity associated with many of the human participants in dog sports, just as in the case of all leisure activities, it is not surprising to find at least a proportion of them committed to their sport to such a level as to constitute serious leisure, in the words of Stebbins (2007). These individuals commit significant amounts of time and money to their leisure pursuits, often sacrificing other aspects of their lives. These people have, albeit to a limited extent, been studied elsewhere (e.g. Baldwin and Norris, 1999; Gillespie *et al.*, 2002; Hultsman, 2013) and it is not the aim of this book to focus on the human participants. Rather, in the case of all these serious leisure participants and committed hobbyists it is important to recognize the implications of their focus for the dogs they own and are responsible for. This is something that has yet to be studied but deserves attention: to examine if, despite being dedicated to their sport and consequently the physical welfare of their dogs, serious leisure devotees in dog sports treat their animals as objects (albeit highly prized ones) or as sentient beings with rights and dignities.

Animal Welfare and Rights in Sport Dogs and Dogs in Sport

There is an ongoing debate about the welfare of the dogs in relation to the long- and ultra-long-distance dog sled races such as the Yukon Quest and Iditarod. When the races are acknowledged as being an extreme test of physical and mental endurance for the human participants the question is asked whether we, as humans, have the right to place dogs in such an extreme environment. This is brought into stark relief by claims that over 100 dogs have died while racing in the Iditarod between its inception and 2008. This, as Mehus-Roes (2009) pointed out, may only be the tip of an iceberg that does not take into account those dogs culled outside of the race as their owners deem them unsuitable for racing as they attempt to breed a team capable of winning.

All the human participants, while undoubtedly taking part for a variety of reasons, still have the option to either not take part or quit at any time. The animal rights position would ask where this option for the dog is. Indeed,

Hood (1996: 307) has stated that: 'Those who seek to stop sled dog racing argue that the dogs are forced to endanger their lives because someone else has made the decision for them to compete in a potentially dangerous activity.' Such questions and concerns, while riling many of the sled dog community, have arguably helped to push up the standards of animal welfare at events such as the Yukon Quest. The result is that Quest and Iditarod rules now require vet checks at each stopping place along the course and that: 'there will be no cruel or inhumane treatment of dogs. No use of whips will be allowed' (Hood, 1996; Firth, 1998: 257). Such rules do not, however, answer the query from the animal rights lobby about the right of the dog to take part or not. The most extreme animal rights position (as seen in Chapter 1) would suggest that no dog should be taking part in any sled dog race as they are only doing so at the behest of their human owners. Yet taking such a position is to arguably miss the reality that many, though not all, dogs who engage in sled dog racing love to do so. Indeed, Hood (1996: 307) has stated that: 'No one has to force a sled dog to race, however – that's what they most enjoy. In fact, it's difficult to prevent a husky from running.'

Here we enter the murky world of attempting to understand the messages that dogs are sending out continually to humans and other animals. We need to find out if the sled dog is 'happy'; not by asking it as we would a human, but by listening to it with all of our senses. The answer that comes back, when we attune ourselves to what the dog is saying, is that it is often happy to run and that we should not therefore prevent it, as doing so results in sled dogs sending out an equally clear message, one of misery at desire unfulfilled. Like Evans (2008) I would suggest that anyone doubting that sled dogs love to run and pull a sled need only step into a dog yard to see how excited and happy dogs get when preparation for a ride begins. My first such experience was outside Thunder Bay in Canada. When I arrived at the yard the dogs were all dozing in, on and around their homes (individual wooden dog houses) and they continued to be relaxed/lazy until the first harnesses appeared. This was the signal for hyper-excitement, in just the same manner as the lead is greeted by the average pet dog as a prelude to a walk. Once the dogs are harnessed up (in the case of my Thunder Bay experience to the front of a quad bike instead of a sled as snow was lacking but mud was in plentiful supply) the joy of the dogs going on the trail meant they set off at speed while those left behind howled their disappointment. Since then, I have witnessed exactly the same happiness among sled dogs in Whistler, Canada, and in Leutasch, Austria. Adopting a welfarist approach, the need is to ensure that when the dog says 'enough', 'no' or 'yes please' we listen rather than misusing our position of power to force it to participate or prevent it from doing so.

The ultra-animal rights position would prevent participation of the dog in sledding. Yet such a position would arguably only lead to the extinction of those dogs who have been specifically bred to pull a sledge. I can see the appeal of such a position: it speaks of the need for humans to stop playing God, something that many people outside the animal rights movement can relate to, as debates continue to rage about genetic engineering. However, the reality is that animals such as sled dogs do exist, and to say that breeding them should cease is to condemn a subspecies of animal to extinction and that is in its own way an example of playing God. Sled dogs exist and if we classify them as sentient beings they have a right to life that negates the option of extinction through lack of breeding related to their lack of participation in sledding. This means that sled dogs are here to stay and if this is recognized then the emphasis must be on their holistic welfare. It is in effect a case of choosing life over an impossible future untouched by humans.

A similar debate to the one above could be had with all of the types of dogs discussed in this chapter. The situation is complicated in many instances by the fact that it is not only the rights and welfare of the dog that is open to debate, but other animals as well, such as the fox in the case of the Foxhound and the hare in the case of the Greyhounds used for coursing. Yet if we recognize the right of the Foxhound to live, for example, then we must also come to terms with the fact that it is a hunting animal whose existence is inexorably tied to the fox hunt and as a consequence to the death of foxes. How both animals can continue to exist requires compromise rather than a prioritizing of one species over another. Furthermore, this compromise must be based around the rights and welfare of all the animals involved rather than the idealized views of humans who objectify these animals.

Then there is the question of dog fighting where an argument may be made for allowing such a sport to ensure the continued existence of dogs who are the central feature of the sport. Following the logic applied to the continued existence of sled dogs, Foxhounds or Greyhounds, how, it may be asked, can we condemn the pit bull to extinction just because human moral values have changed and what society once viewed as entertainment is now widely seen as repugnant? Yet such an argument misses the central point, which is the need to listen to the dog. The question must be asked: do the dogs enjoy fighting; do they like it; do they gain all the healthy mental and physical benefits that are associated with engaging in an activity freely and for enjoyment (i.e. leisure) from it? It has been argued in this section that the answer to such questions in the case of sled dogs (among others) and their sport is 'yes' if they are not pushed beyond their own limits by humans who fail to listen to them. Yet in the case of dog fighting I would suggest the answer is 'no'. Dogs will fight, both inside and outside of a pit or ring, but there is not an enjoyment associated with such an occasion. Rather, humans are utilizing issues of fear, survival, territoriality and dominance (be it for access to food or mating opportunities) that reside within dogs (and many other animals) to goad them into fighting. In other words, just as in the case of hunting and racing dogs, there is a manipulation of the dog by the human, but in this instance it is one in which the dog gains nothing positive in return. The hoped for dominance is a mirage; the possession of a territory and survival (aside from not being killed in the ring by another dog) is at the behest of the human owner. In other words, from an animal rights and an animal welfare perspective, there is nothing in dog fighting for the dog.

If we accept the existence of dogs in sport and that it can be beneficial for them to be involved in such activities we must then look at how to ensure these benefits while minimizing, if not eradicating, the potential for harm to the dogs. As in the case of the Yukon Quest and Iditarod, discussed above, this can necessitate the setting of rules and regulations to ensure dogs are not overly stressed so that the fun of the activity is lost to them. In this vein regular health checks are now a feature of racing Greyhounds at many tracks, though not all, around the world. However, there is also the question of what is to be done with sports dogs after they are no longer able to undertake the sport to the level their owners desire.

With specific reference to Greyhounds, Morris (2009) has suggested that some trainers consider a hound to be unworthy of racing past its fourth birthday, while he himself suggests that with care a Greyhound may successfully race till its seventh year. Either way when it is recognized that Greyhounds can live well past 10 years of age there is clearly the potential for a significant problem. What is to be done with dogs like the racing Greyhounds when they are considered to be past their sporting prime?

Historically the answer has been a very quick and brutal one leading to the death of the dog; its disposal a picture of its status as object or tool and also an indictment of the throwaway consumer society, of utilizing the dog only for as long as it is beneficial to the human to do so. The dog may have enjoyed itself while participating in the sport but to kill it merely because it can no longer work to a standard set or desired by its owner does not speak of animal welfare. Yet care must also be taken here in giving a blanket criticism of the euthanizing of dogs. Here we must delve into the tortured debate about the right to die, which is becoming such a hot and sensitive topic as more humans seek it and societies continue to cringe away from discussing it in a rational manner.

I myself have put a dog to sleep; she was Snuffie (already introduced earlier in this book) and my faithful friend for 9 years. In the end, when she was suffering from cancerous growths in her spine, I had to take the decision (because nobody else could, most especially Snuffie) to end her life when I balanced up the quality of her life. How much pain was she in? Could she still do everything she had loved to do her entire life? Was there any hope that things would get better for her? The answer was an intensely personal one for her and me but in the end it was my decision. I had to take responsibility, because I had the power, and to not use that power to make a decision would have been to act immorally. Here then, animal welfare is at the heart of the debate. It is not a matter of right and wrong but of trying to do the 'right thing'. So let us take this debate back to consider what to do with dogs who have reached the end of the line in a sport as far as their owner is concerned; or having been bred for a sport, have been found to be poorly suited to it. If the answer reveals that it is merely expedient from the owner's perspective to kill the animal, then the welfare of the dog is not being considered and the killing should be deemed immoral. Alternatively, if all the options have been considered and it is deemed in the best interests of the dog to be put down then is this not a case of placing the welfare of the animal at centre stage?

Concerns about the destruction of healthy Greyhounds who either cannot race at top speed or who are poorly disposed to race at the tracks led to the establishment of voluntary organizations dedicated to the rehoming of these animals. The National Greyhound Racing Committee (NGRC) in the UK set up one of the first such organizations (the Retired Greyhound Trust) in 1974,

46 years after the organization itself was created (Johns, 2002). In 2010 this organization successfully rehomed 4247 retired Greyhounds (Greyhound Board of Great Britain, 2010). Yet only 12–15 years ago dog rehoming centres in the UK were full of retired Greyhounds because the general public was unwilling to take them on due to their poor image (that is, a working animal in a muzzle trained to chase and requiring significant amounts of daily exercise). A re-education of the public to point out that Greyhounds are not dangerous (despite the muzzle image) and actually require very little exercise has helped considerably in changing this situation (personal communication with Retired Greyhound Trust, 2012). It is important to note that the Retired Greyhound Trust was only ever intended as a means of dealing with NGRC-registered hounds.

Despite the success stories of rehoming Greyhounds, Mehus-Roes (2009: 102) points out that: 'according to the Humane Society of the United States, about 25 percent of retired Greyhounds are still euthanized each year'. This concern is mirrored by the Retired Greyhound Trust's own statistics that show approximately 9000 Greyhounds retiring from racing each year in the UK compared to the roughly 4000 the Trust rehomes (Retired Greyhound Trust, 2010). These figures suggest that while the Trust (2010: 1) is doing excellent work it is still falling short of its goal to: 'strive for the day when no ex-racing Greyhound is without a good home'. One way of achieving this was noted by the Retired Greyhound Trust in an interview in 2012. It was stated they hoped to see the number of registered tracks in the UK reduce to 17 in the future and the number of Greyhounds registered with GBGB to reach about 6000. They felt that if such levels could be realized then the goal of rehousing all the hounds who are appropriate for rehoming could be achieved. Such a goal however is at odds with the notion put forward by the GBGB in an interview in 2012 that the number of registered tracks was due to expand to 27 in 2013. It is interesting to note that the Trust sees no reason why the British government would ban Greyhound racing and actually sees the best route to ensuring the welfare of the dogs being to ensure the sport is a prosperous one where breeders and trainers are not encouraged to skimp on the costs of animal welfare. This may be seen as another example of compromising in a manner that is defined to maximize the welfare of the Greyhounds.

Attitudes to the Greyhound may be compared with those relating to the Foxhound. In an interview in 2012 one of the UK's leading breeders of Foxhounds was asked what happens to these dogs when they are of no use to the pack. He responded by saying: 'It's more kinder [sic] to put them down than do anything else. They aren't pets, they smell, they stink and all they want to do is going [sic] hunting.' While those who gain entry to the pack (and many will not) may well be able to enjoy the life of the pack and the hunt it will be for only a fraction of the length of time they would naturally live. This is underlined by the point made by the same interviewee that: 'A good hound which lasts more than six or seven seasons is invaluable. I've got some at the moment which are 8 or 9 years old; they're the rare ones. I would say the average is 6 years.' While at first glance it may be shocking to some people to think of healthy dogs being put down, as the Foxhound interviewee noted this is not something that is done simply for the convenience of the owner. Rather, it is done with an eye on the welfare of the dog, who truly is not designed for a life outside of the hunting pack and not rehomeable in the same way as the Greyhound is. It may be a painful reality, but it is a reality nonetheless and the only alternative is to have no Foxhounds at all, or at least none that are bred to hunt. What this debate shows is that welfare considerations can make people find alternatives to the euthanizing of healthy dogs but that it can also, after due consideration, result in euthanasia. There is no one-size-fits-all answer; rather the welfare of dogs and consideration of their rights must be seen at a more individualized level.

In addition to providing some insights into the world of dogs in sport, this chapter has sought to discuss how the sports that dogs are involved in relate to their welfare and dignity. These discussions have been complex and highlight the difficulties of adopting extreme animal rights positions. Instead, they suggest the need for compromise in order to maximize the welfare of dogs in a manner that recognizes their sentience and associated rights. The chapter has also shown how it is dangerous to simply assign labels of 'object' and 'tool' to sports dogs. Instead, there is a need to reach down further and explore the underlying values of the dogs' owners and their relations with their dogs. In this way it is possible to see that many of the owners of these dogs have their welfare at heart in a manner that clearly distinguishes the dogs from inanimate objects or from animals whose owners do not care for or recognize their dogs as sentient beings with inherent rights. The book now moves on from the world of the sports dog to explore the leisured dog, though many of the issues raised in this chapter will be of value to understanding this animal and its relations with humans.

4 Leisured Dogs and Dogs as Leisure Objects

Introduction: Defining Leisure

This chapter focuses on the leisured dog and the dog as leisure object as opposed to the dog as worker or sport dog in the leisure environment. It includes a discussion of whether a dog can truly be leisured or whether it is actually only in the leisure environment at the behest of its owner (i.e. it is a leisure object). The leisured dog is defined as one who is in the leisure environment with its owner but within the context that it is recognized as a sentient being and not an object by its human companion. In contrast, dogs viewed as objects rather than as sentient beings become leisure objects when they are brought into the leisure environment by their owners. The chapter is grounded in the recognition that leisure is defined by the perception of freedom, which is relative as opposed to absolute. Within this context it is proposed that dogs, even as companions or pets of humans, can be leisured although whether they perceive it in the same way as humans is open to debate. Building on this, an integral part of the chapter is concerned with discussing what 'leisure' for a dog is and what are their leisure needs. This chapter is set up to encompass discussion of the leisured dog and the dog as leisure object from both the perspective of the dog and the human, recognizing that there is the potential for significant differences to exist between the two.

Do Dogs Do/Have Leisure?

In America it is estimated that owners spend approximately US$40 billion annually on their pets, buying toys, collars, clothing (mass produced and made by fashion designers), beds and magazines, among other items. These owners also spend time and money taking their pets to parks and beaches, to dog day care and obedience classes (Rudy, 2011). The question is whether any of these activities and/or purchases are actually for the benefit of the dog or the pleasure of the owner. This necessitates two questions: first, is it possible to 'give' an animal leisure? And second, is the leisure experienced through these purchases and behaviour purely experienced by the dog, by the human or by a mixture of the two to varying degrees?

Leisure has been widely defined as the ultimate expression of the self, as a time/space/activity/mental state in which the individual is 'free' to give voice to and seek satisfaction of their own desires (Pieper, 1965; Kelly, 1996). Trying to find such leisure in a situation that is constructed by consumer industries, where the rules and regulations are imposed on the participant from the outside even if they are tacitly accepted by and therefore reaffirmed by the individual, is therefore arguably impossible. Instead, one needs to look outside the realms of leisure controlled by the manipulations of others. One such arena in a human context has been said to be that of 'play'; play being that which is unfettered by rules and regulations and oversight imposed from above by those not involved as an equal in the play of the moment. This does not mean that play does not have rules but that they are a creation of the actors in the moment. As such, play lacks the structure of formal sport whose rules and regulations are imposed on the actors by distant bodies. Instead, play is spontaneous. The nature of play also means that it clearly requires agency and awareness of the self and the other. To be able to engage with another being or beings in a spontaneous manner where fluid relations exist and rules are made up in the moment clearly requires sentience.

The question then is: do dogs play? The answer that comes back very clearly is that they do, like many other animals. In this way not only are dogs seen to have and joyfully engage in leisure but their play also speaks volumes about their sentience (Sanders, 1999; MacFarland and Hediger, 2009; Horowitz, 2009a). This is because, while it is clearly unstructured, the play of dogs is equally clearly associated with rules that are made up in the moment but also learned across differing play situations. Witness when two dogs meet off-leash, there will be the initial rush to get to within physical proximity, followed by a much more cautious approach. Then, when the friendliness of each dog has been determined, will come what has been described as the 'play bow', the indication that the opportunity to play with 'you' (the other dog) would be very welcome. Then witness the moment when both dogs spring into action: there is unabridged fun, enjoyment, sheer joy in the physicality of the moment. The chasing, bowling over, the rough and tumble, all of these are moments and actions of play that can be seen in the dog and across multiple species. Then witness the arrival of a new dog, so the group of two has to reconfigure itself, or reject the advances of the new arrival. If the new dog agrees to the rules in place the games go on; if not, things are disrupted until a new set of rules is established or the new arrival is banished. I would love to show the reader the reality of this play by taking them to my local beach where my dog Gypsy will most likely bump into another regular beach walker. His dog, Honey, will always play with Gypsy and the two will always establish rules for the games in which they engage where dogs take centre stage and owners are generally ignored. Alas, I cannot take every reader to the beach but this is not the end of the world; if you own a dog the answer is easy, take it to your own beach or open space and let it play. If you do not own a dog, just go to any place where dogs gather and watch them play; either way the proof that dogs play and engage in displays of sentience while doing so is right in front of our eyes, just waiting to be seen. Part of the sentience involved in the play of dogs, as Horowitz (2009b) and Bekoff (2004) have noted, is evidenced in how dogs will tailor their attention getting and play behaviour to the abilities of another dog. This demonstrates an awareness of the other, a desire to engage with the other and a level of self-awareness that enables a dog to shape its own abilities to enable it to play with a dog who possesses differing abilities.

Dogs do not only play with other dogs; they also play by themselves, with humans and with a variety of other animals. Attempts to play with different species may not always be successful due to the difficulties of communicating across species, but they can be, and even when they are not the attempt speaks volumes for the sentience of the dog. Witness, for example, within my own house the play that occurs between Gypsy and our often aloof cat (Catkin). There are times when one or other of the two animals will play with the other in a one-sided manner (i.e. when Catkin hides behind a door in the dark to pounce on Gypsy or when Gypsy chases Catkin when the latter has been spooked by a sudden noise). This play, though one-sided, even has rules that the two animals know and have worked out for themselves. Gypsy could easily kill Catkin but never seeks to do so and Catkin could cause serious damage with her claws but refrains from doing so. Then there are moments of mutual play, where both animals will come together to mutually initiate a bout of play. Their communication in these moments speaks of sentience and of an ability, albeit imperfect, to communicate across species. Rooney *et al.* (2001) have also demonstrated how the play between dogs and their human owners is an example of species attempting, not always successfully, to communicate with one another.

It is important to recognize that the play engaged in between dogs, between dogs and other animals, and between dogs and humans is fundamentally different. Indeed, Rooney *et al.* (2000: 247) note that when playing, dogs 'react differently to dog and human play partners'. Irrespective of which species are playing together the displayed play, the underlying motivation for engaging in play and the nature of sensations gained from it will be specific to the participants in the moment of a particular play session. This suggests a level of self-awareness by the play participants as well as an awareness of the nature of the partners involved in a play session and a recognition that not all of these are the same. Following on from this is a recognition that different rules apply to a play session based on the nature of the partner being played with. All this speaks of animal sentience and consciousness. The construction of rules of play by dogs and the resultant manner in which dogs play with others (dogs and non-dogs) suggests, as Bekoff (2004) notes, that dogs possess a sense of morality, a notion of fair play and, as a consequence, an ability to empathise. All of this, of course, speaks of dogs as sentient, conscious beings.

If dogs play then the next question that can be asked is why they play. A similar question has been asked in relation to children and non-canine animals that appear to play. Here there is a significant degree of overlap between human and non-human theories of play. In both instances the role of play as a developmental tool for young human and non-human animals is highlighted (Van Slyck, 2006). Similarly, in both cases the notion that play may simply be engaged in because it is fun is often dismissed and its role in development focused on instead (Carr, 2011). Indeed, within the context of animal play, Horowitz (2009a: 197–198) has stated that: 'One might thus suggest that the function [of play] is to have fun – but this is frowned upon as a true function.' Yet dismissing the fun to be gained from play and instead linking play solely, or even primarily, to evolution of species reduces the actions of individuals engaged in play to those of automatons. This does not mean that play does not and cannot have benefits for the development of young humans and animals but that the value and importance of fun should not be neglected as a driving force and rationale for play. Yet the importance of play as a developmental tool has been used as a justification for those in power (parents and teachers in the case of children and owners in the case of dogs) to control and manipulate play, seeing play engaged in purely for fun as a wasted opportunity for personal development (Carr, 2011).

The provision of sports for dogs can be seen as an attempt to control and manipulate their play, offering dogs the potential for exercise but robbing them of the less constrained reality of play. In a not dissimilar manner we are witnessing the emergence of 'play dates' for dogs where owners deliberately construct an opportunity at a specific time and in a specific setting for their dogs to 'play' together. Katz (2003) notes this is not an uncommon phenomenon in the USA and I have been invited (an offer politely sidestepped) to participate in such an activity. On the one hand, the idea clearly does give dogs often living a sole dog life in a human household an opportunity to interact with another dog; something that dogs in general clearly thoroughly enjoy. Yet there are concerning undercurrents at work here. First, there is the issue that this is a manipulated play where the encounter is under the control of the humans with only specific dogs invited to the party. It is then a poor imitation of the more free-flowing ideal of play where anything can happen. As such it is, while not unstimulating, not as stimulating as it could or should be. Second, it smacks of all that is wrong with anthropomorphizing; in this instance, of viewing and treating the dog as a young child rather than what it really is (i.e. a dog). Despite concerns among those in power about unstructured play, there is plenty of evidence that such activity has significant welfare benefits for children (Kelly, 1996; Valentine and McKendrick, 1997; Frost et al., 2008) and non-human participants (Held and Spinka, 2011). Consequently, just as there have been calls for children to be able to play freely without outside interference (Tuan, 1998; Honore, 2004) it may be argued that dogs should have the same type of opportunity. In both cases it demands recognition of a degree of self-awareness and sentience of the player.

Despite attempts by those in power to manipulate dogs, just like children they are capable of making play out of experiences and items in ways that the creator of the space or item had not planned. In this way dogs are self-empowering, manipulating the world around them for their own enjoyment. Figure 4.1 provides an image of just such an instance where Snuffie was surrounded by her

Fig. 4.1. The basketball-playing dog or the dog at play.

basketballs. I cannot remember where the balls came from but certainly she never played basketball. Rather, like many dogs, it was her pleasure to chase the balls around (both when they were thrown by someone and when she herself threw them) and constantly 'worry' and chew them. In much the same way Gypsy has destroyed a football and a rugby ball.

An important question to ask here is whether exercise is a form of leisure. As humans we are constantly told today about the importance of exercise for our physical and mental well-being. We are advised that specific amounts and types of activity are a requirement of the human body and without them we risk injury, illness and even premature death. In comparison, the focus on exercise for dogs has, traditionally, been on the need for it to prevent boredom and resultant destructive behaviour in dogs. The valid suggestion is that if a dog is left at home alone for several hours at a time (common among urban-dwelling, often dual-income households), it can become bored and destructive if not exercised regularly (King *et al.*, 2009). Exercise has therefore in many ways simply been seen as a way to wear out a dog so that it is content to sleep for a large portion of the day. While this is arguably still the main reason most people exercise their dogs there is a rising trend towards recognizing the physical health benefits of exercise to dogs in the face of a growing obesity epidemic among our pets dogs. Indeed, it has been estimated that in the USA 50% of dogs are overweight (Brown, 2013).

Feeding on increasing concern among owners over the health of their dogs a tech company announced in 2013 that it was to start selling a device to clip to the collar of a dog that would be able to record when a dog was walking, playing or resting. They sell this as an aid to help 'pets live longer and healthier lives' (Fox, 2013), which as anyone who has lost a dog will tell you can only be a good thing. However, it speaks of removing the leisure from the lives of dogs and further controlling their behaviour. Similarly, in 2012 a Japanese company launched a pedometer for dogs (O'Mahony, 2012). We may say it is for their betterment as we as humans know what is best for our dogs, but there is still the issue that this ignores the sentience and rights of the dog. Similarly, the exercise regimes being put in place to reduce obesity in dogs and the dog gyms now available in countries such as the USA (Brown, 2013), while aimed at increasing canine health fail to consider the dog as more than an object. As part of this an estimated 3 million dogs in the USA spent time on treadmills in 2010 (Manning, 2012). In its worst instance taking dogs to gyms and swimming pools for exercise can be seen as an objectification of the dog where the owner is more concerned with what the activity says about their status than about the health of their pet.

Alongside the need for physical exercise for dogs is an increasing recognition of the need for mental stimulation to make for a truly contented animal who is not bored and potentially destructive or antisocial. Indeed, the Dogs Trust (undated: 15) in the UK identified that while 'Exercise is essential to keep your dog fit and in good condition' 'Dogs also need to exercise their brains to be completely happy.'

Whatever the reason for dog exercise it is clear from this discussion that it is not, in a pure sense, a leisure experience as defined in a human context around self-discovery and enjoyment, though it is arguable that the latter can certainly occur during the exercising of dogs. This recognizes that while the human may be exercising the dog to tire it out, prevent destructive behaviour and/or reduce levels of fat, the dog is likely to be engaging in the behaviour simply because it enjoys doing so. One need only note the attentiveness, the wagging tail and air of excitement whenever the dog lead appears to appreciate that what may be seen as exercise by the human owners is an enjoyable leisure activity for the dog. Yet, just as in the case of humans, for it to truly be a leisure experience the dog must surely feel it has freely engaged in the experience; that its participation can be stopped at any time. The perception of freedom is the crucial point here as it allows for willing engagement in the leisure experience.

The classic and most common method of exercise is simply to take the leashed dog for a walk, the duration of which will vary according to the nature of the dog and the available time of the owner. More recently, with the craze for running as a means of keeping fit among humans, many dog owners are to be seen out jogging with their dog, who is either running off-leash with them or, more commonly, attached to them via a lead. A small number of cases have also been reported and seen of dogs being exercised by means of the owners driving their cars along roads with the dog running alongside either off-leash or with the leash attached and held by the owners through an open window. The latter method has been condemned when brought to public attention as a case of animal cruelty where the dog has no control over the speed set, and the danger of being squashed under the moving vehicle is all too apparent.

However a dog is exercised while on a leash, it can and does often have little control over the speed set or the route taken. Study a dog walking off-leash and without the intervention of human commands and you will see it constantly varying its pace, taking frequent stops and apparent diversions to sniff interesting scents, and constantly doubling back on itself. Contrast this with the dog taught never to stop and sniff or scent mark while walking on a leash or the dog forced to run at a constant pace to conform to the exercise regime of its human owner. Exercise is clearly being gained by the dog in these instances, and it mainly gives the appearance of being happy or at least content to be on the leash, but the physicality of the leash obviously severely constrains the freedom of the leisure experience.

The problem of course is that there are two sets of leisure needs involved whenever a dog is exercised. These are the needs of the dog and those of the human. In addition, both needs must be set within the context of the rules and regulations that define the acceptable behaviour of dogs and the appropriate behaviour towards them by humans. Allowing a dog to wander freely in many spaces is not, as will be discussed in Chapter 5, safe or practical. It would also drive the average dog owner to despair to follow a dog on a lead as it chose to define the route and nature of a walk. Consequently, if the leisure potential of the exercising of the dog is to be maximized, it must be an activity that is seen as a compromise of two sets of needs and desires that is set within the boundaries of rules that are outside the immediate control of the participants. In this way all participants may gain leisure, albeit leisure that is compromised. From this perspective the notion forwarded by Rogerson (1991: 22) that: 'Walking a dog on a lead and denying it the right to exercise freely is just plain cruelty' is plainly erroneous. That a dog can be walked cruelly on a lead is without doubt true; but it is equally true that this compromised leisure can and does give enjoyment to both dog and owner if undertaken in a manner that considers the needs of both participants and the wider society and environment in which it is undertaken.

A variation on the theme of exercise and leisure is seen in Fig. 4.2. This picture was taken in 2012 in Hyde Park, London, UK, and features two dogs chasing a remote-control car operated by their owner. The dogs were obviously used to this as a form of exercise and needed no encouragement to chase the vehicle, while the owner was equally obviously a fan of remote-control cars and was happy to drive it around until the dogs were tired. In this way we see a novel coming together of the leisure needs and desires of dogs and owners in a mutually beneficial manner.

So far we have talked exclusively of the leisure of dogs as being active; of them being up and doing things either in play or exercise. However, the

Fig. 4.2. Dogs in Hyde Park, London, UK.

Fig. 4.3. Passive leisure of dogs.

majority of free time (a poor indicator of leisure though something without which it is hard to imagine the richness that is leisure being possible) that humans experience is spent in pursuit of sedentary leisure and the same can be said to be true of dogs. In the sleep and relaxation of dogs, especially on a sunny day, there can be said to be a degree of joy and abandon that draws parallels with the human slumped in a hammock strung between two palm trees on the edge of a golden beach. They exude bliss in a manner that speaks of pleasure fulfilled. That such slumber, as shown in Fig. 4.3, often comes after a period of exercise seems to make the whole experience (of active and passive leisure) all the more enjoyable.

The passive leisure of dogs and the joy they appear to take from it remind us of the need to view leisure as more than a continual, and often apparently desperate, search for fulfilment. In this way, the passive leisure in which dogs engage so contentedly is a lesson for harassed humans to take note of and an example of the concept of slow living (Honore, 2004). This passive behaviour is also another example of how dogs can have leisure.

Dogs and Human Leisure Days/Events

Christmas, Halloween, birthdays and a variety of national holidays can be seen to represent leisure time and leisured opportunities for humans. They are often a time to dress up, give presents, engage in excessive consumption of food and alcohol, and/or meet up with friends and/or relatives. Within the context of the movement of dogs towards becoming a central feature of the family and the giving of human characteristics to them, it is probably little surprise to see that dogs are being given an increasingly central role in these days and even given their own events. It is not uncommon now for the birthdays of dogs to be celebrated by their owners in the same manner that human birthdays are commemorated. At the same time, the giving of Christmas presents to dogs is no longer uncommon and some owners take their pets to see Santa in a manner that used to be reserved for children. Indeed, Herzog (2010) states that 66% of pet owners provide their animals with Christmas presents, something I will admit to doing myself. Do I give the present for the benefit of the dog? No, I must admit that the primary reasons are human-centred. It just seems mean when all the human members of the family are getting presents not to give anything to Gypsy (or Snuffie before her). There is also a logic that in doing so she is distracted with something to chew on while the kids can get down to the serious business of present unwrapping. Does Gypsy mind? Not really, as instead of being ignored and shifted out of the way of the presents as she seeks attention and the kids seek to unwrap things, she is able to enjoy a tasty chew toy or begin the process of disassembling a tennis ball. In this way while the driving force to give her a present may be human-centred at least it is clear she is enjoying what she is getting; really, is it any different to the underlying reasons behind much of the giving of presents that occurs between humans?

The AKC provides evidence to suggest the tradition of dressing up in spooky costumes at Halloween is no longer restricted to humans. One in ten dog owners reported that they could not imagine not dressing their dog up for the night, and nearly half of the study's respondents stated they liked dressing their dog up for Halloween (American Kennel Club, 2005a). Such a claim is supported by Herzog (2010) who suggested that as many as 18% of pet owners dress their animals up for special occasions. While many dog owners undoubtedly engage in this dressing up similarly to the way most parents do with their children (i.e. cheaply), there is a market for extremely high-cost dog costumes. For example, Herzog (2010: 76) identified a web-based pet boutique, *Tea Cups Puppies Boutique*, which offers a '"Garden Party Swarovski Dress" for [US] $3,000.' Aside from this, owners can and do purchase swimsuits, tiaras, wedding dresses, Harley-Davidson outfits and tuxedos, among other things, for their dogs (Herzog, 2010). The common theme that runs throughout the trend for dressing dogs in fancy dress or items of clothing for which they have no 'need' is the objectification of the dog. The argument can be made that these dogs are suffering no 'harm' and that they may well be enjoying the attention they receive from their owners; yet in dressing them up as furry humans these owners are ignoring the dignity of dogs. 'Dignity' is of course a human term and it is clear that dogs, if they consider it at all, feel very differently about dignity compared with humans. However, as a responsible dog owner, the leader in any human–dog relationship, the one in power, it is the responsibility of the human not to trample over the dog's dignity in the rush to meet their own self-indulgent desires for the humanization of their dog.

It is easy to suggest that in including dogs in events and leisured days that are human constructs these animals are being treated as objects, where their needs and welfare are being ignored as the owners dictate what the dogs should do. Yet to apply this view to all the humans and dogs involved in these events and behaviours is an oversimplification. As discussed in Chapter 3, it is not sufficient to judge the extent to which an owner considers the welfare of a dog merely by looking at the activities the dog partakes in. Rather, we need to look at the underlying rationale and how each owner views their dog. In this way it may be argued that it is possible for the individual owner to perceive the rights of their dog and recognize its existence as a sentient being while at the same time participating with it in an event that, on the face of it, appears to objectify the dog.

It is not just the individual owners that need to be looked at to see if their dogs are truly being objectified. Rather, the rationale behind some events and participation in them needs to be considered. For example, the Christian church now offers special services in many locations at which owners may bring along their pets, mainly dogs. This may be seen as another objectification of the dog who is dragged along to a human construct to take part in a service it knows nothing about and about which it cares even less. However, when we look beneath the surface we realize that the provisioning of these services by the church explicitly supports the notion of non-human animals having souls, something that marks a significant shift from the traditional position of the church, which viewed non-human animals as lacking a soul (Coren, 2004). Those owners who attend such services help to give legitimacy to this view and through it support the notion that if these animals are like humans in that they have a soul then they must also have rights and welfare requirements that go beyond mere physical comfort. In this way, what looks on the surface like objectification may actually be seen as empowerment of the dog and recognition of its rights and welfare.

Dog Owners and Dogs in Leisure

Despite everything that has been discussed earlier in this chapter and also in Chapter 3, it is important to note that: 'what most people like to do with their dogs is just hang out with them' (Mehus-Roes, 2009: 29). Put another way, to simply spend some time relaxing in the company of their dog is the biggest leisure activity in which dog owners engage with their pets. The major demand put on the dog, therefore, is for them to be with their owner, something dogs are generally very happy to do. This builds on the concept raised earlier in this chapter of slow leisure: that simply hanging out together can be seen as the most popular form of leisure that owners engage in with their dogs. This is arguably as close as most people get to true leisure; it is an activity and time spent without outwardly directed targets. Yet such experiences run contrary to the notions of recreation that have dominated western society and see such 'down time' as wasted time.

In Chapter 2 it was noted how the working dog has been depicted in idealized images of the leisure environment. Here it is important to note that the leisured dog has also been utilized in the marketing of the leisure space and to reflect on what this says about and how it influences notions of the centrality of the dog to the life of the human family. Within this context, Fig. 4.4 shows pictures that have been utilized in a variety of marketing and information sources (including *Park* magazines, visitor centre displays, visitor leaflets and the Park website) published by the Loch Lomond & The Trossachs National Park in Scotland. In all of these pictures the dog is clearly a central component of the happy family out walking in the countryside, the Scottish countryside in this case. In this way, the dog is a leisure companion of its human owners, a 'with'. The pictures in Fig. 4.4 also clearly highlight what is defined by society as a good, responsible dog owner, someone who has their dog on a leash and therefore under close control in this instance. Similar pictures are common in the marketing of the happy family on holiday, as including not only mum,

Fig. 4.4. Centrality of the pet dog in the leisure experience. (Photos courtesy of Loch Lomond & The Trossachs National Park Authority, UK.)

dad and children, but also the family dog. In all of these cases, the dog is present as an intimate member of the family, sometimes a play friend of the humans, but always central to the unit. The influence of pictures such as those highlighted in Fig. 4.4 on the construction of the holiday environment as dog friendly is discussed in Chapter 5.

Pictures such as those in Fig. 4.4 speak volumes about the social construction of the leisure experiences of dogs and their owners and definitions of the 'good' dog owner. At the same time, they are a reflection of the increasing desire of humans to position the dog as a central component of their lives.

Dogs as Leisure Objects

Following the discussion about whether dogs in leisure are treated as objects, the focus of this section is on dogs who in the leisure experiences of humans, at least at face value, are objectified. These dogs are differentiated from the sport dogs of Chapter 3 in that the leisure experiences they are a part of are clearly not sports. This objectification of the dog is rooted back to the widely held social and legal view of the ownership of animals that effectively categorizes them as objects to be owned (Rudy, 2011) and in many ways treated in a manner that is little different from the way we treat inanimate objects. As in the case of the sports that dogs have and do take part in, there is no room in this book to discuss all of the ways in which dogs are leisure objects. Instead, this section focuses on several examples, using them to discuss the reasons for the objectification of dogs in leisure, and how this sits within the context of animal welfare and the sentience of dogs.

The most problematic discussion in this entire book, for me as the author at least, is the sexual relations between people and dogs that fit either under the heading of bestiality or zoophilia. In largely trying to avoid having to write about this issue for over 2 years I have recognized my own limits as a researcher; there are simply some research topics into which I have no wish to venture. Yet I feel strongly that while most of us feel a repugnance towards such behaviour as that associated with bestiality and zoophilia there is a need to drag this behaviour into the light of day. This should ensure that it gains the discussion and research (with someone with more fortitude than I and the very careful backing and support of their institutional environment) that it requires, like all other aspects of human behaviour about which we would normally prefer to neither see nor hear. Such work is needed in order to fully ensure that the rights and welfare of those in the subordinated positions – those without power, or only limited power – are not endangered. This view mirrors the work of Rosenberger (1968: 9–10) who has stated that: 'Any sexual practice, no matter how perverted or repugnant to our moral senses, is entitled to be placed in the spotlight of scientific discussion, within the bright sunshine of logic and reason.' However, I would distance myself from Rosenberger's overall work, which had no interest at all in the rights or welfare of animals and, especially by contemporary standards, espouses a very sexist viewpoint. Indeed, Rosenberger's (1968: 187) claim that: 'as a rule, bestiality is harmless, even when it is a perversion, in no way endangering the "morals' of "society"' completely misses the point that it is not harm to human society that needs to be at the centre of the stage but the potential for harm to the rights, welfare and dignity of the animals utilized by bestialists and zoophiliacs.

It is arguably the very repugnance that most of society has, or at least displays, for bestiality and zoophilia that inhibits research into it. As in my own case I just cannot stomach researching in the field. Others may well be 'dissuaded' from researching in the field for fear of their own reputation being tainted by association with it. It is therefore not surprising that Beirne (2001: 43) has suggested that: 'To most people, bestiality is a disturbing sexual practice that invites hurried dismissal rather than sustained intellectual inquiry or scholarly reflection.' Not surprisingly, very little research or academic writing has been undertaken on bestiality or zoophilia (Rosenberger, 1968; Munro and Thrusfield, 2005; Beetz, 2005a; Donnan and Magowan, 2010; Grebowicz, 2010), particularly with specific reference to dogs, that has a clear scientific foundation or at the very least is not inherently biased by the beliefs of practitioners. As Beirne (2001: 43) sums up: 'it is remarkable that both moral philosophy and the social sciences have almost completely neglected to study this enduring social practice that has traditionally been viewed with moral, judicial, and aesthetic outrage'.

Bestiality and zoophilia is stigmatized in virtually all contemporary societies and major religions (Ford, 1999). This ensures any participants who engage in this behaviour do so out of sight of the public gaze, unwilling to tell others about their behaviour (Bolliger and Goetschel, 2005), making it doubly difficult for anyone to study. It is extremely difficult to gain access to research participants and is a topic whose study could all too easily stigmatize not just the participants but the researcher as well. However, censuring the latter is no way to assess the extent of a problem or help in arriving at any necessary solutions.

So what exactly is bestiality? Without going into detail it can simply be defined as the sexual coupling of a human with a non-human animal. Zoophilia is differentiated from bestiality, at least in the minds of participants, in that it is supposed to indicate a relationship between an animal and human that goes beyond the merely sexual to become an emotional one as well (Miletski, 2002; Beetz, 2005c). We will explore the implications of the definition of zoophilia later in this section.

Given the hidden nature of and lack of research on zoophilia and bestiality it is impossible to make any precise claims about the extent of the activity in general let alone with specific reference to dogs. Instead, we are required to make do with extremely vague statements such as the following by Miletski (2005: 1): 'Human sexual relations with animals, a behavior known as bestiality, have existed since the dawn of human history in every place and culture in the world,' a point repeated by Beetz (2005a). A similarly vague, though nonetheless disturbing, claim is made by Bolliger and Goetschel (2005) in stating bestiality is an activity that is more widespread than thought. As with virtually all acts of sex it is not just the act that needs to be counted but the extent to which it is viewed through pornography. In this sense bestiality is suggested to be widespread, with sales of static and moving visual material having been spread across North America, Europe and parts of Asia and having now gone global thanks to the all-encompassing nature of the Internet (Ford, 1999; Miletski, 2005). It has also been something engaged in on the screen by the most famous porn star, Linda Lovelace (Miletski, 2005), though whether her participation was willing or otherwise is a matter of strong debate (Ford, 1999) for which there appears to be little conclusive evidence other than the words of the opposing camps.

While it may be viewed as one of the pre-eminent social taboos it is important to recognize that bestiality and zoophilia themselves are not illegal in many countries. Rather, prosecution of cases of such activities are commonly related to any pain and suffering the animals experience as a result of sexual contact with humans (Bolliger and Goetschel, 2005). Indeed, it is claimed that in countries such as Italy, Spain and the Netherlands the selling of bestial pornography is legal (Bolliger and Goetschel, 2005), although Miletski (2002) suggests Denmark is the only place where bestiality videos can be legally produced and distributed; another indicator of the lack of quality data and research on the subject. It can also be argued that laws against bestiality and zoophilia are unnecessary when animals are protected by others that prohibit harm to them by humans. However, while laws designed to protect animals from physical harm are certainly very valuable it is possible, as in Bolliger and Goetschel's (2005) view, that such laws all too often ignore the dignity of the animal.

As far as bestiality is concerned it is clearly the case that the rights of the animal are totally ignored. The animals are nothing more than an object for the sexual satisfaction of the human (Miletski, 2002) and as such it can be said that there is clearly no concern for their rights or welfare beyond that of their continuation and functioning in a manner akin to the longevity desired of a tool. However, zoophilia – on the face of it – may present a more nuanced problem. While mainly, though supposedly not exclusively (Miletski, 2002) entailing a sexual content, a zoophilic relationship is supposed to be just that: a 'relationship', something that is ongoing and based on more than simple sex. Zoophiles, like many people who have a totally platonic relationship with their dog, claim to listen to their animal and to have its welfare and rights at heart. It may or may not be true that they listen, but the acts they engage in are still irresponsible. These people are in a position of responsibility, as is any animal owner. They are required to act only in ways that respect the dignity of the animal. In this way, it may be seen to be wrong to engage in zoophilia as, even if the animal appears willing and to be enjoying itself, these people are still exploiting the animal due to the nature of the power relation between the animal and human. This is not about whether an animal consents to sex with a human but about whether even if it does consent it is still the wrong thing to do. Consequently, Beetz's (2005b: 61) claim that: 'some animals, such as dogs, seem to enjoy the attention provided by the sexual interaction with a human' is irrelevant. It is not just about whether they 'appear to enjoy an activity' but whether we, as creatures capable of independent thought and control, know that such behaviour demeans the dignity and hence the rights and welfare of the animal. In addition to criticizing Beetz, this view stands in opposition to the notion that an animal has given 'permission' for sexual intercourse with a human 'by being passive' (Rosenberger, 1968: 188). Such a view is simply wrong as it totally ignores the dignity of the animal and the power relation in which it is situated where the human is the dominant player. In this way I stand in opposition to the position adopted by Peter Singer in his review of *Dearest Pet: On Bestiality* by Midas Dekkers in which he noted that sex with animals, including the pet dog, can be 'mutually satisfying activities' and that 'Sex with animals does not always involve cruelty' (Boxer, 2001). There are many potential types of 'cruelty' and in this case Singer missed the fact that demeaning the dignity of the dog, even if the dog gives no thought to this, is an act of cruelty.

The position I have adopted is supported by Beirne (1997; 2002: 196) who despite admitting to seeing apparent pleasure being demonstrated by dogs in bestiality videos while being the centre of sexual attention from humans, states: 'I [the author] suggest, simply, that bestiality should be understood as sexual assault.' Beirne focuses on the issue that it is impossible for us as humans to know when a 'yes' from a dog for a sexual relation is truly a 'yes'. Dogs are renowned for reacting positively to just about any show of human attention so it is little surprise to hear of them reacting in an apparently positive manner to human sexual advances. This does not make it right; rather it makes it a case of exploitation and deliberate ignoring of the rights of the dog. This position argues in favour of the idea there do not need to be specific separate laws against bestiality or zoophilia. This is because the focus needs to be on the welfare and rights of the animal and any prohibition against sexual acts by humans with animals needs to be grounded in animal welfare laws. Yet at the same time, and as noted earlier, these laws need to incorporate recognition of the importance of the dignity of animals. Such a view echoes the point made by Bolliger and Goetschel (2005: 41) that: 'Because zoophilia infringes unquestionably upon the sexual integrity of an animal, it above all represents a violation of the dignity of an animal, and thus constitutes a fundamental infringement of an animal's welfare.'

Performing or dancing dogs have a place in the history of the circus but pre-date this institution and have occurred and, to an extent, still do occur outside of this space. Indeed, writing in 1875, Strutt noted the presence of dancing dogs on the streets of the cities of England, though he also pointed out that they were not very popular at the time of his writing. Although talking about performing animals in general, Regan's (2004) point can be applied to dogs who have been trained to give a performance for the amusement of the human spectator. He points out that: 'Many people, especially parents and their children, enjoy watching these performances. The animals make us laugh and sometimes "ooh" and "aah". You have to marvel at what they can do and applaud the skill of the trainers. For most people, it is hard to see what could be wrong with this' (2004: 139). The reason they see nothing wrong is that they view the animal as an object. It helps, especially in the case of the dog, that the performing animal is likely to be giving physical signs of enjoyment, such as a wagging tail, which is actually linked to the potential reward for completing the task rather than for undertaking the task itself.

Looking back at sled dog racing, which was discussed in Chapter 2, it is interesting to reflect on what became of the original dogs who made the serum run to Nome in 1925. The venture clearly won the imagination of the general public and there were people who were quick to exploit this, taking the dogs from working tools to objects of curiosity in the leisure environment in one easy step. Although the journey to Nome had involved many dog teams, to ensure the serum arrived as quickly as possible, it was the team that arrived in Nome led by Balto (the lead dog) upon which the public gaze fixated. The team was taken down to Los Angeles to receive a key (in the shape of a dog bone) to the city and to feature in a movie about the run. Yet their fame was only fleeting and while their handler returned to Alaska the dogs were sold on to become amusements in Los Angeles sideshows before ending up at the zoo in Cleveland. Balto became forever a leisure object when on his death he was stuffed and placed on view in the Museum of Natural History in Cleveland (Onion, 2009).

The experiences of Balto may well be described in today's society as being symptomatic of an ignorance of the rights and welfare of dogs, but they also demonstrate the desire of humans to impose their own rose-tinted version of reality onto the dog and construct its deeds and acts from a human perspective. Such constructions are not unusual and neither is their potential to act as an attraction for the leisured human. In the UK one of the most famous dogs is Greyfriars Bobby in Edinburgh who was supposed to have lain on the grave of his owner and pined away, eventually dying close to his side. The story is one of unrequited loyalty and devotion, an ultimately sad yet also heroic story that exemplifies the traits that humanity most covets in dogs. A statue of Bobby has been erected in Edinburgh and it is now a major tourist attraction, his owner largely forgotten though not the acts with which he is associated. In the constant retelling of such acts we see their reinforcement as authentic in the minds of humanity and the notion of associated traits of devotion, love and loyalty become part of the make-up of all dogs. In this way characters such as Greyfriars Bobby play a role in the cultural construction of the dog (see also Chapter 1). Less famous than Bobby is Bum, whose statue is depicted in Fig. 4.5 and is situated close to Bobby's in Edinburgh. Rather than focusing on the history of the

Fig. 4.5. Bum the Dog in Princes Street Gardens, Edinburgh, UK.

dog, this statue is a representation of the twinning of the cities of Edinburgh and San Diego, where Bum lived. Yet while the statue may represent a political act, the dog itself is said to be similar to Bobby in many ways, in that it represented many of the qualities humans associate with their ideal dog.

Those people who go on holiday without their dogs, for reasons associated with the distance and type of travel being undertaken or the difficulties of finding dog-friendly accommodation, often find themselves missing their presence. In Whistler, Canada, some owners have overcome this situation by volunteering to walk the dogs housed by Whistler Animals Galore (WAG), the local animal rescue shelter. Seeing the benefits of this for a volunteer organization, the dogs and the tourists, WAG now runs a small advertising campaign highlighting the opportunity for tourists to do some dog walking, or for them to come and volunteer some of their holiday time in other ways such as cleaning out the kennels or aiding the socialization of pups and cats. Whistler Tourism and some of the hotels in the resort, such as the Fairmount, have helped to advertise this option. The situation may not be ideal, with the dogs exposed to tourists who come and go, but there is little ideal in a dog rehoming centre beyond the crucially important fact that if such places did not exist the dogs they rescue would likely be dead. However, the walks these dogs gain from tourists do give them valuable exercise and socialization, the latter being good in its own right and a potential aid in the ability of WAG to rehome the dogs. As the Director of WAG recalled, the opportunity to link tourists and dogs also provides a potential avenue for the adoption of a dog. When talking to me in 2012 she told how one tourist had come to walk a dog, fallen in love with it and when he left at the end of his holiday took the dog home with him by plane. The Director also estimated that of the 27,000 visitors WAG receives each year the vast majority are visitors to Whistler. In volunteering to help the animals at WAG it is arguable that these people do not view the dog as an object but as a creature whose welfare is equally important to that of the human involved; it is a sentient being. At the same time, however, these abandoned animals may be viewable as objects, temporarily giving those who have not brought their dog on holiday some canine company or acting as a tourist attraction for other visitors. Clearly, research is needed to begin to fully understand how people visiting places such as WAG view the animals that they are interacting with and the implications of this for their welfare.

The existence of dogs for rent has been noted by Kean (1998) in Japan. Here, the animals can be rented by those who wish to be able to walk a dog, or spend some time with one, but do not feel they have the ability to commit to owning a dog on a full-time basis. What we have in this instance is in effect a 'convenience' dog; one that the humans can use when they want and easily discard without having to feel guilty as they know it will be going back to a safe and secure environment. In some ways the concerns about the welfare of these dogs are similar to those being walked at WAG in Whistler. Dogs are emotional animals who thrive on consistency in their lives; a revolving door of different walking companions/handlers is not designed to help these animals. In the case of WAG such a situation can be said to be better than the alternative where there are insufficient regular volunteers to care for the dogs' needs. However, to deliberately set up a business to hire out dogs is different entirely as it objectifies the dog for no purpose other than the satisfaction of the human client and the profit margin of the business owner. It is, in its own way, another form of animal abuse, an emotional one that tramples on the dignity of the dog.

Dogs have been presented in a huge variety of ways in art, some of which are shown in Fig. 4.6. The position of the dog in art is a complex one that neatly depicts how the position the dog assumes is determined by the perspective of the viewers, be they the owner of the dog, the artist or the viewing public. Many of these individuals may see the dog as an object where the challenge to the artist may be in capturing the essence of the animal and in doing so focusing on the challenge and what it represents rather than on the dog and its sentience, rights and welfare. Similarly, viewers may see the dog as a representation of the ability of the artist, making the dog merely a vehicle through which the artists' abilities are visualized. In contrast, the owner may view the product of artistic endeavour as a physical and permanent manifestation of the dog they loved as a sentient being rather than as an object.

Perhaps the ultimate example of the dog as object is the artificial dog. Traditionally this has been the domain of the stuffed toy, with the original teddy bear having long since been joined by just about every type of animal imaginable in the stuffed range. Among these are dogs (as shown in Fig. 4.7, my first two 'dogs'). They are a physical representation, not just of a real dog, but – probably more significantly – the human idealization of a dog. These stuffed dogs, just like other stuffed animals, are often given names and characters that, while reflecting real dogs, are also heavily laced with human-like characteristics and traits. In this way, they feed on and reflect human desires, the reality of dogs and the social construction of dogs that were discussed in Chapter 1.

Fig. 4.6. Artistic representations of dogs (clockwise from top left: statue in Hohen-werfen, Austria; statue in Waitati, New Zealand; painting of Manhatten Transfer by Eleanor Wilson).

The stuffed toy dog, though, is just one example of the artificial dog. In 1999 Sony began marketing a robotic dog which promised to be interactive, just like a real dog. They were at the forefront of computer developments; in many ways a test bed to allow computer designers to demonstrate their ability to create interactive and lifelike robots. They were also very expensive, selling for US$2000 each (Herzog, 2010). Yet in many ways the robot and stuffed toy dogs are ideal. They can represent everything humanity expects of the dog, all that we have imposed upon the dog, without any of the drawbacks. They will not poo; drop fur everywhere; require food, water or exercise; die; or act in a

Fig. 4.7. Stuffed toy dogs.

socially inappropriate manner at any stage. While these may be the upside of the artificial dog the downside is that they are not living, breathing creatures; as such they are incapable of the empathy (whether it be real or purely in the minds of the besotted human owner) associated with dogs. The fake fur of the stuffed dog may be luxuriant but to stroke it is a poor substitute for the real thing even if the latter is a little smelly and not entirely clean to the touch.

Rights and Welfare of Dogs in Leisure

The growth of sled dog riding as a tourist attraction was noted briefly in Chapter 2. Many winter sports destinations now provide the opportunity to engage in a short sled dog ride in places as diverse geographically as Whistler, British Columbia (where a variety of the 2010 Winter Olympics events were held), and also in Seefeld, Austria (where the 1964 and 1976 Winter Olympics cross-country skiing events were held). The experiences in Whistler are a reflection of the mass-tourism market that this premier ski/snowboard destination is targeting. The rides are relatively short, the routes are standardized to such an extent that the dogs could and probably would undertake the journey without any human guidance and the visitors are offered an obligatory chance to say 'hi' to the puppies at the end of the ride.

The demand for this mass-market type of dog sledding is high and, reflecting on this, an operator in Whistler in the build-up to the 2010 Vancouver Winter Olympic Games sought to exploit a likely upsurge in demand during the games by significantly increasing the number of his dogs. The result, easily seen with the benefit of hindsight, was that after the Games had finished and the tourists had gone home the operator was left with more dogs than he could sustainably keep (Fennell and Sheppard, 2011). In a horrendous (I apologize for the language but no other word really does the point justice, no matter how emotive it is) display of the dog as object the operator gave the job of destroying a significant number of dogs to an employee. The exact number of dogs is difficult to gauge from the coverage given to the case, with reports ranging from a little more than 50 to about 100. The lack of specificity is in itself concerning, as it says little for the value placed by the media on these animals, but whatever the precise figure it was clearly substantial. When the news of the mass killing of these dogs eventually came to light there was moral outrage from a variety of groups in Canada including those who voluntarily rehome unwanted sled dogs. Fennell and Sheppard (2011: 202) claimed that the destruction of the sled dogs 'is obviously a question of morality; morality, or a lack thereof' yet this is only true if the animal is deemed to be more than an object, to have rights and be sentient, something that is still debated in society in general and certainly questionable legally, as discussed elsewhere in this book. It is interesting to note though that, despite so many societies wrapping themselves in a moralistic blanket of animal rights and welfare, the culling of the Huskies in Whistler was virtually totally ignored by the global media. Further evidence of the lack of recognition of the rights of dogs and their position as sentient beings is arguably provided by the sentence eventually passed down by the Canadian authorities to the manager of the sled dog operation where the cull occurred. He received 3 years' probation, a fine of CAN$1500, a 10-year gun ban and 200 hours of community service (Barrett, 2013). This sends out a message that in the eyes of the law the dog remains little more than an object, the property of its human owner who may do with it as he/she pleases. Since the events in Whistler the British Columbia Ministry of Agriculture has moved to instigate a sled dog Code of Practice (2012). It is not my intention to critique this document in any detail; rather I simply want to note its existence as a step in the right direction towards recognizing the rights and welfare of working animals such as the sled dog as being something more than just a worker's tool.

On the basis of the events in Whistler I conducted a series of interviews with sled dog operators in Whistler in 2011 (not with the one found guilty of the mass destruction of dogs), and in 2013 in Austria and Switzerland. The voices that emerge from these interviews reinforce the notion that identifying the activity in which a dog is involved is only one part, and arguably not even the most important part, of finding out whether its welfare and rights are being considered and protected. The operators I spoke to ran various numbers of dogs, from as few as ten to over 30, though none could be said to be large-scale operators. Only the Whistler operator ran sled dogs as her main source of income. In comparison the Swiss operator who had 35 Siberian Huskies decided to run a sled dog tour operation based on the recognition that, having rescued these animals, it was necessary to find a way to ensure that they did not bankrupt the family. In this way the primary rationale for the business had been the feeding and welfare costs associated with the dogs. In comparison another Swiss operator ran her dogs as a leisure experience for herself, offering tours only to a small number of people, in a way never intended to allow her to make a living from it. Meanwhile, the Austrian operator ran his dogs as a small component of an outdoor adventure and team-building company, which, while clearly an income generator, meant the dogs were not a central component of his or his business's economic well-being.

While the businesses and resultant demands on the dogs were diverse, all of the operators had the welfare and interests of the dogs firmly at centre stage. To a large extent the dogs were members of the family and treated as such. Decisions on whether and when to put old dogs to sleep were made on a case-by-case basis that had the welfare of the individual dog at heart rather than any consideration of the financial bottom line. In essence these were all businesses, but they were ethical ones, in which money was not allowed to rule over the lives of the dogs.

All of the operators interviewed clearly saw their dogs as working animals. Indeed, the Swiss operator with 35 Siberian Huskies stated: 'The Husky is born to pull, born to run, born to work.' However, the Austrian operator noted that his sled dogs were both pets and workers:

> of course it's a mixture. I also see them as working dogs so they have to do their job ... but on the other hand I've got four kids and they also like the dogs so from time to time I take one of the dogs to my place and they stay with us, with the family, and so they are not just on their own so they are part of the family and therefore they are also pets of course.

Seeing the dogs as working animals did not stop the operators interviewed showing considerable compassion for their dogs. For example, the Swiss operator with 35 Siberian Huskies, when talking about her oldest dog, said:

> We have one dog ... he is 14 now, last winter no, but the winter before he still worked. He wanted to go with ... he didn't run very fast but he always run, always run. He didn't pull anymore but it doesn't matter, he wanted to go. Now he is old, he's old. He stays with us; he stays here in the group until he has died. He stays with us and he doesn't go away because he worked a lot and he has the right to stay with us until he will die.

Similarly, the Austrian operator discussed how he dealt with the reality of what to do when a working dog got old. He stated:

> what we do and that works pretty fine, I always have some very active dogs, they are in front of the sled they work hard then we have some retired old dogs and we go for a walk with the snowshoes and we do nice hikes also in the summer ... [he talked very emotionally about how you decide when is the time to end the life of the dog] they are not moving anymore, just laying around, it's not their life ... and it's also not right to keep them alive artificially. I think it's much better to say now it's the end. We had a very nice life.

The compassion of the Austrian owner was further exemplified by his identification of his dogs as having 'very beautiful souls'. With compassion firmly at the centre of her relationship with her dogs the Whistler operator stated: 'If I can't afford to give dogs what they deserve I shouldn't be in this job.' The result of her belief was that she worked three jobs during the summers in order to pay the food bills for her dogs.

In the case of all of the sled dog operators I interviewed none of them could be said to have viewed their dogs as simply objects or tools. To all of the interviewees their dogs were clearly seen as individuals with rights, while at the same time being regarded as highly valued tools. The long-distance sled dog competitors interviewed by Kuhl (2011: 35) also appeared to view their dogs in this manner, with one musher quoted as saying: 'The relationship you have with the dogs, individually and as a team, is far away the most critical element to everything about the whole dog sledding experience.' The positioning of sled dogs as tools and animals with rights can feel contradictory at times but it is crucial to understand that in all instances when a decision was necessary the dogs were always seen primarily as sentient beings with rights rather than merely animated tools.

While the operators interviewed took an animal welfarist view of their sled dogs they were all able to provide stories of other operators who fitted the mould of the mass-cull operator in Whistler. For example, the very small-scale operator in Switzerland stated:

> I do not live from that money [earned from running her dogs], I have my shop, where I sell all the material. And I never would like to be in the situation, that I would urgently need the money from the work with the dogs. Here in Switzerland we have now many people, offering Husky Rides and Tours to 'make' money. A lot of people take care very well to their dogs, but also many people just see that they can make money.

The interviewees were not surprised by my failure to gain interviews with operators of that type. Though care must be taken in trying to infer too much from a lack of data it certainly appears damning that some operators did not want to talk in an interview setting that was defined as entailing discussions of animal welfare and animal rights.

Overall, this chapter has sought to demonstrate how dogs, as sentient beings, can and do have leisure. At the same time, the chapter has also shown how dogs can be used as leisure objects and that their leisure and access to it is often controlled by humans. In this way the leisure of dogs is often a compromise but, as will be discussed in more detail in the following chapters, the leisure of their owners can be as well. Just as has been the case elsewhere in this book, this chapter has demonstrated how it is unwise to categorize the position of the dog based simply on the activity it is involved in. Rather, how owners treat their dogs and feel about them needs to be examined alongside their positioning and experiences in the leisure environment to understand the extent to which their sentience and rights are recognized or that they are objectified. Finally, this chapter has highlighted the need to look beyond physical and emotional well-being when considering the welfare of dogs and also to consider their dignity.

5 Providing for the Leisured Dog and Dog as Leisure Object

Introduction: Why Provide for the Leisured Dog and Dog as Leisure Object?

This chapter begins by discussing the physical and psychological benefits to humans and dogs of sharing time and lives, with a specific emphasis on leisure time. As part of this discussion the problems that have been associated with dogs and their owners spending time apart will also be highlighted. Based on this, the scale and diversity of leisure experiences available to dogs and their owners will be highlighted. Recognizing that dogs may require (or owners may wish for) more than simply being allowed into the leisure environments with their owners, this chapter also examines changes in the quality of experiences offered by the leisure industry to dogs and their owners. Analysis of the extent and nature of access to leisure spaces for leisured dogs and dogs as leisure objects will include a discussion of why leisure experiences are and are not accessible to dogs and how owners overcome barriers to access leisure experiences with their dogs. Analysis of the access to leisure spaces available to dogs will include recognition that all dogs are not considered equal in the eyes of society. The entire chapter is situated within the recognition that, as Rudy (2011: 30) states: 'we have never been more focused on the comfort and entertainment of our pets' than we are today.

It is important to differentiate between the provision of services and experiences for dogs and those provided for their owners. In many instances when a range of services and experiences are, on the face of it, being sold to the dog they are in reality being targeted at the human owner. The owner is the one in power, with the financial purse strings, after all, and the commercial providers know this and so target this group rather than the dog. At the same time, however, they know dog owners are seeking to buy for their dogs, or at least for their construction of the dog (how they see their dog and wish themselves and their dog to be seen by society) and therefore need to pander to this at the same time as having the potential to exploit it. This feeds into the social construct of the 'good' dog owner. Not only do many people want to do the best they can for their pet dog; society actually demands it, castigating those who abuse or neglect (both of which are social constructs) their pets and applauding those who are good owners. The pet industry recognizes this and also helps to shape definitions of what a good dog owner is, arguably driving it in a direction that encourages the spending of ever-increasing amounts of money on dogs. The result is that among the products and services identified with dogs many are aimed at the human owner, either for the needs they perceive their dog to have or their own needs to be identified as a good dog owner. In among all this there are, however, products and services that can be said to be beneficial to the dog even if not directly aimed at them.

This chapter and those that follow will talk about boarding kennels and pet hotels, and dog cuisine, the services and products highlighted in relation to owners' desires and perceptions of needs, and dogs' actual needs. However, it is important not to separate these two, recognizing instead that as the relation between pet dog and owner can be a strong one and that the dog is a social construct, it is not possible to fully separate the desires and perception of the owner from the needs and desires of the dog. The material presented in this chapter stems from a variety of secondary and primary sources. The latter includes a series of semi-structured interviews undertaken in the autumn of 2008 with management staff in four of the hotels and a dog day-care centre in Whistler, Canada, as well as one of the mangers of Tourism Whistler.

Illustration of the Scale and Diversity of Leisure Experiences Available to Dogs and Dog Owners

Go into almost any pet shop today and you are likely to be confronted with a diverse array of toys that are ostensibly for dogs. There will be a range of balls to be thrown (and even things to help the owner throw them and save them from having to pick up a slobbery mess when it is returned to be thrown again), various things to act as the focus of a tug of war and many diversions for those dogs who love to chew. The evidence suggests that there is a significant demand for such products, with the AKC stating that on average dog owners in the USA each spend US$217 per year on toys and treats for their dogs (American Kennel Club, undated, b). In addition, there will be a range of collars, leads, clothing items and beds. Many of these items are likely to come with fashion designer labels. As we see people spending ever more money on their pets in general and dogs in particular, and see the same people viewing the dog increasingly as an integral part of the human family and in the process often as a pseudo-human, we have not just seen the evolution of the pet shop but the emergence of luxury stores targeted specifically at the pockets of besotted dog owners. Examples abound of such stores in countries around the world including the Mut Hut Emporium in Canmore, Canada, which states it was formed 'for the sole purpose of realizing the importance of a pets [sic] place in your family' (Mut Hut Pet Emporium Inc., 2011). Other examples were noted in the previous chapter when discussing fancy dress-wear for dogs.

Head to the newsagents and onto the web and you will find magazines and websites aimed at pet dogs, or at least at their owners (Rudy, 2011). You will also find for sale an array of options to tantalize the taste buds of the dog either with pre-made pet cuisine or cookery books extolling the virtues of cooking for your dog and the diverse range of fare you can provide them (this issue will be discussed in detail in Chapter 8). Head into the world and it is possible to find a variety of environments that have been constructed for the pet dog. These include off-leash areas and pet hotels (the latter will be discussed in detail in Chapter 6).

What is clear is that there is a strong economic rationale for companies to be dog-friendly, to benefit from some of the discretionary funds being spent on dogs and to ensure the satisfaction of customers who wish to share their leisure experiences with their dogs. Support for this view is provided by the Kennel Club (undated: 1), which stated, based on their own research, that: 'four out of five businesses claim that their dog-friendly policy has helped them draw in more customers'. The Kennel Club also reported that: '95 percent of people think more businesses and locations should be Open for Dogs, and find the atmosphere more welcoming when dogs are present'. Yet just as is the case with humans some of the most utilized and sought-after leisure experiences for and with dogs are not specifically constructed. Rather, they involve the ability to freely visit the beach or countryside. Indeed, it has been estimated that today approximately one in five visits to the Scottish countryside for leisure purposes are made by people who take their dogs with them (Anonymous, 2005).

Facilitating dog access to leisure experiences

At the same time as we have witnessed the acceptance of the dog as a member of the family we have seen an increase in the desire among owners to take their dogs with them while engaging in leisure. The result, according to Rice (1968) was that by the 1960s in the USA it was not uncommon to see humans and their dogs in holiday resorts and nightlife centres. The same is certainly true today in many countries, where dogs are to be found exploring urban centres and stopping at pubs, restaurants and cafes, just as can be seen in Fig. 5.1.

With the increasingly central position of the dog in the human family it is not surprising to find an increasing number of people wishing to take their pet on holiday with them (Menn et al., 2010). Such an activity has been greatly aided in the UK by the removal of quarantine regulations, designed to prevent the importation of rabies to the country, and their replacement by pet passports (the Pet Travel Scheme) that effectively allow dogs and their owners to travel to and from the UK at liberty.

Carr and Cohen (2009) reported that one of the main reasons people wish to take their dog on holiday with them is that it is a member of the family. It is therefore not surprising that in 2007 the AKC reported that 40% of dog owners in the USA seek out dog-friendly accommodation when booking their holidays

Fig. 5.1. Dogs and owners exploring café culture in Seefeld, Austria.

(Humane Research Council, 2010). The scale of demand for dog-friendly hotel accommodation was exemplified in an interview with one of the management team of the Hilton in Whistler in 2008 who stated there could be between 20 and 30 dogs staying in the hotel at the weekends during the peak summer months (with the hotel having 288 rooms in total). In addition to the apparent significance of the dog-friendly holiday market it appears to be one of the fastest-growing segments of the tourism market (World Travel Market, 2007).

Recognizing the potential of providing accommodation that allows for dogs and even caters to them (or more accurately what their owners perceive to be their needs) many operators are now providing for this growing market (Weaver and Lawton, 2010 in Backer, 2012). Indeed, in a report published in 2007 the World Travel Market claimed that in the UK: 'hotels are currently the only sector [of the tourism industry] where players cater enthusiastically to the needs of visitors with pets' (9). Yet even here the number of accommodation providers that allow dogs in their rooms is small relative to the overall number of providers. That the number of dog-friendly accommodation providers is small in comparison to the demand was highlighted by Carr and Cohen (2009) whose study in Brisbane, Australia, reported that while many dog owners wished to take their pets on holiday with them they often found it difficult to locate suitable accommodation. Similarly, Bly (2012) reported that over 40% of dog owners in the USA have stated that it is difficult to find pet-friendly holiday accommodation. It is therefore probably no surprise that Hill and Bowling (2007) noted that 41% of American dog owners have reported smuggling their dog into tourism accommodation at some point. Carr and Cohen

(2009) found some respondents felt that finding accommodation for them and their dogs was so difficult that they chose not to go on holiday at all rather than have to leave their dogs behind.

The idea of allowing dogs into holiday accommodation raises the issues of what is identified as 'appropriate' accommodation and dog-related behaviour and by whom. This needs situating within the context of the centralizing of the dog in the family, which is arguably leading to increasing numbers of humans letting their dogs lead much of their lives inside the family home, and even sleep in the same bed as their owners. Indeed, the American Veterinary Medical Association (2012) has reported that 51% of owners in America let their pets sleep on their bed frequently and that only 22% say they never do this. With specific reference to dogs, Katz (2003: 14) suggested that: 'Fifty per cent of dogs now sleep in their owners' bedrooms, and half of those sleep on their owners' beds.' In comparison, Voith et al. (1992) reported that only 45% of their American respondents stated their dogs were never allowed to sleep on their owners' bed. These expectations of 'normalcy' on behalf of the dog owners arguably colour their expectations of what is acceptable accommodation for them and their dogs while they are on holiday. Figure 5.2 depicts both the social acceptance that many owners now allow their dogs to sleep in their bed and the willingness of hotels, the Valhalla Inn chain in this instance, to cater to this. In this way the advert reaffirms the normalcy of dogs sleeping in beds with their owners as an integral part of the human family and encourages such positioning of the dog. In contradiction to the image in Fig. 5.2, dog behaviourists and health experts continue to state that the dog in the bed is neither an acceptable nor even a desirable situation.

The nature of what is offered for dogs in an accommodation unit varies widely across operators and both within and across countries. An example of the lengths some accommodation providers are willing to go to in catering for dogs and their owners is provided in Fig. 5.3, which shows the welcome pack

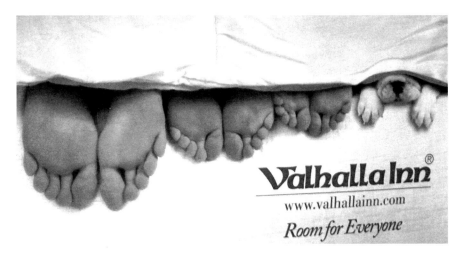

Fig. 5.2. Poster in Thunder Bay airport, 2008.

Fig. 5.3. Whistler, Hilton hotel dog welcome pack.

provided to dogs and their owners upon arrival at the Hilton Hotel in Whistler, Canada, in 2008. The pack, at the top of the picture, was filled with all the other goodies displayed and after being emptied out is designed to be used as a water bowl for the dog. In addition, the hotel provided things such as a dog leash, a chew in the form of a toothbrush, a small bag of treats and some wet wipes for dogs so owners could clean off any muddy paws. Yet such welcome packs as those provided by the Hilton are but the tip of the iceberg when it comes to the potential offerings in hotels for dogs. For example, Herzog (2010: 76) states that in the Sarasota Ritz it is now possible to pick from four different massages for your dog ('the Swedish Pet Massage, the Full Body Relaxation Massage, the Invigorating Sports Massages, and the gentler Senior Pet Massage') at a cost of US$130. In addition to allowing guests to bring their dogs with them, in 2008 the Fairmount Chateau in Whistler offered food menus for dogs prepared by the hotel's executive chef, including a vegetarian option. Items included French toast, and egg and gizzard pudding for breakfast (at CAN$8 each) and rice and bean, and lamb and rice stew for lunch or dinner (at CAN$10 each).

The Hilton is not the only hotel in Whistler that promotes itself as being dog friendly; indeed as the picture in Fig. 5.4 shows one of the pre-eminent hotels in the resort, the Fairmount Chateau, openly accepts dogs as guests and has no problem with them being walked through the lobby. An important point to note here is how all of the other occupants of the lobby paid no attention at all to the dog. There was no shock in seeing the dog in this situation; it was to all present something 'normal' and therefore totally unworthy of attention.

Fig. 5.4. Lobby of Fairmount Chateau, Whistler, Canada (2008).

In January, 2005, a study was undertaken of five Internet sites[1] and two guidebooks (*Australian Dogs on Holiday*, McGill (2002) and *Holidaying with Dogs*, Dennis (2000)) dedicated to advertising self-defined dog-friendly accommodation in Australia. These sources represented all of the major websites and guidebooks advertising dog-friendly holiday lodgings in Australia at the time of the study. A total of 1149 accommodation providers and 824 camping-only facilities (it was unclear what the nature of the accommodation offered by 170 of the advertisers was) advertised themselves in these books and Internet sites. The aim of the study was to assess the nature of what these operators were offering to dogs, or more accurately to the owners of the dogs.

Analysis of the advertisements in the dog-friendly accommodation guidebooks and Internet sites clearly shows a wide variety in the nature of what is offered to dogs and the rules imposed upon them and their owners. At one extreme there is a group of units that could best be identified as offering 'dog heaven'. This type of unit promises to provide every possible delight for their canine visitors and their advertisements clearly show the operators' willingness to happily accept dogs with human guests. For example, the advert for a self-catering unit in Victoria states, 'I get pampered!! When we arrive, a comfy bed is waiting for me beside the wood fire, with my own special towels, shiny bowls and yummy treats. Outside is my own private courtyard complete with a well appointed kennel, just in case I want to catch up on some sleep while my parents go out.' This advert clearly positions the dog as a central part of the human family and anthropomorphism is prevalent. The peak of dog friendliness is perhaps expressed in the following quotation from the advertisement of a bed and breakfast unit in New South Wales:

the two resident Labradors are always ready to show visiting dogs around their backyard – 60 acres of native bush and pasture with plenty of room to run. There is also a dog swimming pool (dam), Arrin the horse to talk to and a doggie bed to snuggle into at night next to the wood fire. Blankets, sheets and towels are supplied for each guest dog as well as silver service bowls and special treats on arrival.

In total, only 14 operators stated they provided special bowls, gifts and/or bedding for dogs.

At the opposite extreme, there were a number of advertisements within the dog-friendly accommodation guidebooks and Internet sites that may be defined as being very dog-unfriendly. Such providers tended to advertise a variety of barriers and restrictions dogs and their owners would face during their vacation. For example, a self-catering and campsite provider in Queensland stated in its advert that: 'we do allow pets on a very restrictive basis'. Furthermore, a self-catering and campsite unit in New South Wales stated in its advert that dogs are not allowed 'during Christmas and Easter school holidays, not in cabins or on verandas at any time'. In a more extreme advert a campsite in New South Wales stated dogs were to be 'taken out of park for toilet needs'. In addition, another accommodation provider in New South Wales stated in their advert that: 'female dogs should be de-sexed or at least guaranteed not to come on heat during the holiday'. One of the most extreme dog-unfriendly adverts was by a self-catering and campsite unit based in Victoria, which stated dogs were only allowed 'at management's discretion, not allowed in onsite accommodation or amenities, not allowed at all during peak periods, must be on-leash, and not left unattended'. In total, 42 accommodation providers only allowed dogs outside of the peak tourism periods and three required dogs to be de-sexed. These rules and regulations may, of course, be argued to have been put in place for the benefit of non-dog-owning guests, an issue that will be discussed in more detail later in this chapter.

It is interesting to note that although pet dogs are increasingly being allowed inside the family house, only 354 of the accommodation providers studied in Australia stated this was an option. In contrast, 806 stated that dogs were only allowed outside of the accommodation unit. Of those operators that reported allowing dogs inside, 73 stated they were not allowed on furniture and/or in certain rooms. In comparison, hotels such as the Hilton in Whistler, as well as providing beds for dogs in their owners' rooms, have no specific rules about where the dog should sleep, effectively enabling it to sleep on its owners' bed if they wish.

While accommodation providers may increasingly be allowing dogs into their premises, it appears that the majority are not charging for this service. While some charge an extra cleaning service this is not the same as charging for the use of the room. Indeed, all the hotels interviewed in Whistler in 2008 stated they only charged a room cleaning fee if people wished to bring their dog/s with them. The need for this additional fee was related to the extra time and effort required to ensure the removal of all dog hair from a room, something that all respondents identified as being needed to ensure that the next guests in the room did not have an allergic reaction. For example, the interviewee for the Crystal Lodge in Whistler stated that: 'You have to appreciate of course that people do have allergies so they do steam clean the rugs, they completely strip all the bedding and curtains and everything so that its ridden of any sort of dog dander or hair.' The point was often made that this extra charge barely covered the cleaning cost and did not pay for the treats the dogs received during their stay. Yet there was never any suggestion that extra charges should be levied against dog owners. The reasoning extends to the identification of the dog as an integral member of the family. Thus, the logic was that as hotels often do not charge extra for children to stay with their parents, and that these children often receive small welcome gifts, the same should apply in the case of dogs. This is exemplified by the Crystal Lodge interviewee who stated: 'I think we like to consider it [the dog] part of their family because that's how I treat my dogs so … I know a lot of managers [in Whistler], it's just a part of someone's family and to us I think it would almost be like charging for their children.'

Yet it may be argued that accommodation providers are missing out on a potential revenue stream given the centrality of dogs to many owners' lives. How much are these operators potentially missing out on? Possibly more than 30% of the standard price according to the World Travel Market (2007). This claim is supported by Carr and Cohen (2009) who reported that 13% of their dog-owning respondents stated they were willing to pay over 25% of the cost of a holiday without a dog in order to be able to take their pet with them.

Recognizing not just that there are an increasing number of dogs and therefore people exercising their pets in urbanized areas and popular rural settings, but that the general public does not wish to see or even worse step in any dog poo, many public authorities around the world are now providing free dog poo bags to owners (Fig. 5.5). The need for such bags is starkly illustrated by an estimate from the late 1980s that in the UK the dog population at the time produced 1 million kilos of poo every day (Council for Science and Society, 1988). When it is recognized that the dog population has expanded since then (see Chapter 1) the scale of the problem becomes apparent. Indeed, as shown by an AKC study in 2005, the main complaint of those not owning dogs in relation to dog owners is that all too often they leave their dogs' poo wherever it falls (American Kennel Club, 2005b). That concern among the general public with the poo left behind by dogs in public spaces is not just a feature of western countries is exemplified by a news article from India in 2012 noting the concern of citizens in Pune regarding dog excrement left on hill trails (Anonymous, 2012b).

Dog poo bag dispensers are generally located at various points in urban areas, and along known popular walking routes, together with appropriate bins for the disposal of full bags. Similar bags have been provided outside some hotels where dogs are allowed to stay, as in the case of the Hilton Hotel in Whistler, Canada (Fig. 5.5). The provisioning of dog poo bags is often backed up by rules and regulations that allow authorities to fine those owners who do not pick up after their dog, though proving which dog has left a mess behind is far from easy. There have also been attempts to make the picking up of dog poo, and placing it in an appropriate bin, a central component of the social construction of a good dog owner. This behaviour is by no means a foregone conclusion; it is evident in a variety of places as divergent as Canada, the UK

Fig. 5.5. Dog poo bag dispensers (top row, left to right: Hilton Hotel, Whistler, Canada; Hermitage, Scotland; Lake Louise, Canada; bottom row, left to right: Hochfelden, France; Leutasch, Austria; Vienna, Austria).

and New Zealand that some owners are picking up the poo in a plastic bag and then simply throwing said bag into the bushes along the edge of the pavement. An example of this constructing of the good dog owner is provided by the Scottish Outdoor Access Code, which extols readers to 'remove faeces left by your dog in a public open place' (Anonymous, 2005: 43). While these steps to encourage people to remove the poo deposited by their dogs may not have been entirely successful the manager interviewed in the Loch Lomond and Trossachs National Park in Scotland in 2008 stated that the provision of bags and bins, along with appropriate governmental legislation, had made a significant difference in reducing the amount of dog poo left behind.

As well as the provision of dog poo bags and public by-laws to encourage responsible behaviour there have been some attempts to provide dog toilets: specific areas where dogs are supposed to be encouraged to do their business while walking in public spaces. The one in Fig. 5.6 is located just outside the grounds of the Palace of Versailles. While highlighting that another toilet was

Fig. 5.6. Public dog toilet in Versailles, France.

provided in Toulouse, France, the Council for Science and Society (1988) stated that such experiments had not been a success.

Dogs, just like humans, require regular access to water to prevent dehydration. Yet, when out in public, dogs can find it difficult to access such refreshment, particularly in urban areas and more sculpted landscapes, where poorly drained surfaces and associated puddles are considered a blot on the landscape. Recognizing this most basic of needs for dogs many human leisure destinations are now offering water stops for dogs, as seen in Fig. 5.7. Most commonly these are associated with bars, cafes and restaurants which allow dogs on their premises (either inside, or more commonly, outside). The extension from offering free water to human guests to providing the same for dogs is something that involves only a minimal cost but whose benefits are potentially significant. It appears to have begun with the provision of a communal drinking bowl but more recently individual bowls are starting to appear. This not only raises the quality of the service in the eyes of the human owner but also means the dogs are more likely to drink from the bowls as they do not smell of other, potentially more dominant, dogs. The businesses gain the satisfaction of the human customers who view their dogs as important members of their families. They are likely to become repeat clients and give positive word-of-mouth recommendations to their friends and relatives, and both of these outcomes are highly desired by the service industry sector. Yet such offerings are not only restricted to food outlets and can include other settings such as historic parks and gardens. In each case the emphasis is on ensuring the satisfaction of the human through providing a basic service for the dog.

It is all well and good offering tourists and their dogs a variety of facilities in the leisure environment but there is clearly a need to ensure both groups can actually get to these experiences if they and the leisure industry are to benefit. This obviously requires that dogs should be able to access appropriate modes of transportation. Yet access to public transport for dogs is not a widespread phenomenon, with buses and trains often banning them. This situation

Fig. 5.7. Catering to the liquid needs of dogs (from left to right; Chenonceau, France; Vienna, Austria; Isle of Arran, Scotland).

is exemplified by public ground transport in the UK which the World Travel Market (2007: 9) stated:

> tolerate[s] pets at best. National Rail accepts dogs, cats and other small animals on board and the Caledonian Sleeper from London to Fort William, operated by First ScotRail, allows dogs and cats to accompany their owners in the sleeper cars for a £40 surcharge. However, there remains no transportation or tour operator service offering packages specifically targeted towards this consumer group.

The Associated Press (2012) also noted that in the USA dogs are not allowed on Amtrak trains or Greyhound coaches.

The problems with taking dogs on public transport noted by the World Travel Market (2007) are not universal. Many western European countries allow dogs who are under control to travel with their owners on buses and trains (Coppinger and Coppinger, 2001). For example, in Austria dogs are allowed on both modes of transport as long as they are on a lead and wearing a muzzle. Muzzles may not be something that dogs appreciate wearing but they provide a visual assurance to non-dog-owning travellers and in doing so allow dogs and their owners to travel on public transport. As a result, in my journeys through Austria in 2013 it was common to see dogs on public transport and nobody remarked at the sight of them or gave any indication there was anything untoward or unusual in the sight. Figure 5.8 shows that dogs are also allowed on the London Underground and buses (personal communication with Kennel Club, 2012).

Dogs are increasingly being transported by air, with most airlines now willing to take them, as seen in Table 5.1 (the data presented in this table were collected in December 2013 from the websites of the airlines listed). The data show that while all the airlines are willing to transport dogs in their cargo space only 13 of the 24 studied were willing to allow pet dogs in the passenger compartment, and one airline, Air China, provided no information on its policy. The presence of dogs in the passenger compartment is not a new phenomenon; Szasz (1968) noted that TWA (Trans World Airlines, which has since merged with American Airlines) allowed small dogs in the cabins of its aeroplanes.

Fig. 5.8. Dog on London Underground (2007). (Photo courtesy of David Scott.)

The same size restriction exists today though the specific weight differs across airlines, with a maximum ranging between 5 and 8 kg. The weight is really only a guide as, no matter what its weight, the dog must be small enough to fit comfortably into a cage or carrier beneath the seat in front of the passenger (Stapen, 2013b); anyone who has ever been on a plane will know this is a very small space even for a small dog. Those dogs not small enough to fit in the cabin are consigned to the cargo hold in pet-carrying boxes. Some of the airlines stress that the baggage hold where dogs will be located is pressurized (e.g. Air Canada and United Airlines), while others point out that pets in their cargo holds will experience air conditioning (e.g. Lufthansa and Singapore Airlines) but such information is often not available on the airline websites. KLM is the only airline of those listed in Table 5.1 to state that the area of the hold in which pets are transported will be heated. The absence of information regarding the conditions animals are likely to encounter in the hold of a plane does not necessarily mean that certain things, such as heating and oxygen, will not be available but the absence of the information can do nothing to reassure owners wishing to fly with their dog.

Several airlines name specific breeds the carriers will not transport in a cabin or hold; this includes fighting dogs and brachycephalic (snub-nosed, short-snout or flat-face) dogs who are deemed to be prone to breathing diffi-culties. Each airline has its own policy regarding the prices it charges for the

Table 5.1. Airline policy regarding the transportation of dogs.

Airline	Service dogs allowed	Service dogs allowed free of charge	Dogs allowed in cabin	Dogs allowed in baggage hold
Air New Zealand	Yes	Yes	No	Yes
Qantas	Yes	Yes	No	Yes
British Airways	Yes	Yes	Yes	Yes
United Airlines	Yes	Yes	Yes	Yes
Emirates	Yes	Yes	No	Yes
Lufthansa	Yes	Yes	Yes	Yes
Air Canada	Yes	Yes	Yes	Yes
South African Airways	Yes	Yes	No	Yes
Air China	No information provided			
Cathay Pacific	Yes	Permit fee required; no other costs noted	No	Yes
All Nippon Airways	Yes	Yes	No	Yes
Korean Air	Yes	Yes	Yes	Yes
Malaysia Airways	Yes	Yes	No	Yes
Singapore Airlines	Yes	Yes	No	Yes
Air France	Yes	Yes	Yes	Yes
Alitalia	Yes	Yes	Yes	Yes
KLM	Yes	Yes	Yes	Yes
Aeroflot	Yes	Yes	Yes	Yes
Iberia	Yes	Yes	Yes	Yes
Saudi Arabian Airlines	Yes	Yes	Yes	Yes
Aerolineas Argentinas	Yes	Yes	No	Yes
Latam Airlines Group	Yes	Yes	No	Yes
El Al	Yes	Yes	Yes	Yes
Japan Airlines	Yes	Yes	Yes	No

transportation of dogs, the details of which are beyond analysis in this book. However, with the exception of guide and other service dogs, the transportation of dogs incurs a generally not insubstantial cost.

It is difficult to obtain data to determine the number of dogs flying, though according to Associated Press (2012) 2 million pets and other animals are transported by air each year in the USA. It is even more difficult to obtain data for those animals that die or go missing while flying. However, there are reports of dogs freezing to death in the cargo hold. For example, in 2011 it was reported that a dog on a flight from Russia to the USA had frozen to death in the cargo hold of the plan carrying it (Breyer, 2011). Breyer also reported that between 2005 and 2009, 224 dogs were reported lost, killed or injured while being carried by airlines based in the USA. Given these figures it is not surprising that a study conducted in the USA found that 75% of the respondents did not trust airlines to take care of their pets (Stapen, 2013a). While more accurate data are needed to identify how many dogs fly each year and what harm, if any, comes to them it is important to remember that while it is clearly not without risks the vast majority of those animals that are transported in planes do so without significant injury or worse. Furthermore, it is important to remember that compared to the number of dogs currently kept as pets very few actually travel by air. For those dogs who do fly it is now possible for them to learn to get used to the idea before engaging in the reality of it. A company in the USA offers the opportunity for dogs to undertake simulated flight experiences at US$349 a go (Associated Press, 2013).

What can be seen from everything discussed in this section is that the dog is increasingly able to access a wide array of leisure experiences to such an extent that the sign in Fig. 5.9 has become the norm rather than the exception in many countries. However, when investigating this image further, we find it is often true that dogs are being allowed into spaces and experiences not for their benefit but to cater to the desires and perceptions of their owners.

The Health and Safety of Dogs in the Leisure Environment

Just as humans face a variety of potential risks in the leisure environment, so do dogs. These risks begin with the journey to the leisure environment, as noted in the previous section with specific reference to aeroplanes. Within the private automobile the safety of the dog occupies a poor second place to concerns about the safety of human passengers. While there are laws concerning the wearing of seatbelts for humans, no such requirements exist for dogs even though they are at least as likely as a human to end up being seriously injured in the case

Fig. 5.9. A welcoming sign.

of a crash. There is now, however, a variety of products on the market that help owners to minimize the potential for injury to their dog in the event of a crash.

As we see more people wishing to take and actually taking their dogs with them on holidays we are arguably seeing dogs, and by default their owners, potentially exposed to greater health risks. For example, Menn *et al.* (2010) have pointed out that people travelling with their dogs across international borders for holidays results in the exposure of these animals to pathogens and/or diseases not found in their home environment. On a more localized scale the same is true in environments such as rural Australia, where a wide variety of dangers exists including the paralysis tick. In this instance, taking an urban-living dog into the rural hinterland may seem like an ideal holiday for all the family, but it does come with heightened risks.

Dogs and water are seen by society in general to have a natural partnership, and dogs are widely perceived as loving to swim and splash in open waters. While it does indeed seem to be true that many dogs love the water it is beginning to be recognized that, just like humans, dogs are quite capable of drowning. Consequently, we now see life jackets for dogs being marketed. On the one hand this may be positioned as being symptomatic of everything bad about anthropomorphism but on the other it can be seen as an indicator of the value and welfare of dogs featuring more strongly in the minds of owners in particular and humans in general. In addition, it is now possible to buy boots, sunscreen and sunglasses for dogs, among other items. The boots depicted in Fig. 5.10 are specifically

Fig. 5.10. Dog hiking boots.

designed to prevent dogs cutting their paws when out hiking with their owners and are also commonly utilized to prevent injury to the paws of sled dogs. What these boots are not is a fashion accessory that can be added to a dog in a similar manner to the various outfits that can be added to a Barbie doll. The former have the welfare of the dog at heart while the latter are concerned with the objectification of the dog for the benefit of the fashion-conscious human owner. Sunscreen for furless dogs is about the welfare of the dog rather than the owner, as (in theory) are sunglasses, though trying to persuade a dog to wear them is no easy task. Even a dog jacket, which can easily be seen as nothing more than a fashion accessory, can be a necessity for the welfare of the dog. The idea that a moderate fur cover is sufficient to keep a dog warm when out for a walk in the winter, especially for the many urban pet dogs who are used to living in the family home, is a rather unsympathetic one that ignores the notion that dogs may actually, just like humans, feel the cold. If owners are disabused of such a belief then the provision of jackets for dogs becomes a matter of the animal's welfare.

Alongside protective clothing and other items for dogs in the leisure experience there is an increasing recognition of the value and importance of pet insurance. The result is that an array of companies now provides pet insurance that covers a variety of veterinary expenses. More recently, with the growth in the number of people taking their dogs on holiday with them, pet travel insurance has begun to be offered, with the first such policy being advertised in the UK in 1999. These insurances offer a similar set of safeguards to dogs as human travel insurance does to their owners, including emergency repatriation and extended care if the dog is too ill to travel after the holiday comes to an end (Dogs Trust, undated). On reflection, the taking out of pet travel insurance seems as logical as having travel insurance for a human yet it is questionable how many owners take this step. Indeed, speaking about the launch of the first pet travel insurance scheme in the UK in 1999, the head of sales and marketing for the scheme stated that only 1 million pets were insured in the UK at the time and that he 'would be astounded if more than 2,000 took travel cover' (Jenkins, 1999).

Geographical, temporal and cultural constraints on provision and access

Arguably the biggest current debate surrounding dogs and their owners is whether the former should be allowed into wilderness or natural landscapes. For example, they are banned from accessing national parks in countries such as New Zealand and Australia for fear of their potential impact on the indigenous wildlife, much of which is already under severe strain due to the impact of introduced species and the encroachment of human developments on their natural environments. In a personal e-mail communication with the New South Wales National Parks and Wildlife Service in Australia in 2002 it reported that the smell of dogs and their urine and poo can deter wildlife from using an area, while these deposits can also contain infectious diseases, and add nutrients to soil and thereby increase the spread of invasive plant life. Other reasons provided by the New South Wales National Parks and Wildlife Service for banning dogs from national parks extended to the notion that: 'Dogs are predators – being domesticated does not change this' and that dogs, even when on-leash, can escape and result in the establishment/growth of feral dog populations. Finally, the New South Wales National Parks and Wildlife Service identified: 'Barking and other canine behaviour such as biting and jumping can annoy or injure other park users' as reasons for banning them.

The potential impact of pet dogs taken into areas of indigenous wildlife is shown graphically in the marketing material presented in Fig. 5.11. The emotiveness highlighted in the figure is repeated by the Department of Conservation and Land Management (2002) in their explanation for the banning of dogs from national parks in Western Australia. 'There are several reasons why dogs and other pets shouldn't be in national parks and other reserves. They jump on children, create chaos in dangerous areas such as cliff tops, gorges and the water's edge; foul public picnic areas, chase wildlife and disrupt gatherings.'

Even in countries such as Canada where dogs are allowed into national parks there is fierce debate as to whether this should be allowed to continue. Against this backdrop it is interesting to see that LaBelle (1993: 2) argued: 'Dogs inflict less damage on the wilderness than any other pack [carrying] animal because they eat only the food they carry and cause no erosion to the trail.' This claim is clarified by LaBelle's statement that dogs need to be on a leash at all times and that aggressive or difficult dogs have no place in the back country or wilderness to ensure they do not threaten human users of the space or wildlife. While talking specifically about using a dog as a pack animal the points made can easily be applied to dogs in general. The need for dogs to be on-leash was strongly championed in an interview with the National Park Warden's office in Banff in 2008. The view was made that in an ideal world dogs would not be allowed in national parks in Canada as there was too much potential for them to run off-leash and in the process to disturb, injure or kill the wildlife. While claiming that such incidences were an everyday occurrence in the Banff National Park the interviewee pointed out that the majority of the problems were with local dog owners rather than visitors to the park. Such a reality was arguably due to the lack of any off-leash exercise areas for dogs in

Fig. 5.11. Promoting the prevention of dogs accessing environments that are home to indigenous wildlife in Queensland, Australia.

the park in general or the township of Banff in particular. Yet while wishing for the banning of dogs the interviewee admitted that dogs did have a positive role to play in discouraging wildlife from entering the township where it may come into conflict with humans and potentially be injured. The problem then shifted to having to differentiate between the positive and negative harassment of wildlife, something that is potentially difficult to differentiate between in the eyes of the public.

The points made by LaBelle, while arguably true, are also an oversimplification of a much more complex reality. A dog does not have to be off-leash or even out of control to potentially adversely affect wildlife, as noted above. The problem is that, as admitted by the New South Wales National Parks and Wildlife Service in my communication with them: 'many of the reasons [for banning dogs from national parks] … are based on common sense. I have not been able to find specific research on this or on any public response to the pet restriction in National Parks.' Basing public policy on guesswork and preconceptions rather than on valid research is only ever likely to result in continuation of the status quo, irrespective of whether such a situation is correct or beneficial to all those involved (human and otherwise).

It is interesting to compare the messages about not taking dogs into national parks or the banning of them from such spaces with the message that has consistently been promoted in the case of one of the UK's most popular national parks, the Lake District. An analysis was undertaken of the tourism brochures produced by the Keswick Tourism Association between the early 1900s and 2008, Keswick being the self-proclaimed 'Heart of the Lake District'. In these brochures the pet dog has consistently been portrayed enjoying the walks and lakeshore experiences on offer in this National Park since 1988, as exemplified in Fig. 5.12. The pet dogs have always been shown with their family, in a style that depicts the centrality of the dog to the family leisure in a way similar to that noted in Fig. 4.4 in Chapter 4. The portrayal of the dog in this manner since the late 1980s dovetails with the increasing centrality of the pet dog in the family. In terms of access to the national park, the message in these photos is clear: well-behaved dogs are very welcome. All the dogs pictured in the brochures were either on-leash, or if they were off-leash (and more than half the dogs pictured were) then they were under close control. The presence of pet dogs in the UK's national parks was underlined in an interview with one of the managers of the Loch Lomond and Trossachs National Park in 2008 in which she responded that it was 'taken as read' that dog owners use the national park with their pets and that it was 'an automatic assumption' that dogs are allowed into the UK's national parks. This speaks of a cultural mindset regarding the dog and national parks rather than just a set of rules and regulations.

Where dogs are not banned from natural landscapes their owners are generally asked to act responsibly and ensure their dogs are under control. Consequently, it is common at the start of walking tracks where dogs are allowed for signs to be set up (such as those in Fig. 5.13) reminding dog owners of the need to keep their dog on a leash; sometimes this is accompanied by an explanation of the necessity of this to try not only to enforce rules of good behaviour but to provide a logical explanation for them. The theory is that this education of the visitor will

2006

2002

1999

1996

Fig. 5.12. Pet dogs in brochures promoting Keswick, in the English Lake District National Park, UK. (Photographs courtesy of Keswick Tourism Association, UK.)

Fig. 5.13. Please keep your dog under control (from left to right, Kananaskis, Canada; Salzburg, Austria).

aid uptake and acceptance of the rules and regulations. What constitutes 'under control', which assumes a dog is off-leash, or even 'on-leash' can be problematic, though, and require explanation. Leashes come in all sorts of lengths, including extendable ones that can see the dog on-leash but at a considerable distance from its owner. Consequently, generally speaking, 'under control' can be said to mean that the dog 'is able to respond to your [the owners'] commands and is kept close at heel' (Anonymous, 2005: 43).

In some rural/wilderness areas we see extra restrictions being placed on dogs at specific times of year, particularly when wildlife are breeding and/or moulting and are therefore particularly vulnerable. So, during the breeding period for ground-nesting birds in Scotland dog owners are asked to be especially careful; either avoiding such areas altogether or ensuring their dog is under control or on-leash (Anonymous, 2005). A similar suggestion is made in New Zealand regarding beaches which are known as sites where penguins go to moult. If an owner fails to take note of this advice in New Zealand and their dog kills or injures a penguin then they face the prospect of 'up to three years' of imprisonment or fines of up to NZ$20,000 and an order for destruction of the dog' (Fox, 2012).

In rural areas where pasture farming has traditionally been the dominant feature of the local economy there has been a long running battle between farmers and dog owners visiting these places with their pets. The concern from farmers is that pet dogs, generally nowhere near as highly trained as their working dog relatives on the farms, will disturb and potentially kill the livestock; something that is especially concerning during lambing season. Indeed, it is stated within the Scottish Outdoor Access Code that: 'many farmers and land managers, have concerns about dogs when they are not under proper control as this can cause serious problems, including worrying of and injury to livestock' (Anonymous, 2005: 42). Consequently, there is a strong message for those visiting farming regions with their dogs that includes the fact that farmers have the right in places such as the UK to shoot dogs they feel are worrying their animals.

The beach is also an arena of potential conflict regarding the access of dogs and their owners (Holmberg, 2013). The banning of dogs from specific beaches either entirely or during peak summer months (Fig. 5.14) is not uncommon. In other cases dogs are required to be on a leash at all times. The reasons for such restrictions vary but are based around the needs and desires of the human

Fig. 5.14. Dog access to beaches (from left to right, the Okanagan Valley, Canada; Lyme Regis, UK).

population who wish to enjoy the beach without the harassment of dogs and the potential mess left behind by them. In addition, they are banned from other beaches, either temporally or permanently, because of their potential to harm wildlife (as noted above). The task of trying to balance the rights and desires of dog owners to take their pets to beaches, and of those who wish to experience the beach without being bothered by dogs, is a thankless one for local authorities where pleasing everyone is plainly impossible. A not uncommon tactic employed is to classify all beaches within a locale as dog friendly or off-limits to dogs and advertise them accordingly. The key, of course, is ensuring that all of those people who wish to access dog- and non-dog-friendly beaches can do so in order to make sure they are not adversely impacted upon by any zoning decisions.

The urban and semi-urban playing field or sports pitch is another area where there is the potential for conflict between dog owners and other users of these spaces. The Scottish Outdoor Access Code encourages dog owners not to 'allow your dog to run onto sports pitches, playing fields or play areas when these are in use' (Anonymous, 2005: 44). Yet the obvious problem of a dog on a pitch during a game of rugby or football is not the only one associated with their use of such spaces. The leaving of a dog poo, either by wilful neglect or simply missing the event while the dog is running off-leash is arguably especially problematic on a sports field where the potential not just to step in a poo but to fall in one is all too real. Which dog owner can claim to have picked up every poo their dog has ever done? I would have to admit to probably having missed a fair number when my dogs have run off-leash at the beach, especially on dark mornings when a black dog is almost invisible. Hence we see conflicts arising between sports users of these spaces and dog owners who often rightly point out that they represent one of the few open spaces in urban areas where dogs have the potential to run off-leash.

Dogs are widely banned from access to shops, irrespective of the goods on sale within, but this is not universally the case. Rather, in some locations dogs are specifically invited into shops, as seen in Fig. 5.15, while in others they are not prohibited but neither are they actively encouraged to enter. Why differences exist in terms of the access allowed to dogs and their owners can be guessed at in relation to the goods sold in a shop and the potential for wagging

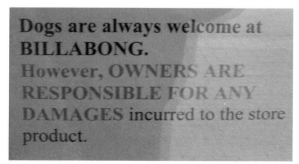 

Fig. 5.15. Dog access to shops (from left to right: Whistler, Canada; Devon, UK).

tails to cause untold damage but more factual based analysis is not possible due to a dearth of research on the subject.

A similar case to shops exists in relation to restaurants, cafes, pubs and other sites where food for humans is produced and consumed, with some operators allowing dogs in, others barring them entirely and many allowing them in outside areas only. It is important when dealing with the issue of dogs and food premises to note it is not necessarily against the law for dogs to enter such places. For example, in the UK the law is solely concerned with ensuring the hygiene of food outlets (Wedderburn, 2012), something that is not automatically imperilled by the presence of a dog in a dining area. The reasons then for not allowing dogs in food serving premises or only allowing them outside of such places appear to have more to do with culture or misconceptions about dogs. The perceived potential for dogs to disturb other guests may also be a reason for banning them partially or wholly from food outlets. Once again, more detailed analysis of the reasons is not possible due to a lack of research on the subject.

Even in hotels that are clearly dog friendly, such as those located in Whistler, Canada, that were discussed earlier in this chapter, there are rules and regulations regarding the behaviour of dogs and their owners and spaces where the former are banned from entering. Within the Whistler hotels dogs were generally not allowed to be left in the rooms by themselves. Yet in cases where this rule was broken there was a tendency to aid the dog rather than to implement draconian punishments. For example, the Hilton interviewee stated: 'on occasions we've gone up to the room and picked up the pet and just brought him down to the lobby and let him hang out in the front office till the owners come back and that's usually worse case scenario'. Such a move speaks volumes about the perception by the hotel of the dog as an integral member of the human family and therefore the level of care and attention that should be bestowed upon it as a guest of the hotel.

Some, but not all, of the hotels in Whistler stated they had pet-free floors in the building, while others had rooms specifically set aside for those holidaying with their dogs. While part of the reasoning for this provision was to minimize disturbance to other guests there was a strong emphasis on ensuring that anyone suffering from allergic reactions to dogs would not suffer. The banning of dogs from the pool area of hotels was explained by the Hilton interviewee who noted it had nothing to do with health and hygiene but was simply due to the potential of dog fur to clog the pool filters.

There was a general view from all of the interview participants in the Whistler hotels that the dogs who stayed in their hotels tended to be well behaved, with complaints from other guests rare, and inappropriate behaviour by dogs – or more accurately their owners – minimal. Where complaints did occur there was an emphasis placed on attempting to educate these visitors about the efforts of the hotel to ensure that hygiene levels and the health of human guests were not adversely affected. Failing this, there was recognition of the impossibility of pleasing everyone and consequently an acceptance that a small percentage of people will always find something to complain about and that was no reason to change the dog-friendly policy of the hotels. The acceptance of dogs in hotels in Whistler, which extended to having no size limits on dogs allowed at any of the hotels interviewed, seems to be the result of several factors including public demand, the willingness of staff to have dogs in the hotel and the dog-friendly nature of the whole of Whistler. This is exemplified in the following quotation from the interview conducted at the Crystal Lodge:

> most of our management team has dogs and I know I struggle myself trying to find accommodation with it so I'm glad that we are [dog friendly] and it's just Whistler itself, the town, everyone seems to have a dog and the trails are all accustomed to it, the lakes or beaches are welcoming of dogs.

The cultural mindset in Whistler of dog friendliness was confirmed in an interview with Whistler Tourism, which identified the town as having always been a dog-friendly one even before it became a major outdoor adventure leisure and tourism destination.

Not All Dogs are Equal: Socially Acceptable and Socially Unacceptable Dogs

The presence of stray dogs is of increasing concern in a variety of tourism environments. They are viewed by tourists as a potential health threat and a source of dissatisfaction with the holiday experience that may result in tourists choosing to holiday elsewhere in the future (Webster, 2013). Solving the problem of stray dogs is not something that is solely the responsibility of the leisure industry and certainly it cannot be undertaken in isolation from the wider society. The most widespread and traditional method is to round up such animals and either kill or rehome the dogs depending on their state and nature. This method may be an ongoing one in many locations but at other destinations it may be boosted at certain times in an effort to rid specific areas of stray dogs prior to major events or peak holiday seasons. In these instances the emphasis may be on culling rather than rehoming these dogs. The effectiveness of such a programme in dealing with stray dog populations is questioned by Webster (2013), with the suggestion that it may even increase populations in the medium term. This is because culls result in access to greater resources for a smaller number of dogs, resulting in a population explosion. It is also likely, in an age of increasing concern about the rights and welfare of animals among the general public, that if news of any stray dog culls in the build-up to summer holiday seasons or mega-events reaches the general population there will be a public backlash against destinations associated with such activities. The extent of such a backlash and its impact on the profitability of associated tourist destinations and/or events is, however, unknown at this time.

Other tactics have seen the tourism industry recognize the benefits (both social and economic) of its involvement in programmes such as those run by Cats and Dogs International (CANDi) which focus on the de-sexing of dogs in developing regions of the world as a means of reducing the stray dog population. Tourism industry partners include hotel chains, local hotel operators and airlines such as Air Transat, a Canadian holiday travel airline (Webster, 2013; CANDi, 2013).

While there are occasional reports of the slaughter of dogs as part of the beautification of tourist destinations, as in the case of the Ukraine in the run up to that country's hosting of the Euro 2012 soccer championships (Osborn, 2011), factual data and detailed analysis are generally lacking. Only by rectifying this situation can the scale of the problem and potential solutions that deal with the complex reality of balancing human welfare, economics and the rights and welfare of dogs be arrived at.

It is not only stray dogs who are less socially acceptable. The pit bull has earned an unenviable reputation as a fierce and aggressive animal in general society, due to its use in dog fighting, and as a result it is not uncommon to see it banned in places where other dogs are allowed. For example, when interviewed in 2008 the Delta hotel in Whistler, Canada, stated that the pit bull was the only type of dog it did not allow guests to bring into its premises. As is the case in many instances reality does not necessarily match perception. Yes, there is no denying that pit bulls can be aggressive, but then again so can all dogs, especially when they are trained to be. However, a well-trained and socialized pit bull is arguably no more dangerous than any other type of dog.

The position of the assistance dog

The assistance dog, when it is working, is clearly a tool that enables the human handler to experience life in a manner that would otherwise be impossible. It is recognition of this that has given rise to the virtually universal laws that give guide dogs for the blind (as the iconic assistance dog) access to every public space, including all those where ordinary dogs are banned. More recently other types of assistance dogs have gained similar rights of access.

Despite these laws the stories of exclusion, or of second-rate access to leisure spaces and experiences offered to guide dog handlers due to the presence of their dogs continue to circulate (Small et al., 2012). The barring of people with guide dogs from shops and restaurants is, Sanders (1999) suggested, due mainly to people's ignorance of the laws that enable such access. Such a view was confirmed in an interview with Guide Dogs for the Blind in the UK in 2012. Ignorance of the law as an excuse for barring guide dogs from leisure experiences was also noted by Small et al. (2012) in a study of disabled people in Australia, although they also noted the open flouting of the law. Whether it is a case of ignorance of the law or breaking of the law the situation misses the deeper point that people feel the need to bar access to guide dogs in particular and assistance dogs in general in the first place. Such barring is arguably not due to application of laws that ban non-assistance dogs from such spaces but from social constructions of dogs as being animals that do not belong in shops and restaurants due to their lack of cleanliness or their potential to disrupt, a view confirmed in my interview with the Guide Dogs for the Blind in 2012. This construction stands at odds with the highly trained nature of assistance dogs.

The social and legal rules governing the access of service dogs to spaces where other dogs are barred is exemplified by the airline industry. As Table 5.1 demonstrates, all but one of the airlines studied state on their website that service dogs are allowed to travel with their handler in the passenger cabin at no extra cost. Unlike small pet dogs, who are allowed to travel in the same space, the service dogs do not need to go in a crate. While on the surface this may look like a case of open access at work, a more detailed examination shows that service dog handlers still face a variety of barriers and potential discriminations. Some airlines state the dog must be positioned on an absorbent mat throughout the flight (e.g. Air New Zealand and Singapore Airlines), the logistics of which are clearly unrealistic. Furthermore, while allowing service dogs on their flights, Aeroflot states: 'Passengers travelling with guide dogs are provided with seats at the rear of the cabin.' This effectively consigns service dogs and their handlers to the worst seats on the plane, which is arguably a clear example of discrimination. Acknowledging that most service dogs are large breeds, such as Retrievers and Labradors, the suggestion that these animals should sit in the legroom space of their handler (the standard position noted on the websites of the airlines listed in Table 5.1) is another unrealistic proposition. While it may be suggested that a way around this is to allow the dog to sit on a seat next to their handler, some airlines specifically state this is not allowed (e.g. Korean Airlines, Singapore Airlines, Aerolineas Argentinas and South African Airways). Finally, while certification of the status of a dog as a service animal is arguably justifiable and easily obtained by handlers, Cathay Pacific identifies specific permit requirements for anyone wishing to travel with their service dog that look intimidating to this ob-server and as such come across as nothing other than a barrier to travel.

It is worth noting that while guide dogs in particular and assistance dogs in general may be able to travel anywhere, in theory at least, organizations such as Guide Dogs for the Blind in the UK and Assistance Dogs International actually discourage handlers from taking their dogs with them on international trips. This relates to the physical stress it can place on dogs, the problem of what to do in the event of an injury to the dog and the fact that taking the dog outside of its normal environment can negate its potential to perform its duties, placing the handler in potential danger and exposing the dog to mental stress (personal interviews with both organizations in 2012). This once again brings home the difference between the social construction of dogs, assistance dogs in this case, and the reality of these dogs. They are intelligent and highly trained animals but they are not automatically able to transfer their knowledge and training from one environment to another. In other words, they are not the 'super' dogs that society often portrays them as. This is not to say assistance dogs are not wonderful, but to recognize their limits, and therefore that we should not set them up to fail by expecting too much of them.

Unfortunately, while work has begun to be undertaken looking at the issue of disability and access for the disabled to tourism, leisure and hospitality ser-vices and spaces, such work seems to have ignored the question of guide dogs in particular and assistance dogs more generally (i.e. Darcy, 2003; Shaw and Coles, 2004; Yau et al., 2004; Daniels et al., 2005; Daruwalla and Darcy, 2005). Given the wildly differing needs of disabled people, and the specific differences of those who seek to enter tourism, leisure and hospitality spaces not just by themselves but with an assistance dog, there is arguably a need to develop research focused on specific disabled groups, the guide dog community among them.

With guide dogs legally allowed anywhere in most countries it has been suggested that regular dog owners who wish to take their dogs into places such as restaurants and the cabins of airplanes have begun to 'disguise' their pets as service dogs. A quick search of amazon.com for 'service dog vests' shows it is easy to buy such a product without the need to prove either the purchaser's disabled status or the position of their dog as a service one. The Americans with Disabilities Act 'prohibit[s] questioning a person about their disability and from asking for evidence of a service dog's certification' (Arnold, 2013), which neatly allows pet dog owners to abuse the provisions made for service dogs. Yet even if these laws were not in place it is socially inappropriate to question people's disability so unlikely to happen. Aside from being ethically questionable to abuse the rules designed for service dogs and their handlers, this behaviour has the potential to give service dogs a bad reputation, with most pet dogs nowhere near as highly trained and therefore as socially responsible as the service dogs.

Controlling Leisured Dogs and Their Owners

Humans are expected to behave in a responsible way; it is the only way in which any society can function in a sustainable manner. We must do no harm (as broadly defined) and while this message is ingrained in us by moral guardians of society (which includes parents, teachers and religious leaders, among others) it is enforced when necessary by legal processes. Healthy, fully functioning adults and to a lesser extent children (a complex term whose definition is discussed in detail in Carr (2011) but for the purpose of this discussion can simply be viewed as anyone under 18 years of age, while offering apologies to any teenagers who feel offended at being defined as a child), are not only expected to behave responsibly but are also viewed as being responsible for their actions. In other words they are deemed to have agency. In comparison, if seen as objects then dogs cannot be expected to have agency and therefore cannot be expected to be responsible for their actions as these actions must be the product of the owner of the object. Even if we reject the notion of the dog as an object and see it as a sentient being, as I do, it is unfair to say that it should be solely responsible for its actions. By recognizing the sentience of the dog we are not saying it should be seen as an equal to humans, or that it should be able to understand all the intricacies of human social rules, for this latter is clearly not possible in just the same way that humans fail to understand all the intricacies of the social rules of the world of dogs. Rather, it is clearly incumbent on human owners to ensure their dogs behave appropriately when out in human society. Consequently, it is right that as Sanders (1999: 31) stated: '[if] the dog misbehaves or fails to perform in line with public expectations, the owner usually is held responsible'.

Rules and regulations may be established for the control of dogs and their owners in the public space, such as those noted earlier in this chapter. However, arguably the strongest control can be, and is, brought to bear by the weight of social expectation. Fail to control your dog in an appropriate manner in public and it is not just the law that will potentially be broken. Rather, the status of the owner as a 'good' and/or 'responsible' dog owner will be brought into question. Because of the recognition of the agency of the human this goes beyond just the individual as dog owner, extending to the questioning of their right to be defined as a good and responsible member of society. It is through this social castigation that we see the strongest potential for control over the behaviour of dogs.

Owners whose position as a good owner and member of society is brought into question by the inappropriate behaviour of their dog must attempt to rectify the situation to re-establish their position (Sanders, 1999). The stigmatization is not confined entirely to the human, though, with negative dog behaviour leading to the identification of the offending animal as a 'bad' dog as well. This clearly recognizes at least partial agency by the animal, because objects cannot be labelled as 'bad' as a result of the actions to which they are put by their owners.

While the stigmatization as a bad owner may deter some people from allowing their dogs to behave in an inappropriate manner or from doing so themselves it is clear that by itself this is not sufficient. Laws and their enforcement are required to lend weight to the social labelling. Such laws are increasingly being felt at the same time as more people are owning pet dogs and seeing them as a central component of their families and leisure experiences. The reason is the actions of the few which are resulting in the destruction of flora, harassment and killing of wildlife and other animals, the pestering and intimidation of other dogs and non-dog-owning humans using the same space, and the leaving behind of dog poo where it can pose a health hazard as well as ending up on clothing and shoes or even in the hands of children too young to know better (Mehus-Roes, 2009).

Overall, this chapter has sought to demonstrate how dogs and their owners are provided for in the leisure experience and how their access to leisure spaces and resultant behaviour is influenced and controlled. In doing so, the chapter has highlighted a range of examples while doubtlessly not covering everything. For example, a detailed discussion of off-leash dog parks would have been wonderful to include but even in a book dedicated to dogs and leisure there is simply not space for everything. The offerings for dogs and their owners in the leisure experience, as shown in this chapter, speak volumes about the social construction of the dog and its current positioning at the heart of the human family. They also speak of the identification of the needs and welfare of dogs by owners and the wider society. Finally, the chapter reinforces the point made in Chapter 4, that the leisure of dogs and their owners is often a matter of compromise, something that can be said to be true of the leisure of all humans. It is a compromise between the needs and desires of dogs, their owners and wider society.

Note

[1] dogs4sale.com.au (2005) Holiday with dogs. www.dogs4sale.com.au/Holiday_with_Dogs.htm, accessed 25 July 2014.
Doggy Holiday (2005) Doggy holiday: Take your dog with you on holiday. www.doggyholiday.com, accessed 25 July 2014.
Holidaying With Dogs (2005) Dog friendly places to stay.
www.holidayingwithdogs.com.au/listings, accessed 25 July 2014.
Pets Playground (2005) Pet friendly holidays. http://petsplayground.com.au, accessed 10 January 2005. Please note this website is no longer operational.
TakeAbreak.com.au (2005) Holidaying with Pets. www.takeabreak.com.au/HolidayingwithPets.htm accessed 25 July 2014.

6 The Boarding Kennel and Dog Day-care Centre: Dog Holidays

Introduction: Defining the Dog Holiday

This chapter explores the history, scale and nature of boarding kennels and dog day-care centres. Associated with these businesses, the chapter also discusses the professional pet-sitting industry. This analysis is set within the recognition of the changing nature of human–dog relations and the values associated with pet dogs by their owners/human companions and society in general. The chapter builds on work in Chapter 4 that discusses the nature of leisure for dogs and examines their leisure needs. Based on the recognition of the changing position of dogs in society in general, and within individual families and human perceptions of the leisure needs of dogs, this chapter discusses the potential future for the boarding kennel, dog day-care and pet-sitting industries.

The History, Nature and Scale of Boarding Kennels

Figure 6.1 shows the number of boarding kennels for dogs operating in Vancouver, Canada, from 1947 to 2011. The data were collected from advertisements placed in the Vancouver Yellow Pages and show that the first boarding kennel began advertising itself in 1948. It is important to distinguish between boarding and breeding kennels as in the Yellow Pages both types of kennel were placed under the same heading ('kennels'). The graph shows both those kennels that clearly advertised themselves as offering boarding services, and a combination of these and other kennels whose specific function could not be determined from the advertisement. Figure 6.1 clearly shows there has been a significant increase in the number of boarding kennels operating in the Vancouver area since the end of the Second World War. This growth in the number of boarding kennels dovetails with the increasing number of households owning at least one dog in countries such as Canada. However, this

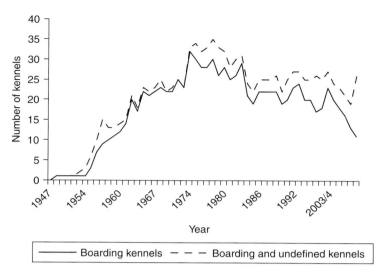

Fig. 6.1. Trends in boarding kennels in Vancouver, Canada, between 1947 and 2011.

growth does not explain the reason for boarding kennels. They originated out of a need for people to be able to place their dog somewhere while they went on holiday, reflecting both the historic difficulties associated with taking a dog on holiday and the lack of desire to do so; changes to both being a relatively recent phenomenon, as noted earlier in the book.

The reasons for the apparent decline in the number of boarding kennels since the mid-1980s and especially in recent years are not easily defined and clearly more research is needed to give a definitive explanation. However, it must be remembered that the numbers shown in Fig. 6.1 are of operators advertising in the Yellow Pages. As more diverse sources of advertising have become available, with the advent of social media and the Internet, it is possible that operators have turned to these outlets and abandoned the Yellow Pages. It is also possible that the trend represents a maturation of the industry. A further issue is that from 1993 the Yellow Pages added a separate 'Pet Care Services' section (which had been formerly known as 'Pet Exercising Service' and 'Pet Exercising and Feeding Service' and periodically appeared in the Yellow Pages but with very few operators listed), which has grown rapidly in terms of the numbers of operators it lists. Some of these operators, included in Fig. 6.1, specifically state they offer boarding services. Others offer a wide range of services including dog poo removal, dog grooming and dog day care (a more detailed discussion of these establishments is provided later in this chapter). As in the case of the kennel advertisements, many of the Pet Care Services advertisements do not specify the services they offer; indeed there were 29 such operators advertised in the 2010/11 Yellow Pages. It is not unlikely that at least some of these operators do offer boarding services and if that is the case it would potentially at least partially halt or even reverse the decline noted in Fig. 6.1. Another explanation for the apparent decline in boarding kennel numbers in Vancouver is the increasing number of people who take their dogs on holiday with them and the associated increase in pet-friendly holiday accommodation offerings, as noted in Chapter 5. This trend may be reducing demand for boarding kennels sufficiently to be driving some out of business.

The traditional image of the boarding kennel is of a series of cages made of wire with concrete floors for easy cleaning. Dogs may be housed separately but equally likely may be grouped together in a relatively small area enclosed by chain link fencing with potentially a roof on top. If there is any exercise area to be had it is likely to be uninspiring and its access limited. This is the home for the dog who is not taken away on holiday with its owners. It is a convenient place to dispose of the dog while the humans enjoy their holiday as obviously it cannot be left at home to fend for itself. The notion of the dog fending for itself is something that various authorities in countries with a history of high dog ownership have sought to define as socially unacceptable. The result is that when the owners go on holiday and either do not wish to or cannot take the dog with them the kennels are the standard alternative.

Though the original image of dog kennels may have been barren, by the 1970s this was already changing in the USA where Edwards Benning (1976) spoke of the development of the 'poochie penthouse' with four-poster beds, shoes for chewing on, wall-to-wall carpeting and whatever food the guest ate at home, along with plenty of open space to run in. This evolution has continued to the point today where the traditional kennels have been consigned to history and the pet hotel is more the norm. It is important to note the change in the name from kennel to hotel. The latter of course has traditionally been a human space; one associated with holidays and all the positive, enjoyable moments linked in the minds of humans and the views of society (rightly or wrongly) with such experiences. By identifying as a pet hotel rather than as a kennel, operators are selling themselves not as somewhere to abandon a pet dog while the human family enjoys itself but as somewhere a dog will want to go and where it will have a very enjoyable time. In this way these organizations are feeding on and reinforcing the ideas that dogs are a central part of the human family and that they have needs and desires akin to their human owners. Examples abound of these hotels which advertise themselves like Ruth's Pet Hotel (Anonymous, 2014) does as 'home away from home for your dog'. Some pet hotels are now offering a variety of add-ons that are reflections of the same trends in hotels for humans. For example, Herzog (2010: 76) reported that it was possible for a dog to stay in a pet hotel in Los Angeles where they can spend an hour in a 'Zen Den', which is advertised as a 'simple Eastern retreat for your dog to relax and indulge'. In addition to pet hotels, developing on from the notion of summer camp for children that was developed in North America and remains a central feature of the summer period of many children in the continent, it is now possible to send your dog to camp. Indeed, one operator in Vancouver, Canada, advertises itself under the label 'kennels' in the Yellow Pages with the slogan: 'Going on Vacation? Send your dog to camp.' This is playing on the notion of summer camp for kids and the social construction of a 'good' parent as one who ensures their child goes to such a camp (Carr, 2011). In this way the company is intimating that a 'good' dog owner will send their pet to a camp.

Further analysis of the boarding kennel adverts placed in the Vancouver Yellow Pages between 1948 and 2010–2011 confirms that there has been a significant change in the nature of these operations over time. The original kennels were fairly utilitarian by contemporary standards. In 1948 the advertising stretched only as far as noting that dogs would have access to indoor and outdoor runs, though even at this stage heated accommodation was on offer.

As early as 1955 we see a shift in the nature of the advertisements used by dog kennel operators as they begin to appeal to the idea of the pet dog as a member of the human family. This is seen with one kennel advertising itself as 'the country club for city dogs' in this year. This tag line borrows from human marketing and branding in the leisure and tourism sector and is suggestive of luxury and leisure rather than a convenient dropping-off spot for dogs while their owners enjoy a vacation. The notion of the boarding kennel as a place where dogs could experience a holiday was pushed to the fore in the following tag line that was used in the advertising of a kennel in 1967: 'Where holidays are happy days.' The 'country club' was followed by the hotel (in 1962) then the 'rancho' (in 1966), 'inn' (1978) and 'villa' (1978). More recent additions to the marketing lexicon of dog boarding kennels in Vancouver are 'camp' (in 1988), 'ranch' (in 2003), 'rural adventure' (in 2003) and 'urban escape' (in 2004).

The boarding kennels of Vancouver have not only used a variety of terms to suggest the boarding kennel as a place where a dog can enjoy a holiday rather than as a dumping ground for temporarily unwanted pets. Rather, they have advertised themselves as providing a variety of facilities and services, all of which have been marketed to dog owners arguably to reassure these people that their dogs will enjoy the kennel experience and as a result assuage the guilt owners may otherwise feel at preventing the dog from holidaying with the family. Consequently, in 1959 there was the first reference made to a kennel offering a large field (of 7 acres) for dogs to exercise in. Subsequent adverts of similarly large fields emphasized them as spaces for dogs to enjoy and explore, such as that of one company in 1962 that said it offered '50 exciting acres'. This was the first link between dogs and enjoyment of the countryside used by kennels and has more recently morphed into the offering of camps for dogs, such as 'Camp canine – A fun holiday for your dog', which appeared in 1988. It is worth noting, however, that while ideas of space and countryside have persisted since they entered the marketing imagery of boarding kennels, the large open field has not been a persistent feature. Rather, it had gone by 1977 and did not reappear until 2004. While it is important to recognize that all of the material presented in the Yellow Pages is marketing, rather than a list of all available features, it could be suggested that the apparently less than wholesale buy-in of the kennel industry to the large field as a feature of their operations relates to the difficulties and dangers associated with large numbers of dogs running free in a large space. While the idealized image of a dog running free across a natural landscape may appeal to many owners the reality of dealing with a large pack of off-leash dogs is something very different.

Other more persistent features of kennels in the Vancouver area since their introduction have been the covered run (first seen in 1965) and the provision of exercise for pets (first seen in 1962). The idea of the dog as an individual also came to the fore in 1966 when the provision of individual care/attention for each dog was first marketed. The idea that the kennel and any adjacent run should be clean or hygienic was first marketed in 1959 and reached its peak in 1985 with the marketing of a boarding kennel as 'hospital clean'.

It may be suggested that many of the facilities that kennels have advertised themselves as offering are a reflection of the nature of how dogs were and are treated in the family home. This is supported by the advertising of the kennel as a 'home away from home', which first appeared in the Vancouver Yellow Pages in 1962. Such a view is furthered by the marketing of a kennel in 1970 as being air conditioned, while 1975 saw the first kennel stating that it provided music in its kennels, and one in 1987 provided a picture of one of its canine guests enjoying the luxury of a television in its kennel. It is not only the fixtures and fittings that have been used to show the boarding kennel as a home away from home or a holiday destination for dogs. Rather, the food on offer has also been used, with the notion that dogs will receive 'excellent cuisine' being introduced in 1970. The individual attention to each dog was also highlighted by the marketing of 'individual diet[s]' for the first time in 1980.

The question to be asked in the case of all these facilities and services for dogs in boarding kennels is who they are being aimed at. Are they truly for the dog, or are they for an owner who feels guilty at leaving their dog in kennels while they go on holiday? As a possible extension of this latter view, but also distinct from it, are the facilities offered at the luxury pet motels for owners who view their dogs as being little different from human children? Such a perspective is arguably catered to by an operator in the USA who now offers to read stories to the dogs before they go to sleep (Lammi, 2013) in a manner akin to the good parent reading their child a bedtime story. The view that these services are for owners rather than dogs is supported by the manager of a dog day-care centre in Whistler, Canada, who was interviewed in 2008. When asked about changes in dog kennels she stated:

> They're definitely different than they used to be. Cause, you know, it used to be kennels … rows and rows of cages and that sort of thing and now … what people demand when they leave their pets is totally different … is indoor/outdoor play at all times so their dog has a private run but that also that they have social play hours and the quality of care of the facility, having staff stay on, is like 24-hour care.

A pet motel in the Brazilian city of Belo Horizonte provides a different example of the provision of services that may have the dog as a central feature but is actually marketed towards the human owner. In this case the motel is actual a 'love hotel' where dogs are taken by their owners for sexual liaisons with other dogs. It is the equivalent of the love hotel for humans that has a long history in many locations around the world. As Romero (2012) noted: 'Whether dogs like Harley [one of the motel's guests] actually need a romantic curtained-off suite to breed seems beside the point. Some dog owners simply like the concept of a love motel for their amorous pets and are willing to pay about [US]$50 for each session.' That the rights, welfare and dignity of the dog are a poor second to the desires of their owners in the context of this operator is arguably clear as they offer artificial insemination services to those dogs who fail to become pregnant as a result of a meeting in the love motel. This opens the debate about the rights and dignity of the animal and raises the suggestion of rape in the animal arena. While we need to be careful to avoid placing human conceptualizations of consent and rape onto dogs, the artificial insemination of dogs or any other animal clearly robs them of dignity and ignores their sentience. There is no question of the dog being able to resist, or to decline to be inseminated. Instead, the dog is treated as nothing more than an object whose pregnancy is desired by the human owner.

Pet Sitters

Today, the kennels are no longer viewed as the only alternative for those owners who cannot or do not wish to take their dog on holiday with them. Rather, it is possible to hire a professional pet sitter who will either take your dog into their own home or, not uncommonly at an additional fee, will care for both your dog and house, allowing the former to remain in its home. The research does not exist at this time to clearly quantify the scale of the demand for pet sitters and the industry catering to it but it is interesting to note the claim by Mackenzie (2008: 3), that: 'Hiring a petsitter is often considered a necessity and not a luxury... Nowadays pet owners would no more leave their pet alone than they would a child.' The industry has played on the notion that a pet sitter is the thing that a 'good' pet owner will invest in when they cannot take their dog on holiday with them. Indeed, one pet-sitting company operating in Vancouver, Canada, in 1987 advertised itself in the Yellow Pages by stating that: 'When the whole family is looking forward to vacation – except the pet – The 'Critter Sitter' provides daily home care and security checks for pets... For pets who prefer to stay at home.' Just to reinforce the point the advert included a sketch of a dog happily curled up, the picture of contentment.

An indicator of the scale of the pet-sitting industry may be seen in Fig. 6.2, which shows the number of companies advertising their services in the Vancouver Yellow Pages. That this industry is a more recent phenomenon than the boarding kennel is clear in that the first operator was recorded in 1987. The graph shows three distinct forms of pet sitting, with one option including a person living with the dog in the owner's home, another seeing the dog taken to the pet sitter's home and a final option where the dog is left in the owner's home and visited regularly by the operator. The data presented in the graph also suggest that the pet-sitting industry may not be viable in the longer term, with numbers declining in recent years; as noted earlier, though, this may be due not to a decline in operators but rather to their abandonment of traditional marketing outlets such as the Yellow Pages in the face of the growth in social media and the Internet.

Another indicator of the scale of the dog-boarding and pet-sitting industry is provided by the Australian Companion Animal Council (2010), which estimated that dog owners in Australia spent AUS$375 million in 2009 on these services for their dogs. This money was spread across an estimated 1241 kennels. In comparison, in New Zealand dog owners were estimated to spend

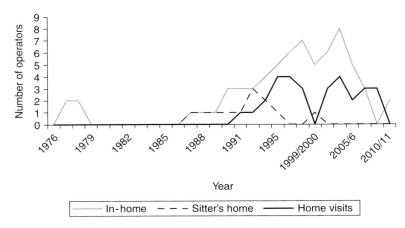

Fig. 6.2. Dog-sitting companies in Vancouver, Canada.

NZ$45 million each year on dog boarding, dog day care and walking services. This was spread across 59 pet-minding and 72 pet-boarding operators in 2011 (New Zealand Companion Animal Council, 2011). Given the scale of money involved with the dog-boarding industry, as broadly defined, it is not surprising to see the number of providers of these services in a place such as Vancouver. Providing boarding kennels and offering to house-sit pet dogs is obviously a lucrative business.

The Dog Day-care Centre

The dog day-care centre or, as it is often advertised, 'the doggy day-care centre' is presented by the industry as an opportunity for a dog to have a leisure experience among other dogs. Yet the origin of the dog day-care operation arguably had little to do with providing entertainment for dogs and was more concerned with exploiting those people living in cities who did not wish to leave their dog in their apartment or townhouse during the day while they were at work. In this way the dog day-care centre was like the early boarding kennel, a dumping ground for the inconvenient pet. As data extracted from the Yellow Pages of Vancouver, Canada show, the dog day-care centre is a relatively recent phenomenon, with the first advertising itself in this outlet in 1995. It is however also a rapidly growing industry with 13 companies advertising their dog day-care centres in Vancouver by 2011.

The dog day-care operators tend to advertise themselves in a very anthropomorphic manner that reflects, feeds on and in the process confirms the humanization of the dog at the centre of the human family. The language used by dog day-care centres also draws a strong link between these spaces and the day-care centres of children, in the process exploiting and reinforcing the link between children and dogs and also furthering the humanization of the dog. This is arguably why we often see them referred to as 'doggy' rather than 'dog' day-care centres. Within the adverts provided by dog day-care centres in Vancouver's Yellow Pages the terms 'supervised play', 'play areas' (as opposed to exercise areas), 'comfy nap area', 'field trips' and 'K9 play-school' have all been used. In addition, they have been described as offering environments that are fun and safe for dogs where treats and chew toys will be available.

It is not only the advertising of dog day-care centres that speaks of the anthropomorphization of dogs, but also how these businesses are run. For example, the manager of a dog day-care centre in Whistler, Canada, was interviewed in 2008 and responded to being asked if dogs were ever kennelled by stating:

> there's two little side areas [as well as the main area] that if there's stressed behaviours that happen then they might get a little time out in one of the quiet areas but they can still see the other dogs... We don't use kennels or crates or anything unless an owner specifies ... they say: 'oh, my dog likes a little time out in his kennel' so then we can put the kennel on the floor in one of the quiet areas. Their dog can have a little 5 minute, if they want it, but otherwise no, it's happy. They get to play and run about and enjoy each other's company.

This followed on from her stating that the operation: 'was opened up under the concept that nobody can leave their dogs in a hotel room during the day but everyone wants to go skiing and everything so you need somewhere for them to come play and so this is their sort of holiday'.

Perhaps the ultimate anthropomorphization used by the dog day-care op-erators is the offering of sleepovers for dogs by one operator in Vancouver for the first time in 1997. What is really on offer is a form of boarding but it is humanized in this terminology to pander to the views of the human owner and the manner in which they treat their dog. Another example of the nature of dog day-care facilities is provided by Alpine Dogs K9 Adventures based in Whistler, Canada. The invitation to the dogs is for them to 'join the pack!' The implicit message here is that owners who do not allow their dogs to experi-ence such offerings are depriving them of the opportunity to be part of a dog pack; one filled (if the pictures in the company's poster are to be believed) with happy and friendly dogs. Consequently, the marketing imagery presented by dog day-care centres feeds on and helps to define what a 'good' dog owner is. In this sense it is someone who gives their dog all the experiences that a dog day-care centre can offer rather than leaving it at home. Even if an owner stays at home with the dog they may fail to meet this industry-informed definition of a good dog owner as they may simply allow or encourage the dog to snooze the day away rather than engage in all the activities a dog day-care centre can offer. This links back to the discussion of the leisure of dogs in Chapter 4. The notion that the happiness of the dog is at the core of the dog day-care op-eration is highlighted by one company in Vancouver that advertised owners would 'Pick-up a happy tired pet' at the end of the day. As in the case of day-care centres for children, dog owners therefore get to feel the glow of making their dog feel happy while also benefitting from a tired dog who does not require additional exercise.

Who is the Customer?

All of the advertisements for dog kennels, pet hotels, pet-sitting services and dog day-care centres, among others, are clearly aimed at least primarily at humans. After all, it is only the human who can read or decipher the meaning of the pictures. The services being offered are also clearly partially for the benefit of the human dog owner. Such services and the purchasing of them may provide owners with relief from guilt at not being able to spend as much time with their dog as they would like or take them on holiday. Indeed, in a study conducted in the USA it was found that 72% of respondents felt guilty about not taking their dog on holiday with them (Stapen, 2013a). In this way, the facilities offered at boarding kennels can become focused on reassuring the owner that they need not be guilty at leaving their dog behind. The result can be a confusing of the needs of dogs with the desires of owners (Wyndham, 2003). However, if we continue to stand by the position that dogs are sentient beings and consequently active social actors then we have to recognize that they can also be customers in the sense that they at least have the potential to directly influence the purchases made ostensibly on their behalf by their owners. In this instance there is a strong similarity between children who have no funds to become the customer themselves but who are able to influence the purchases their parents make (Carr, 2011).

Evidence that dogs enjoy their time at kennels, with pet sitters, or in dog day-care centres is provided by their owners. For example, in a study undertaken in Brisbane, Australia, Carr and Cohen (2009) found that those owners making use of these facilities reported their dogs were very happy with the situation. Indeed, one respondent in this study, the owner of a Labrador–Kelpie cross, said: 'We do not take our dog on holidays with us. He goes to his friend's house during this time. He has a great time with the other dog for company.' Similarly, a Miniature Schnauzer's owner stated: 'I never take the dog on holidays. He thoroughly enjoys staying with one particular friend.' A colleague of mine at the University of Otago similarly makes use of a local boarding kennel for her dog, who seems to love the kennel and thoroughly enjoys going there. Personally, my dogs have always been left either with friends or someone has moved into my house to sit the dog (as well as the cat, chickens and ducks more recently). Why? To be honest I have felt guilty at 'abandoning' my dog (I used to think the cat did not really care who was around as long as it was fed but I am even beginning to doubt that. As for the chickens and ducks, while they are most comfortable being cared for by my daughter I think they cope pretty well when we go on holiday and leave them to the care of someone else). Yet it is clear that despite the sad brown eyes as you close the door on your dog and the happy way that she greets you upon your return that in the intervening time she has not been moping around the house in a depressed state and has, instead, been thoroughly enjoying herself. In this way the guilt is a purely human thing that the dog does not seek to help develop or benefit from. In the same way, assuaging the guilt is purely for the benefit of the human and not the dog.

Such a view is supported by the operator of a pet kennel service in Switzerland who stated in an interview in 2013 that:

> Every dog who comes to us or every cat who comes to us is the most, the dearest to them [the owners] and they think that they [the pets] will cry if the owner goes away 'my dog will cry, my dog will suffer' and we say: 'no, he won't' they don't believe it. They don't believe it. We are trying to tell them, if your dog doesn't see you; doesn't smell you and doesn't hear you, you don't exist for him [and they say] 'no' [in shocked tones]. 'Yes.' They don't believe it. They give a t-shirt, not washed so he [dog] doesn't cry, 'the dog doesn't cry cause he has my t-shirt'. And then we say, 'not a good idea. He smells you and he can't find you; that's worse' and most people understand, they say they understand [I don't think she believes them – Author]. If they understand here [pointing at heart] I'm not sure. And if they come back, they are sad that the dog is still in good health, it's just eaten and everything was ok. They are sad, they are sad that we had no problem with their dog.

Building on Chapter 5, this one has shown further evidence of the diverse range of services available for dogs in a leisure context. Many of these services were developed, initially at least, to cater to the needs of the human owners to either have a place they could leave their dogs while they went on holiday or to work or where someone could give their dog the exercise it needed. Since then these services have developed to cater both to the needs of dogs and their needs as constructed by their human owners and society in general. In this way, these services are a reflection of the shifting position of dogs in relation to humans and their increasingly central position in the human family and the associated humanization of the dog. The result is that on the one hand the services noted in this chapter can be viewed as another manifestation of the objectification of dogs, while on the other hand they can clearly be seen as seriously considering the rights and welfare of dogs. Consequently, as suggested elsewhere in this book, it is important to look beyond generalizations to see whether individual services and the owners taking advantage of them are objectifying the dog or if they have the welfare of these animals at heart.

7 Dogs as Cuisine

Introduction: Food, Cuisine and Leisure

This chapter is based on the recognition of the culturally defined status of dogs, the taboo surrounding the eating of dog meat in many contemporary societies and the propensity for all of this to change over time and space. The chapter provides a discussion of the extent and nature of the consumption of dog meat as cuisine and the reasons behind it. This includes an analysis of how the consumption of dog meat is constructed as deviant and how this can drive changes in the nature of socially acceptable cuisine. The eating of dog meat is, though, not the only way in which the dog is utilized in human cuisine. In recognition of this the chapter examines the position of the dog in the marketing and branding of alcohol and food production and consumption industries.

Within this chapter cuisine is seen to be differentiated from food. The latter is defined as being required by the body for its survival. In this way, food is valued purely for its nutritional value. Cuisine clearly also has a nutritional value, and its consumption will sustain the body in just the same manner as food. However, cuisine, unlike food, is also instilled with social and cultural values. Consequently the consumption of cuisine (the act that ultimately turns food into cuisine) represents a demonstration of, assumption of and reaffirmation of these social and cultural values. In that the consumption of cuisine is more than a matter of survival (indeed, survival may not even be the primary reason for the consumption of cuisine), it has an inherent link to leisure. In this way it is not just that the consumption of cuisine can take place in leisure but that it can be leisure in and of itself.

The History and Geography of Dogs as Cuisine

Many parts of Asia have long been associated with the utilization of dog as a part of human cuisine. Indeed, it has been suggested that the presence of dog meat in Chinese cuisine can be traced back to circa 500 BC (Hopkins, 2005). When visiting China in the 13th century Marco Polo noted the presence of dog on the menu (Dunlop, 2008). That he is supposed to have done so with distaste is equally important as it demonstrates that while dog meat was a part of Asian cuisine it was clearly not part of western European cuisine. This does not mean dog has not been eaten in the history of Europe but rather, as noted by Adamson (2002: 2) in relation to medieval Greece, while dog meat was eaten it was: 'not held in high esteem' and consequently cannot be seen as part of cuisine. Writing on the same era, Meens (2002) painted a similar picture in Ireland with the consumption of dog not unheard of but not seen as 'proper' food, being a food of last resort during times of famine instead. Yet Hopkins (2005) identified a French cookbook from 1870 that included recipes for numerous dishes containing dog meat. More recently, Schwabe (1979) has noted the eating of dog meat in Switzerland, something that Podberscek (2009) also noted as having been reported occurring in 1996. What this shows is not just that dog meat has been widely consumed but that its consumption is a contested arena, an issue that will be returned to later in this chapter.

There is also a long history of the consumption of dog meat in Polynesian culture (Hopkins, 2005; Haden, 2009), across Latin America (Fogle, 1983) and among the native American Indians (Hopkins, 2005; Herzog, 2010). With specific reference to the Aztec civilization, Herzog (2010) suggested that they deliberately bred a hairless dog for the purpose of human consumption. In the case of Polynesia Hopkins (2005) identified the serving of between 200 and 400 dogs as part of large feasts given by royalty in Hawaii with attendees including sailors from the UK and USA.

Today, many Chinese continue to consume dog as cuisine (Hare and Woods, 2013) and many Europeans and other westerners remain as distasteful and shocked at the practice as Polo was. Indeed, Herzog (2010: 185) pointed out that: 'For most Americans, the idea of consuming dog meat is particularly repulsive.' However, it is worth noting that in the 17th century the ruling Manchu Dynasty banned the consumption of dog meat, stating that its consumption was barbarian (Hopkins, 2005). This did not, however, stop the eating of dog as it was a deeply embedded cultural practice. Similarly, despite being banned in Hong Kong since 1950 the consumption of dog continues, and enforcement of the ban, according to Hopkins (2005) is a rarity. The eating of dog as cuisine also continues in the Philippines, despite having been against the law since 1998. Similarly, dog is still consumed in the Congo Basin (Herzog, 2010) and there have been sporadic reports of the practice in New Zealand among the Pacific Island and Asian populations. Indeed, while such reports have prompted outcry from organizations such as the Society for the Prevention of Cruelty to Animals (SPCA) it is important to note that it is not illegal to eat dog meat in New Zealand as long as the killing of the dog is done in a humane manner that prevents suffering (Fox, 2009). Other countries where dog meat is on the menu today include Cambodia, Thailand and Vietnam (Podberscek, 2009).

While clearly dog cuisine is not restricted to Asia it is within this region of the world that it is most common and where the provisioning of the demand is big business. Herzog (2010) and Podberscek (2009) have claimed that approximately 16 million dogs are consumed each year in this region. These dogs are often raised for the purpose of consumption in conditions that are akin in many ways to the battery chicken farms that protestors in the West have long campaigned against. I do not have any photos of my own of the conditions in which these animals are kept or transported to market in but there are plenty on the Internet for those who wish to view them. I encourage doing so because it is a reality that needs to be seen rather than brushed to one side and hidden in the shadows because it does not appeal to one's sensitivities.

The boundary between food and cuisine is porous and can change over time. In this way we can see how dog meat eaten to prevent starvation in the absence of other types of energy is a food. In contrast, dog meat that is eaten for a reason other than the nutrition required to sustain the human body can be seen as cuisine. It may entail the eating of dog for reasons of taste or texture but will also include culturally grounded reasons. It is as a food of necessity that Fogle (1983) suggested the eating of dog in regions such as the Far East and Latin America originated and that it only later morphed into a piece of cuisine when the need to eat it passed but the consumption continued.

Dogs as Cuisine: Why and Why Not

One of the reasons behind the eating of dog meat in Asian countries is, according to Hopkins (2005), the belief that it warms the blood, has a variety of medicinal benefits and can enhance virility. The medicinal qualities of dog meat have also been identified by Herzog as one of the reasons for its consumption in China and South Korea. In comparison, in the case of some of the indigenous American Indians it seems that dog may have been consumed as part of sacred ceremonies (Hopkins, 2005).

Dunlop (2008) has suggested that the consumption of dog meat in China relates to a traditional lack of differentiation between pets and edible creatures among the population. There is, however, evidence that this situation is changing in China and other Asian countries as more people in these nations begin to adopt a more western view of dogs as pets and companions. This moves them from being a nameless object into a position where they become a named, individual, member of the human family. By giving a dog a name and letting it into the life of the family as well as the space of the family (i.e. the house) the animal becomes something that cannot be eaten, its consumption being a cultural taboo (Herzog, 2010). The adoption of what has been traditionally a very western view of the dog by an increasing number of people living in Asia may be related to similar reasons identified in Chapter 1 where the rise of the dog to its current position in relation to many western families was discussed. The result is, in the case of South Korea, that many people: 'are increasingly ambivalent about eating dogs, and a recent poll found that 55% of adults disapproved of eating canine flesh' (Herzog, 2010: 187). A similar process appears to be occurring in China where there have been reports of activists seeking to disrupt, if not stop, a festival dedicated to the consumption of dog meat in the city of Yulin in southern China. The festival is estimated to attract as many as 10,000 people and features live dogs who are brought into the city for the festival being killed, skinned and cooked on site (AFP, 2013). Attempts to disrupt the Yulin festival followed the cancellation by local authorities of the Jinhua Hutou Dog Meat Festival in China in 2011 (Wong, 2011).

Changes in social opinion do not occur overnight and the case of dog cuisine is an excellent example. While a majority of South Koreans may now disapprove of the consumption of dog meat, most still do not wish to see the practice outlawed (Herzog, 2010). Despite the rising popularity of pet dogs in many Asian countries it is important to realize that here and in other cultures with a history of eating dog meat the consumption of dog as cuisine and the keeping of dogs as pets actually has a long history of coexistence (Herzog, 2010). Those dogs to be kept as pets have been clearly differentiated from those to be eaten, treated in many ways as two different species despite all the anatomical evidence to the contrary. However, the balance between pet and source of food in Asia has arguably been disrupted with the increasing numbers of people now seeing dogs as pets though it also may be being driven by a desire to conform to western notions of appropriate cuisine and standards of animal welfare and rights. A westernization of Asian values and a desire to appear 'civilized' (i.e. westernized) appears to be behind the consideration of the Chinese government in 2010 to ban the eating of dog. Certainly, it moved to hide such consumption from international visitors by removing dog meat from restaurant menus during the 2008 Beijing Olympic Games (Chang, 2010), a move that the South Korean authorities had also authorized during the 1988 Seoul Olympics (Knight and Herzog, 2009). Whatever the cause, it is clear that there is a rising wave of disgust at the notion of the consumption of dog meat as cuisine in Asia among Asian people.

Herzog (2010: 187) has suggested that: 'Humans don't eat animals they despise and they don't eat animals they dote on.' Clearly in this context the pet dog fits into the doting category. Equally clearly a variety of civilizations and cultures have seen, and continue to see, nothing to despise in the dog and have therefore eaten it. In a contemporary western context there is a culturally rooted despising of rodents such as rats and mice and of bugs such as cockroaches and spiders. The result is that westerners would not normally entertain the idea of eating any of these animals as cuisine. Other cultures place the dog into the same category, not consuming it because it is despised, constructed by human culture as an unclean animal. This view is ingrained in religions such as Islam and Hinduism. This, Herzog (2010: 187) explained, is why 'dog eating is uncommon in India and most of the Middle East'.

It is important to recognize that the identification of the consumption of dogs or any other animal as appropriate or taboo is a cultural construct. Consequently, attempts to ban the eating of dog, which are themselves based on cultural values, can be seen as the imposition of one set of cultural values over another. Such attempts are generally met with significant resistance; not necessarily because of attempts to stop a certain practice or behaviour but for the interference in cultural beliefs and values that such attempts represent. This was seen in 2009 in New Zealand when the reported eating of a dog by members of one ethnic group led to calls for the banning of such practice. In response, the calls were castigated as ignoring the rights of ethnic groups who, through their cultural beliefs and values, saw nothing wrong in consuming dogs (Fox, 2009). The question that needs to be asked at this point is if the cultural rights of humans outweigh the rights of dogs. At the same time we must also ask in an open and frank manner what is really the difference between eating dog and any other animal.

If there is no difference between eating dogs and any other animal then we must either accept that eating any meat that requires the killing of an animal is wrong or accept that all meats, irrespective of the animal they come from, are equally open to consumption. The former view can either be human-centric in that it opposes eating meat on moral grounds, or animal-centric as it opposes eating meat because doing so adversely impacts on the rights of animals. The answer can only come from setting aside human cultural values and examining the nutritional requirements of humans as omnivores, and the sentience of animals, which in turn leads to the need to look at their welfare, rights and dignity. When we do this we see that not all animals are the same; they may all have sentience but it is to varying degrees that mean that their welfare requirements and conceptualizations of suffering are very different across the species. It is within this context that the eating of dog can be seen as problematic. This is a species with, as discussed in Chapter 1, a high level of awareness – of sentience – that is able to feel and display a range of emotions and that has a strong bond with humans. The killing of such an animal, as with virtually any animal, can be done 'humanely' (i.e. quickly so as not to give time for stress or pain to be felt); but can the raising of such animals be done without harming dogs? Given the nature of the dog as an animal that has developed a strong social bond with humans the removal of such bonds within the context of dogs raised as food can be said to cause suffering and reduce the dogs' quality of life. In this way the consumption of dog meat as cuisine becomes unethical. It may be differentiated in this way from cows, pigs, sheep and other farm animals that may be bred in a free-range manner just like dogs but do not suffer in the same way as dogs from a lack of human contact. If we prefer to suggest no animal should be eaten as to avoid animal suffering or abuse of their dignity then we have to live with the consequence that yet again we as humans are playing God. Just as determining which animals should be bred and when they should be killed can easily be accused of acting like God, determining which animals should not be bred is just the same. So I would argue that the answer lies somewhere in between, where life for all involved is a compromise, where the rights and needs of individual species are examined and appropriate boundaries set for the treatment of animals that maximize their welfare and quality of life. Within this context we are talking about animals as including humans as consumers and others as potentially consumed.

Yet it is also important to recognize that the decision to apply thoughts about the welfare, rights and sentience of animals to creatures such as dogs is an inherently cultural one. In this way it is impossible to fully strip away social and cultural values from debates about the consumption of animals, in-cluding dogs. So while I believe that the rights of animals should outweigh the cultural values of any society I also recognize that this is itself a cultur-ally constructed view.

If there is a demand, and there certainly appears to be, for dog meat then there will always be a supply. The danger is that as the consumption of dog meat becomes viewed as morally repugnant around the world the production of it is driven underground, into the dark corners of society where oversight is absent and criminality can thrive. In these circumstances the quality of life of dogs destined for the dinner table can go from bad to worse. Driven far enough in this direction the providers can turn to stealing pet dogs and in doing so en-tirely remove the hassle of breeding and raising dogs. In Asia evidence already exists of the stealing and smuggling of dogs in their thousands for consumption from Thailand and into Vietnam and Laos (O'Brien, 2013).

The Dog as Marketing Icon in Human Cuisine

The dog has been utilized in the marketing of a variety of foods and bev-erages for human consumption. With specific reference to alcohol there are a range of beers that have incorporated dogs into their labels. A re-view of beers and breweries on the Internet that utilize dogs, or terms com-monly associated with dogs, in marketing and branding was undertaken in November 2013. The search was confined to commercial operators rather than amateur enthusiasts though the distinction between the two is prob-lematic, with many operators best described as microbreweries. The term 'dog beer' was used to search in Google and the first 20 pages of results were checked and relevant home websites visited. Other breed-specific search terms were used (i.e. 'Labrador' 'Terrier', 'Collie', 'Retriever', 'Spaniel', 'Akita', 'Samoyed', 'Dalmatian', 'Dachshund', 'Doberman', 'Chow Chow', 'Weimaraner', 'Shih-Tzu', 'Beagle', 'Whippet', 'Setter', 'Pit Bull', 'Husky', Rottweiler', 'Corgi' and 'Poodle') as well as the term 'hound', 'canine' and 'mutt', and the first five pages of Google results checked for each term. The results highlighted in Appendix 1 show that 30 breweries were found to have utilized the dog as the central focus of their branding. These breweries, and a couple of others that do not have the dog as a feature of their corporate brand, produce a total of 145 different beers, all of which are marketed using a dog or a feature commonly associated with dogs. All of the brewers were asked in November 2013 if they could explain the reasoning behind the naming of their brewery and/or beers after a dog or something related to a dog. A common explanation was that the company had been named after the owner's dog, which is in its own way a demonstration of the strength of the bond between people and their dogs in the contemporary era. For example, the Black Husky Brewing Company stated: 'there was never any thought to any other name for us. Some of our dogs are no longer with us, and the brewery gives us an opportunity to honor them and the place they held and continue to hold in our lives' (personal communication, 2013).

The utilization of dogs in the marketing and branding of beer is exemplified in Fig. 7.1. The use of a dog to advertise Tag Lag beer (which came on-tap and in a bottle) is given in the meaning ascribed (on the back of the bottle) to the beer. It is defined as meaning: 'without thought for the consequence: at speed: carefree'. In this way the dog, and particularly one with at least a passing resemblance to a Border Collie, becomes an ideal marketing image with its construction by society as an animal capable of carefree play which appears to be without thought for any consequence, and which always acts at speed. Yet there is also a nobility to the dog in general, and the Collie in particular, that allows it to get away with this image in a manner that the drunken human cannot. So the picture, while hinting at the freedom to be gained from drunkenness, also assures consumers that they will still be viewed as loveable and loyal individuals capable of diligent and intelligent work. A similar use of the notion of dogs was utilized by one of the breweries named after a dog; the company was called Old Brown Dog because: 'the image certainly evokes a sense of loyal, familiarity and companionship, a sense of comfort, really. All of these are positive associations for a beer. It's also helpful that there seems to be a strong link between craft beer drinkers, craft beer brewers and dogs' (personal communication, 2013).

In contrast to notions of devotion and loyalty, potentially spiced up by a little devil-may-care, Colley's Dog in Fig. 7.1 is said to represent the spirit of a man hanged for his role in the murder of two people accused of witchcraft that wanders the place of his death in the form of a huge black dog (personal communication, 2013). Yet even here we see some artistic licence being applied. The mythological story speaks of a scary scenario and a fearsome dog yet the picture of the dog in Fig. 7.1 shows a less than huge dog and one with a happy, smiling face; it suggests the dog as a friend and companion of humans. In this way the beer neatly gives the consumer a grounding in local mythology that

Fig. 7.1. Dogs in beer marketing and branding. (From: left, Barngates Brewery, UK; right: Tring Brewery, UK.)

speaks to the place-specific nature of the beer in contrast to the faceless, globalized, homogeneous beers of the mega-breweries. At the same time it also proclaims its warmth and friendliness through the nature of the dog depicted on the bottle.

It is not only beer that has a close association with dogs, but also the pubs in which this drink has traditionally been served. A study of the pubs listed on the UK's *Good Pub Guide* website (www.thegoodpubguide.co.uk) in November 2013[1] showed there were 374 pubs that were either named entirely after a dog or had a dog featuring in their name. This figure does not, of course, include pubs whose exterior signs may include a dog, even if the name of the pub does not make reference to one. Table 7.1 shows that among the 374 pubs, hounds featured most commonly, while over 100 simply referred to 'dog' in their name. Among this latter group of pubs a total of 11 was known simply as 'Dog' or 'The Dog'. The results in Table 7.1 are interesting in that they show that only a very limited range of breeds of dogs have been specifically utilized in the naming of pubs in the UK.

Linking back to Chapter 2, it is important to note how the names of many of the pubs in the UK that feature dogs are associated with the traditional sports that dogs have been involved in. The prominence of the Greyhound in the names of pubs needs further analysis of the signs outside these pubs to see the specific nature of the Greyhounds and the activities they are engaged in. Only by conducting such work will it be possible to see how the different sports that Greyhounds have been involved in have been utilized and depicted in the naming of the pubs. There is, however, a clear link between the pubs named after dogs and the use of dogs in blood sports. For example, Table 7.2 highlights the link between dogs and fox hunting, with over 80 pubs named the Fox and Hound, or a derivative thereof.

The link between dogs and blood sports in the names of pubs is further underlined by the fact that nine pubs named the Dog and Gun were identified. Despite being outlawed in the UK for almost 200 years there are still even two pubs that hark back to the era of bull-baiting through their name, the Dog

Table 7.1. Types of dogs depicted in British pub names.

Type of dog	Number of pubs
Hounds	160
Dog	117
Greyhounds	88
Beagle	2
Boar Hound	1
Basset Hound	1
Golden Retriever	1
Springer Spaniel	1
Terriers	1
Yorkshire Terrier	1
Bull Terrier	1

Table 7.2. Other animals linked with dogs in British pub names.

Animals	Number of pubs
Fox	87
Hare	67
Partridge	23
Duck	12
Stag	5
Pheasant	3
Bull	2
Badger	2
Horse	2
Huntsman	2
Hedgehog	1
Quail	1

and Bull. The naming of pubs in a manner that links to blood sports such as bull-baiting stems from the fact that such activities were organized by pubs, being put on by the proprietor as a form of entertainment to draw in the crowds (Jennings, 2007). In this manner references to ducks in a pub name often relate to the provision of duck hunting as a pub entertainment. In this instance the duck was placed in a pond outside the pub with its wings clipped to prevent it flying away and a pack of dogs set upon it (Brown, 2003; Jack, 2009). Such is the strength of the link between some pubs and blood sports that it has been noted that even when such events were outlawed in the UK there were still instances of landlords hosting them. For example, Jennings (2007) noted that: 'In November 1841, for example, Samuel Hird of the Rock Inn in George Street, Bradford was convicted of allowing the baiting of a fox and a badger in the brew-house. And in that same district another beerhouse landlord received three months [in jail] in 1861 for staging a dog fight in an upstairs room.'

Even where blood sports occurred outside of pubs they often had an intimate link to these spaces. Hence in Fig. 7.2 we can see huntsmen in the Lake District, in the UK, gathering at the start of a hunt outside the local pub, a common sight associated with fox hunts. Coursing and duck hunting also have a close link to the rural pub (Jennings, 2007). Indeed, such is the link between fox hunting and pubs that the emblem for Tetley's Brewery is a red-coated huntsman (Brown, 2003). The data presented in Table 7.2 show there is a longstanding and intimate link between dog sports and the drinking of alcohol. In many ways such a link may be seen as the forerunner of the link we see in contemporary societies between human sport and alcohol consumption and reflects the notion that most contemporary sports are intimately linked to the pub (Brown, 2003).

While the traditional sporting use of dogs is a very strong feature of the names of pubs that include dogs in them, there are a few that speak to the other aspects of the dog that have been discussed earlier in this book. For example, there are the Lazy Dog and the Laughing Dog pubs, as well as the Dancing

Fig. 7.2. Fox hunt gathering in the Lake District, UK (circa 1910s). (From: Keswick Tourism Association, UK.)

Dog Saloon. Are the names of these pubs a more recent phenomenon than their blood sport-related brethren, and do they reflect the changing dominant position of the dog in human society? Such questions are certainly worthy of an answer but I do not have one at the present time.

The dog has not only been a feature of alcohol-related marketing. Gromit, of Wallace and Gromit fame, has also been put to use by the producers of Wensleydale cheese to promote its products. This is clearly related to the addiction Wallace has to cheese and the fact that they live (if plasticine characters can be said to 'live') in Yorkshire, UK, of which Wensleydale is a part. During a visit to the UK in 2008 it was clear that Wallace and Gromit were not only promoting Wensleydale cheese but also the cheese factory as a tourist attraction. Fliers advertising such visits feature these two characters prominently, arguably even more prominently than the cow that has long been an integral part of the emblem of Wensleydale cheese.

Looking at Fig. 7.3 it is also interesting to see how the dog is used in the depiction of the notion of the family meal. This could be said to be linked to and reinforce the notion of the dog at the centre of the human family. Here is the dog effectively asking: 'where is the rest of the family?' Not only does this reinforce the position of the dog in the human family; it does the same to the anthropomorphic view epitomized by Lassie that dogs care for their human family members, worry when they are not taking care of themselves and seek to address such situations.

Overall, this chapter clearly shows how the dog has been positioned as a central feature of human cuisine, both as a foodstuff and a branding agent. The uses of the dog in cuisine and the changes in these uses over time speak of the way the dog has been constructed by human society and the relationship it has with humans.

Fig. 7.3. Dog and the family dinner. (Copyright © 2010 Herald Press, Scottdale, Pa. 15683 USA. Used with permission.)

Note

[1] The search was undertaken using all of the following terms: 'dog', 'hound', 'Terrier', 'Retriever', 'Beagle', 'Husky', 'Boxer', 'Rottweiler', 'Border Collie', 'Dachshund', 'Dalmatian', 'Poodle', 'Spaniel' and 'Corgi'.

8 Dog Cuisine

Introduction: Differentiating Dog Food From Dog Cuisine

This chapter focuses on the consumption of cuisine by dogs, a phenomenon that is based on the sociocultural construction of the dog. The focus here is not on the provision of food for dogs that is simply related to their calorific needs to prevent starvation. Rather, it examines the cuisine that is provided to pander to the taste buds of dogs, or those their owners perceive them to have, and the ethical concerns of their owners. The link between dog cuisine and leisure is similar to that noted in the previous chapter though in this case it is not just, or even primarily, the dog gaining leisure from the consumption of cuisine but also the owner gaining leisure from the preparation of the cuisine and their dog's consumption of it. The importance of cuisine for dogs to the lives of dogs and their owners is underlined by Rudy (2011: 30) who pointed to the growing popularity of vegan diets for domesticated pets and the 'wildly popular BARF (biologically appropriate raw food, i.e. mostly raw meat and ground-up bones)'. Herzog (2010: 75) also highlighted the importance of dog cuisine in the contemporary era as he suggests that over 20% of dog owners now cook 'special meals' for their pet dogs. This chapter charts the growth of cuisine for dogs and examines the reasons behind this process, along with the implications for the health of dogs.

The Growth and Nature of Dog Cuisine

A reflection of the demand among dog owners for cuisine for their pets is seen in the number and diversity of books that have been published on the topic. A search of the online book store Amazon (via its British website) using the terms 'dog cuisine', 'dog baking' and 'dog cooking' conducted in October 2013, found 125 different books dedicated to helping dog owners provide cuisine for their pets. The titles of all of these books and the year in which they were published can be found in Appendix 2. This total only includes books where cooking and baking and the provision of cuisine for dogs were the central or sole focus. It does not include the wide range of books that now exists on the general health and welfare of dogs; these often dedicate a portion of their length to the preparation of cuisine for dogs. Given the fact that Amazon is (among other things) a bookseller rather than a storage site of all books,[1] care needs to be taken in trying to examine any growth in the number of dog cuisine books over time based on data from this site. However, based on the information available via Amazon it appears that the number of books being published on this topic is increasing.

The earliest book dedicated to dog cuisine that I have been able to locate after searching through Google Books, Amazon (the UK and American versions) and the British Library was published in 1964 and is entitled *The Secret of Cooking for DOGS*. Among all of the books listed in Appendix 2, *The Good Food Cookbook For Dogs: 50 Homemade Recipes for Health and Happiness* by Twichell Roberts (2004) is symptomatic. It has chapters on stews and casseroles, gravies and sauces, savoury snacks, sweet treats, party and holiday food, ethnic specialties and special diets for special needs. That all the chapter titles in Twichell Roberts' book sound as though they relate to human food is an illustration of the anthropomorphization that is going on in and through these books. This is reinforced through the existence of books such as *Recipes for Dogs: Kosher*. No dog is Jewish; they do not need Kosher food; rather, this is a case of humans imposing their values onto dogs and in the process humanizing as well as objectifying them or at the very least paying lip service to their sentience.

The books are clearly aimed at providing dog cuisine but are written in a manner that speaks of human cuisine, of human norms and of human desires for their pets. In this way it may be suggested that the needs and desires of the dog are often missing. Dogs are, by and large, garbage disposal units on four legs that will eat virtually anything and do not care if it has a fancy name or is presented in a 'haute cuisine' manner. The affectations of human cuisine highlighted in many of these books are aimed more at the human than the dog, which is not surprising, since it is the former who holds the purse strings and is therefore the one who is going to be responsible for the purchase of the book.

The nature of the relationship between people and their dogs and the increasingly central position they occupy in the human family is graphically depicted in the titles of the books. There are titles such as *My Dog Says I'm a Great Cook!*, *Canine Cooking: Cooking Made Easy for Your Furry Family Member*, *Elliot's Favorite Treats: Have Your Person Make these 30 Tail-Wagging Treats For You Today!*, and *One For You & One For Me: Desserts for Humans and Dogs*. In these titles we see the illustration of the potential for dogs to talk to their owners, to tell them that they want cuisine and not just kibble. We also see them being situated as a central member of the human family, one whose only difference is based on the amount of fur they possess. In this way these books are helping to anthropomorphize the dog in the eyes of the public.

It is not only cookbooks that have been developed to provide dog cuisine. The pet food industry has also branched out to provide cuisine for dogs rather than just kibble. Just like the cookbooks, these meals have a distinctly anthropomorphic taste to them that is arguably designed to pander to dog owners' perceptions and desires rather than the needs of the dog. So, it is now possible to give your dog *Shredded Duck Entrée* from Fromm which is advertised as including free-range, hand-shredded duck simmered in natural duck broth; it comes with potatoes, peas and carrots. It is no wonder that, as Herzog (2010) noted, this is a meal that is advertised as being of human quality; it is certainly from the description something that would not disgrace a restaurant menu. Similarly, it is now possible to purchase frozen yogurt for dogs (in flavours such as peanut butter–banana–carob, chicken–plantain and tuna–carrot), made, according to the manufacturer, using only human-quality ingredients (Murray, 2013). The notion of 'cuisine' for dogs can be seen to be culturally specific through the example of whale meat sold for dog consumption in Japan. The argument is made that this product was aimed at owners seeking to demonstrate their status rather than to benefit the dogs and it is easy to see why when the cost was £4 for only 60 g of meat (Demetriou, 2013). The whale meat case is yet another example of the objectification of the dog. Interestingly, the owner of the outlet selling the whale meat for dogs in Japan abandoned the enterprise, stating: 'it's not worth selling the product if it risks disturbing some people' (Demetriou, 2013).

To wash all this cuisine down, why not give your dog a bottle of beer, or some PetRefresh Bottled Water (Herzog, 2010)? As part of the Internet search for 'dog beer' noted in Chapter 7 all of the beers for dogs identified by Google were recorded. The search found five companies that are currently producing beer for dogs; their names and locations are noted in Table 8.1. It is important to note that, while these companies are all selling a liquid that they have labelled as beer, there is no alcoholic content in it, nor is it carbonated. In fact, the descriptions of these beers indicates they are closer to liquid dog food than beer, though many do contain barley whose inclusion in the ingredients is noted by the manufacturers as the link to beer. One of the objectives of the beers is clearly to do the dog no harm but the manufacturers are also clearly marketing their product to the owners of dogs and pandering to their anthropomorphic, human-centred desires rather than to the dogs. This is exemplified by Dog Beer (Australia), which proclaims on its website that thanks to their beer: 'Now you can pay back your dog for all that unconditional love. Now you can finally shout your best friend a beer' (Paws Point, undated). This tendency reaches a zenith with Sniffing Butt Dog Bone Brewery, which provides three

Table 8.1. Manufacturers of beer for dogs and location of brewery.

Sniffing Butt Dog Bone Brewery	Canada
Dawg Grog	USA
Bowser Beer	USA
Dog Beer	Brazil
Dog Beer	Australia

different beers: Wheaten Terrier Wit, Indian Puppy Ale and Pug Porter. All three beers are described in the kind of detail normally associated with real ale human connoisseurs, waxing lyrical about the impact of the drinks on the taste buds of the consumer. For example, the Wheaten Terrier Wit is marketed as being: 'brewed in the Belgian Wit Bone tradition: with raw wheat and oats, and steeped in peanut butter. Its pale golden color with a bit of cloudy haze produces unfiltered layers of complex, nuanced flavors that evolve once it's poured into your dog's bowl, and finishes crisp to refresh the palate' (Sniffing Butt Dog Bone Brewery, undated).

As noted in an article by Greenebaum (2004), making cuisine or buying cuisine or beer for a dog from a pet shop or online are no longer the only options for dog owners. In her study based in the USA, Greenebaum highlighted the existence of a bakery for dogs where the products are made on site and are all for consumption by dogs. The arguments put forward about this bakery and the people who frequent it speak volumes about who the bakery is really aimed at. It is not aimed at the dog but at the human owner who wishes to see themself as a good dog owner who views their dog as a central component of the family, as a baby or best friend, but certainly not 'just' as a dog. Here we see the potential for the worst excesses of anthropomorphism and the objectification of the dog in a way that prevents its own expression of self and fails to take into consideration its dignity. The transference is made from a dog owner dedicated to ensuring their animal has a high-quality, nutritious diet free from potentially harmful additives to the owner concerned more with their own image as constructed through their dog and what they give it.

In addition to dog bakeries, as noted in Chapter 5, it is now possible when staying in some hotels to order cuisine for your dog; and a pet food manufacturer recently teamed up with a chain of pubs in the UK to begin offering meals for dogs in these premises. Such a partnership speaks volumes about their entrepreneurial spirit as it enabled the food manufacturer to extend sales at the same time as advertising its products that are for sale in supermarkets. At the same time the pub chain recognized the potential to raise customer satisfaction among dog owners, especially as the food was to be free in the trial (Bachelor, 2010). Unfortunately, it has not proved possible to determine if the trial was successful or taken up on a more permanent basis.

The Reasons Behind the Growth in Dog Cuisine

One suggestion for the recent trend towards cooking and preparing cuisine for dogs rather than relying on simply feeding them dog kibble or tinned dog food is that owners are becoming concerned about the content of such processed foods in a manner that is akin to concern about processed human foods. Underlying this is a desire to ensure that in enabling dogs to eat 'healthy' food they will live a longer and more pain-free life (Anson, 1989; Walsh, 2007; Everest, 2010). There is, therefore, just as in the case of the proponents of healthy eating in humans, an emphasis on improving the quality of life of dogs by encouraging owners to feed them home-made cuisine rather than mass-produced food.

At its most extreme, the shift to cooking for dogs is a reaction against reports of dead dogs featuring in kibble for dogs (O'Grady, 2007; Rivera, 2009; Landers, 2013). Such concerns are highlighted and arguably added to by publications such as *The Dog Food Doctrine* by Riley (2012) in which he seeks to explore exactly what goes into dog kibble and tinned dog food, the two traditional staples of food for dogs. It is important to reflect for a moment on what we mean by dogs featuring in dog food. It does not mean chunks of meat in a style akin to the dog cuisine noted in the previous chapter; rather, if dogs feature in dog food, it is within meat- and bone-meal that has been rendered from a range of carcasses, including, potentially, those of dogs.

While many people may be disgusted at the idea of dogs being a component of mass-produced dog food, a moment of reflection is needed to examine why this reality may exist. Pictures and wordage on kibble bags and dog-food tins may suggest that they contain tender, succulent steak or juicy chicken. Undoubtedly they may, but as Landers (2013) pointed out the cost of kibble ensures that there will be far more cheap food sources in the mix. That dog should feature in kibble is unsurprising if depressing; what other destination is there for the numerous unwanted dogs who fill pounds and shelters to overflowing? As humans we are depressingly guilty of seeking cheap food for ourselves and our dogs while desiring high-quality food. The result is a fallacy that we buy into because we have no wish to examine the alternative. We are equally guilty of creating a situation where the only solution to huge numbers of unwanted dogs is for them to be put down. If we want to remove dog from the menu of other dogs, with the same level of angst discussed in Chapter 7 when looking at human consumption of dog meat, then we need as a society to accept that dog food should not be so cheap. Also, in societies screaming their love of dogs, we need to give homes to the unwanted dogs rather than allowing the continuation of puppy farms and searching for the idealized breed standard and then discarding dogs when they become a nuisance; practices which are just another example of our throwaway society. Yet before we get carried away there is also a need to call for research that clearly shows the presence or absence of dog meat in dog food; something that is unlikely to be easy to undertake successfully. This is especially important when the claim by Coppinger and Coppinger (2001: 233) that pet food manufacturers: 'have to be buying not only the same ingredients, but the same quality of ingredients. They are not searching around for the lowest-quality waste products. They are locked into obtaining a consistent quality and constant supply' is taken into account. This process is related to the need to ensure the well-being of pets that is necessary to retain the loyalty of the pet owners who buy the food for their pets and questions the potential inclusion of dog in dog food.

Nestle's (2008) book focused on the mass recall in 2007 of dog and cat food by a Canadian producer due to it being contaminated with melamine, and arguably it also reflects and adds to public concern about the content of dog kibble. Indeed, this event is often mentioned as the primary motivator for writing books about dog cuisine and for urging people to start cooking for their dogs rather than buying processed foods (e.g. Fortunato, 2007; Cooper, 2012). While confirming the recent growth in the popularity of preparing and cooking food for pet dogs as a result of concern about mass-produced dog food, Mitchell (2013) suggested the beginning of this trend can actually be traced back 25 years. That a book entitled *Feeding Fido: All About Good Nutrition and Cooking for Your Dog, Including Recipes, Special Diets and Tail Wagger Treats* was published in 1982 suggests that this trend can be traced back even further. It has now resulted in a raft of dog cuisine books focusing on providing recipes that avoid the inclusion of potentially harmful ingredients (irrespective of when they were added to the food chain). Consequently, we see book titles such as *Natural Food Recipes for Healthy Dogs, Three Dog Bakery Cookbook: Over 50 Recipes for All-Natural Treats for Your Dog, The Natural Food Pet Cookbook: Healthful Recipes for Dogs and Cats, The Organic Dog Biscuit Book* and *The Wheat-Free Dog Treat Recipe Book*. The pet food industry has responded to the changing desires among dog owners to begin to provide 'all-natural' and organic foods (Herzog, 2010).

In the case of humans the adoption of a healthy eating lifestyle is because we as individuals take on board the associated science and decide to make a conscious effort to consume food that we are told will improve our health. If we are parents, we encourage (or, to varying degrees, force) our children to adopt similar consumption patterns and practices in the knowledge that by doing so we are being 'good' parents and increasing the life expectancy and daily health of our offspring. In a similar way, by determining to offer our dogs healthy food we are able to self-identify as 'good' dog owners. As the adult human we are in a position of responsibility, we can argue, to impose these decisions because we have the mental ability to make an informed decision. This is true to an extent; dogs will happily devour foodstuffs that clearly are not going to do their long- or even short-term health any good at all if left to their own devices. However, the intention behind the decisions of the dog owner needs to be right to justify such behaviour. The welfare of the dog must be foremost in the mind of the human rather than simply placing the dog on a diet similar to that of the human for the benefit of the human (be it their moral stance or the fact that they then feel another creature is with them on the journey to healthy eating; this can be cruel to one whose taste buds have become accustomed and even addicted to the convenience food so widely available). The idea of the journey to healthy eating being one that can be undertaken jointly is promoted in the book entitled *Dinner with Rover – Delicious, Nutritious Meals for You and Your Dog to Share*. Here we have another example of the dog being viewed as a sentient being or object based not on the actions of the owner but the underlying rationale for the action.

The trend towards vegetarian dog food also reflects a concern about the ingredients in mass-produced dog food, though not about the ingredients per se but rather the abuse of animals that are produced in factory-farming procedures to fill the bags of dog kibble (Rivera, 2009). The notion of vegetarian dog cuisine takes us into the realm of debates about whether dogs, just like humans, are naturally vegetarians when everything about the structure of the teeth of both species indicates they are omnivores who have a strong affinity with meat. Indeed, Rothgerber (2013) goes so far as to identify the dog as a natural carnivore. It is important to remember that debates about vegetarianism and the ethics of killing and eating animals are human debates driven by human desires and human concepts of morality and ethical behaviour. Dogs have no qualms about consuming an animal or a product that has, however directly or indirectly, come from an animal. So, when we impose human conceptualizations of vegetarianism on dogs (via books such as the *Simple Little Vegan Dog Book*) we are disempowering dogs, treating them as things incapable of deciding for themselves rather than as sentient beings. At the same time, of course, if we allow our dogs to eat meat, or meat-based products we are, however indirectly, supporting the meat industry and all the potential for cruelty and suffering that entails.

Rothgerber (2013) positioned the problem of whether to feed a pet dog meat or meat-based products at the intersection of conflicting desires among humans to ensure animals do not suffer by being part of the food chain on one hand and a desire to ensure the health of the pet through the consumption of an appropriate meat-based diet on the other hand. While an important consideration, it misses the point that there is also the need to recognize the rights of the dog; to avoid simply imposing human values on it. However, if we do this for the dog, then surely we must also do it for the animals destined to end up in the food bowl of the dog. When looking at such a situation in the wild between predator and prey we may say that we will step back and simply let nature take its course. I will leave that ethical and philosophical debate for another time and place. However, the same decision cannot be made in an industrialized agricultural industry where there is no 'wild' and 'nature' does not simply 'follow its course'. Rather, the dominant position has simply been that humans are by nature the rulers of the planet and everything on it. From this standpoint it is only natural that we are killing huge numbers of animals to feed ourselves and our pets. Such a view is abhorrent from whichever angle it is examined and I personally therefore cast it aside. So this leaves us doomed no matter which option we choose; the reality is that if we are going to feed an omnivore or carnivore then other animals will die. The necessity is to stand up to this responsibility and accept it as the price humans pay for being capable of conscious and ethical thought. Personally, I feel that attempting to provide animals such as dogs with vegetarian diets is simply attempting to assuage our own guilt at the expense of imposing our beliefs on the dog; yet it may be argued that doing so is simply another compromise and one that while potentially impinging on the rights of the dog at least means fewer animals are killed. However, that only shifts the ethical debate elsewhere, because lowering demand for meat will not lead to more animals being left alive but to fewer animals being born, as humans also control that.

Another reason given for providing a dog with cuisine may be seen as stepping over a line into the realm of anthropomorphism but clearly aligns with the changing view of the dog as being no longer merely an animal but rather a member of the family. This reason has been highlighted by Mehanna (2007: 5), who when explaining why to cook for your dog stated: 'Cooking is an act of love; it nurtures and bonds.' She went on to state: 'He'll [the dog] love you and your cooking because he knows you do it just for him.' The notion that cooking for your dog can aid the bonding between it and its owner is reinforced by

Morrison (2012). The notion that the dog will thank you for your efforts in the kitchen and can 'speak to' its human owner to identify the cuisine they desire is played on and reinforced by the book titles discussed earlier in this chapter.

The act of cooking for your dog has also been identified as a pleasurable leisure experience for the human owner. This coincides with the construction of cooking for humans as enjoyable: a leisure experience. It is a view promoted by Leslie (2004: 11) who stated: 'I've put this book together for all humans of like mind – those who love their dogs so much, that a little extra work on their behalf is a pleasure, rather than a chore.' This of course then feeds back into the debate of whether the dog is being seen as a leisure object or a sentient being. In Leslie's case she clearly viewed it as the latter, but an over-anthropomorphization by the human owner could easily see such cooking being undertaken for human-centred reasons where the dog does become an object.

In line with many contemporary cook books and associated television programmes aimed at human consumption, the idea of cooking for dogs rather than buying processed foods has been identified as a potential cost-saving exercise (Jones, 2011). Certainly, making cuisine for your dog, just like making cuisine for your human family, is likely to be the cheaper option. However, attempting to make food for dogs that is cheaper than kibble is likely to be a far more difficult feat for the reasons discussed earlier in this chapter.

It is all too easy to shake your head at those people slaving for hours in the kitchen to produce home-made cuisine for their dogs and to see kibble not just as an easy alternative but the source of a balanced diet. However, it is worth remembering, as Anson (1989) pointed out, that mass-produced dog food is a relatively new phenomenon (indeed, Purina is identified as the first producer of dog kibble less than 70 years ago, according to Eckhardt et al. (2006)) and the notion that it is good for dogs is the product of ongoing marketing campaigns by kibble producers.

This chapter has provided a discussion of the cuisine options available for dogs (and for owners to cook and feed to their dogs). It has shown how the area of dog cuisine contains myriad philosophical and ethical issues that encompass the rights not just of dogs but of all other animals. The chapter has also discussed how, in common with virtually all the other leisure experiences noted in this book, the provision of cuisine for dogs can either be related to the objectification of the dog or be based on the recognition of its rights as a sentient being.

Note

[1] The British Library is supposed to fit more into this category but it was found that Amazon was a far better source of information about dog cuisine books.

9 Conclusions

Introduction

The aim of this chapter is to draw together the issues that have been raised throughout the book and chart a potential future for research on dogs in leisure, as broadly defined to encompass sport, recreation, tourism and hospitality. Before setting out on this final journey it is, I think, important to admit – as has been noted elsewhere in these chapters – that far from covering all aspects of dogs in the leisure experience the book has attempted to examine the issues that underlie the position of dogs in the leisure experience and the nature of the leisure to which they are exposed. This has undoubtedly meant that many dog experiences have not been discussed. While it is depressing to think that even after nearly 80,000 words there is so much left to be written about dogs and leisure I hope this book offers a conceptual and theoretical foundation on which further writings can be based. This chapter, like all those that have gone before it, is based on the recognition of the dog as a sentient being. As noted in Chapter 1, this has implications for the recognition of the rights and welfare of the dog.

Within this chapter we return to the recognition that all dogs and their leisure experiences are culturally constructed and prone to change across space and time which reflect wider changes in social attitudes concerning animal rights and sentience. Reflecting on the history and current nature of dogs in the leisure experience this chapter will discuss likely future trends relating to dogs and the type of leisure they are exposed to and positioned in by humans and potential reasons for these trends.

Building on earlier discussions relating to anthropomorphism elsewhere in this book this chapter will consider how best to address the future potential areas of dog-related research. This will include a discussion of how to listen to the voice of the dog and how to convince a potentially sceptical audience that it is the voice of the dog, rather than a human-defined imaginary voice, that is being heard and reported.

The Rights, Welfare and Dignity of Dogs

Within this book I have attempted to stress the various debates about the rights and welfare of dogs that have raged (and still do rage) across societies. In this context, the dog in leisure has been seen to adopt a variety of roles including tool, object and leisured individual. It is easy to link rights, dignity and welfare to these roles in a fairly arbitrary manner and yet to do so is to miss a much more nuanced reality. For example, we could simply say that the animal tool is an entity whose rights, dignity and welfare is ignored by humans as it is in the leisure arena for the use of humans. However, if we dig a little deeper we see that not all dogs who are effectively a tool in the leisure experiences of humans are equal. Some are indeed without rights, and concern for their welfare and dignity is dubious at best. For others, however, their welfare and rights are of significant, even paramount, concern for the humans who are utilizing them in the leisure environment. A similarly complex reality can be said to exist for dogs who appear at first glance to be leisured beings. It is, therefore, important to look beyond the place the dog fills in the leisure experience to examine the position and values of the human owner and the voice of the dog. Only by fully listening to both the dog and human owner, can we truly assess the welfare of the individual dog rather than simply trying to generalize at the level of the leisure activity in which they are engaged.

The notion of dignity has emerged through the writing of this book, when I was initially focused on issues of sentience, rights and welfare. As has been argued earlier, especially in relation to bestiality and zoophilia in Chapter 4, dignity is clearly a human construct and one that humans care far more about than dogs. While this may be true it does not excuse humans from ignoring the dignity of dogs; failure to consider it is clearly a form of abuse in my mind, or at the least misuse of a dog. Therefore, I suggest that considerations of animal rights and welfare need to include thought of the dignity of animals.

In any consideration of the welfare of dogs in relation to leisure in particular and life in general thought must be given to 'power'. It is clear that dogs do not have the same level and type of power as humans and also that they do not need the same in order for their welfare and dignity to be assured. The abuse of this power can allow humans to utilize dogs as they wish in the leisure experience. The human is clearly the hegemonic powerbroker and as such dog welfare is almost exclusively at the behest of humans. This means, as noted in Chapter 1, that dog welfare in leisure becomes a matter of the ethical and moral behaviour of humans; of ensuring that the power of humans is utilized in a manner that allows dogs to be dogs in a manner that considers their welfare within a sustainable setting.

'Compromise' has, throughout this book, been identified as key not just to the recognition of the rights and welfare of dogs but to the implementation of these in the leisure experience. Recognizing the rights and welfare of the dog has implications for how it is positioned and used in the leisure experience; it also implies that dogs have the right to leisure of their own. This reality is set within the broader reality of the wider society and environment (incorporating flora and fauna, both wild and domesticated). Consequently, it must be recognized that whenever we talk of the rights and welfare of dogs there will be broad repercussions across the human and non-human landscape. Therefore, even after recognizing the rights and welfare of dogs based on their existence as sentient beings rather than as objects, we must recognize that their experiences in leisure – as in life more broadly – are a compromise both of their own selves, their owners', and the human and non-human world in which they live. In this way the experience of dogs in leisure is really no different from that of humans. We may like to think of leisure as being closely associated with the notion of 'freedom' and certainly the academic field of leisure studies has long been closely associated with this; however, there is broad recognition that the freedom on offer in leisure is relative, socially structured and sanctioned, and bought into and actioned by the individual. In this way, the leisure of the individual human is always a compromise. If we recognize the centrality of compromise to leisure then the emphasis shifts to ensuring that as intimated in the word 'compromise' all the actors have a degree of agency, a degree of self-determination. The complexity of the reality of compromised leisure is seen in the discussion in Chapter 3 about Foxhounds.

Compromise opens up a can of ethical and moral worms that dispels the clean and simple solutions espoused by the animal rights extremists noted in Chapter 1. Rather, it highlights the reality of the complexity of the nuanced world in which we all live. This is not to say that the extremists have no place in society or role to play. Far from it: such people are an important, potentially vital, driving force. They are part of the mechanism that ensures a healthy society is constantly critically re-assessing itself and in the process reinventing itself.

When we are seeking to highlight the rights and welfare of dogs and to treat them as sentient beings it is vital that we remember that they are 'dogs'. While this may appear easy – after all, they generally look and sound like dogs – it is actually very difficult given that the dog, and all that it means to be a dog, is a construction of human society. We as humans have all too often constructed the dog and imagined its capabilities with little thought about the dogs themselves. Instead, we are often guilty, with reference to everything really and not just dogs, of seeing what we want to see. In this way when we talk of the dog as a sentient being with rights we must recognize the potential for harm that this can do. In recognizing the sentience of the dog we have raised expectations of the dog, which is potentially unfair. The dog is still a dog; it is not a human just because, like a human, it is a sentient being. The danger of recognizing the welfare needs and rights of dogs yet failing to truly understand the dog is summed up by Budiansky (2000: 10), who stated: 'Dogs that are treated as furry little people who ought to love and be grateful to us for the muffins they are baked and the little birthday hats they are forced to wear are not happy dogs, for they invariably suffer the consequences of our unrealistic expectations.' In this way we can see well-meaning people causing potential suffering by having the best of intentions.

Future Trends in Dogs in Leisure, Tourism and Hospitality

It was noted in Chapter 3 that while the sports that dogs take part in/are used in have changed and evolved over time most, if not all, of these sports are still actively participated in today. Some have shifted from being mainstream activities that were widely accepted across all levels of society to a position where they are now deemed socially unacceptable, sometimes even illegal, and as a result take place in the dark recesses of society. The important point to note here is that they still continue. At the same time, other leisure activities have emerged that are based on the abilities of dogs and the social setting in which dogs exist at the time. Within this context, the shifting emphasis that has seen the dog become ever more recognized as a part of the human family and considered as a sentient being with associated rights and welfare concerns has at least partially driven the changes we have seen in the nature of the leisure experiences of dogs. Yet it is not just the experiences that have changed but also how dogs are being perceived and treated within them. Consequently, we still see the existence of sports such as sled dog racing, but we see more emphasis today on the welfare of these animals than in the past and we see more, though certainly not all, participants treating their dogs as sentient beings.

The blood sports in general, and dog fighting in particular, are likely to be increasingly pushed to the margins and castigated by society. In comparison, the non-blood sports are unlikely to go away though the pressure on them to ensure the wellness of their dogs will increase. Will we see the end of dog fighting? Unfortunately, I do not think so in the foreseeable future. While more people are recognizing dogs as sentient beings with rights there are still too many in the world with no compassion for their dogs and only interested in what they can offer. The popularity of dogs for sports, with agility and fly ball as just the tip of the iceberg, will clearly continue to grow and it will be for society, participants and the sports' organizing bodies to ensure the welfare of the dogs is not compromised by over-ambitious owners.

Away from the world of sport I would suggest there is likely to be an increasing desire among dog owners to take their dogs into all the leisure environments available to them and to provide them with leisure experiences that have previously been the domain of humans. From an industry point of view there are clearly profits to be made here in catering to these desires that are driven by the centralizing of the dog in the family. Yet this increasing desire is likely to continue to fuel potential conflict between dog owners and non-dog owners, placing pressure on finite resources and demanding that everyone should be willing to compromise on their leisure desires and ideals.

My final thought in this section relates to dogs as cuisine. It is clear that the global trend is towards viewing the dog as a sentient being and one that is a core member of the human family. These views stand in opposition to the idea of eating dog as cuisine and are the driving forces against the experience in Asia at the current time. This trend is only likely to continue to gather pace and in the process push the consumption of dog meat to the margins and into the dark. Yet, just as in the case of dog fighting, it is unlikely to stop the eating of dog meat entirely, especially when voices for the preservation of traditional cultural values are added to the debate.

Future Research on Dogs in Leisure

When I initially thought of writing this book, and even when I started writing it after signing the book contract, I thought – perhaps naively – that I would be able to cover everything I wanted to say, and even had some trepidation about meeting my own imposed word limits and targets. Such a view was consigned to the bin within a month of beginning to write as I drew together all the materials I had amassed. I realized there would be no hope of doing much more than scraping the surface of all the issues and nuances related to dogs in leisure. Consequently, it is fair to say that most of the issues raised in the book are in need of more work and that many facets of dogs in leisure did not even make it into the book. I can only highlight these areas to anyone with the time, energy and commitment to look into them.

The dog off-leash park is a space in which there is a need for further research. The parks allow dogs to socialize together and to gain exercise off the leash, a space that can be very rare for dogs living in urban areas. These parks are also a space where dog owners can come together to socialize. Yet while dog parks may on the surface seem to be ideal, they are not without potential problems or concerns. The most obvious concern relates to the potential for dog fights and the associated injuries incurred by dogs and owners who step in to try and break up a fight or defend their dog. How such fights occur, how owners respond to them and how local authorities view them are all questions that need addressing to ensure that the benefits of dog off-leash parks are maximized in a sustainable manner.

The myriad magazines dedicated to dogs are also in need of concerted attention. Some are dedicated to specific dog sports (e.g. *Dog & Driver* and *Mushing*, which are both focused on dog sledding; *Dogs in Review*, which is dedicated to dog shows; and *Dog World*, which focuses on dog trials and shows), while others are more generic (e.g. *Dog Fancy, Dogs for Kids, The Bark*, and *Modern Dog*). Questions about the market for these magazines, what they say about the position of dogs in society and how they influence the nature of leisure experiences dogs are involved with and exposed to all need answering.

There is an ongoing commitment to examine volunteering in leisure and tourism, yet to date this work appears to have largely neglected volunteer work in relation to dogs. Such a dearth of research arguably needs rectifying given the significant numbers of people who devote at least a proportion of their free time to volunteering with various dog-related organizations. For example, in the UK the Retired Greyhound Trust (2010) is helped in its work by over 1000 volunteers. The number of people who voluntarily devote some of their free time to helping with the work of the various incarnations of the SPCA throughout the world is even larger. Questions of why these people volunteer to help animals in general, and dogs in particular, need answering along with questions about the effects these people have on the welfare of the animals concerned.

Another area in need of investigation is the craze for grooming dogs (via a mixture of paints and clippers) to look like something they obviously are not. The popular press is littered with examples of dog Yodas and tigers, among many others (see Hall, 2013, for examples). This arguably falls under the umbrella of what has been labelled as 'creative grooming'. That this activity has the potential to objectify the dog is clearly illustrated in the following quotation from the owner of a grooming company in the USA: '"People love it – it's hilarious," says Holland, who recently dyed a Louisiana State University fan's Golden Retriever to look like a tiger. "It's a good form of expression. People can't wait for their friends and family to see it"' (Bath, 2012).

One of the trends looked at in this book (see Chapter 6) has been the emergence of dog day-care centres to cater to dogs, or at least to pander to dog owners whose dogs spend a significant amount of time 'home alone' as their human family members go to work or other places where the dog cannot accompany them. A new option for these dogs and their owners is DogTV, which is now on offer via cable in the USA. The channel supposedly shows programmes deliberately constructed to cater to dogs, with colours and sounds altered to appeal to the canine viewer rather than the human (Anonymous, 2012c). Whether dogs actually watch this television channel and what they get out of doing so are interesting, yet apparently unanswered, questions. Other similarly interesting questions include how dog owners feel about this type of dog entertainment, how utilizing it compares to the use of the television as an attention substitute used by busy parents of children and all the associated so-cial queries about the 'good' parent and the health of the child, or dog.

Smith (2011) has argued that the illegal nature of dog fighting means that it is unethical to undertake primary research on the topic. I certainly agree that it makes it difficult, and potentially dangerous, to do so and that the latter means many university ethics panels may seek to deny ethical clearance for such work. Nevertheless, personally, I cannot agree that the research area itself is unethical. Far from it; personally, I would argue that it is unethical of us to not conduct pri-mary research wherever it is needed to help address social problems such as dog fighting, bestiality or zoophilia, as well as other illegal or morally questionable activities involving dogs (or any other animal, including humans, for that matter).

I am not seeking to encourage academics to take unacceptable risks, but for all those involved to recognize that sometimes risks need to be taken for the benefit of society. Idealistically perhaps, I believe this is one of the fundamental reasons universities exist. Academics can and should be a voice of the con-science of society but can only justifiably be so if they are able to conduct the necessary research. The key then becomes awareness of risks and the under-taking of risks deemed to be necessary with eyes wide open. Will the research conducted by academics into illegal activities lead to criminal convictions of individuals? Such an outcome should never be the aim of the researcher as that is the clearly defined role of the police. Is it possible, though, that this will be an outcome of the research? Yes, I would have to say it is and that whether the individual researcher decides to cooperate with the police forces and/or other legal bodies will be something they will have to deal with on an individual case-by-case basis. This is a 'messy' position, rather than the clear-cut version preferred by lawyers and those with much to lose in a case of litigation, but perhaps it is the morally right perspective. The job of ethics committees, in my opinion, should not be to stop these researchers, but to offer them all the pro-tection possible and for society to do likewise.

Listening to Dogs

If we are to fully answer the questions raised in this book and truly understand the leisure experiences of dogs then it is necessary to listen to them. In this listening it is important to view them both as individuals and as a member of the 'with', the human–dog partnership, noted in Chapter 1. Bekoff (2007) and McConnell (2005) rightly pointed out that it is difficult to be able to have a conversation with another species, to understand what animals are saying to us. Similarly, Silverman (1997: 171) pointed out that: 'Putting oneself "in the animal's place" [to try to understand them] is a formidable task.' However, as Bekoff (2007) also pointed out, in our interactions with a variety of species (and most notably dogs) we daily prove that – while it may not be perfect – if we are willing to listen to one another we can converse, not necessarily as between humans, but nevertheless in a way that enables us to share space in close physical proximity with them. Before we worry whether this is an 'anthropomorphic' view or not, let us reflect for a minute on what we mean by this term. Is it that any research that seeks to understand the 'other' (be it within the bounds of humanity or across the fictitious human–animal divide) through anything other than a positivistic, reductionist philosophy is anthropomorphic, for imposing the values of the researcher on the researched? Certainly this seems to be the foundation of the taboo against anthropomorphism that Varsava (2013) saw as still pervading contemporary thinking in academia. Rather, I would suggest that in its positive guise, anthropomorphism is about trying to understand the 'other' outside the rigid and limiting bounds of positivistic scientific analysis. In this it is differentiated from the negative guise of anthropomorphism that imposes human thinking on animal behaviour, needs, rights and welfare. The difficulty is that the boundary between the negative and positive guises of anthropomorphism is not definitive but rather fuzzy and it can be easy to step from one to the other or accuse someone erroneously of negative or positive anthropomorphism. Personally, I am not interested in debating without end on the meaning of anthropomorphism. Rather than worrying about whether research into dogs should adopt an anthropomorphic perspective or avoid such an approach, it is more important to worry about listening to dogs, just as we must listen to the human 'other' to understand them. This recognizes that the negative side of anthropomorphism is as limiting as the positivistic approach to studying animals, as neither listens to them by engaging with them as sentient beings in a manner that at least blurs the rigidly constructed differentiation between animals and humans. In this way I agree with Mitchell (1997: 152) who stated that:

> the use of anthropomorphism per se to examine nonhuman psychology is necessarily neither good nor bad for scientific understanding. . . Having said that, I wish to argue that anthropomorphism can be problematic when it is presupposed to the extent that a scientist fails to examine or be concerned with the evidence needed to support the anthropomorphism.

This dovetails nicely with Guthrie's (1997) view that the problem lies not in attributing a likeness between animals and humans, but in doing so without supporting evidence. The question then shifts to what can validly be defined as 'evidence'.

To the scientist grounded in positivistic thinking 'evidence' can only be that which stems from tests that are devoid of human bias and easily repeatable. In effect, we are looking here at the ideal scientific laboratory, where the complexities of a social world can be removed and dissections of it tested in isolated and controlled settings. We will leave aside the fundamental fact that such evidence is itself grounded in the human bias that constructs this epistemological standpoint. Rather, it is simply necessary to recognize that in the contemporary world of the social sciences a plethora of different epistemologies exist that give credence to a variety of definitions of evidence that go far beyond the confines of positivism. The one unifying factor in all these 'ways of knowing' is that they seek to do so outside of the laboratory, preferring instead to study in society with all of the inherent complexities, contradictions and fuzziness that entails. If such approaches have validity for human-centred research – and they do – then the same can and should be said for research that crosses the species barrier.

Understanding the 'other' has arguably always been the prime interest of social scientists. It sits at the core of sociology, anthropology and human geography, among other disciplines. This does not mean that researchers have always listened, or listened well or in the right way, but that they have always tried. The 'other' is labelled as such because it is different, different from the researcher who from a post-modern perspective is different to everyone, if only by degrees. Consequently, human-to-human conversation is fraught with misunderstandings that stem from different verbal and written languages, differences in body language and different standpoints that lead to differing interpretations of verbal and non-verbal messages. Certainly, it is easier to understand what another human is trying to say than another species, but if understanding the 'other' human is possible (though always grounded in the context of the interpreter) then so should be understanding across species as long as minds are kept open for possible explanations and anthropomorphic biases avoided whenever possible. This post-modernistic approach fits well with Bekoff's (2007: 42) statement that: 'It is essential that we try to take the animals' point of view.' This follows on from a similar rallying call by Gerald Durrell (1976: 37) who stated: 'it is important, especially when criticizing, to look at things from the animal's point of view and not your own'. Here the emphasis is on 'trying' in an open and honest manner that recognizes all the potential pitfalls and biases inherent to the individual engaged in the process and moves on to undertake the work rather than abandon the task because of these issues. In this way I agree with Horowitz's (2009a: 31) point that: 'A perfect translation of every wag and woof may elude us, but simply looking closely will reveal a surprising amount.' Following this route leads to agreement with Sanders (1999: 5) that: 'the conventional sociological view that the interactions between people and companion animals are qualitatively different from those between human social actors is, to put it mildly, open to serious debate'.

This book has been written in English as it is the only language that I am sufficiently conversant in to be able to use to any great extent. In using English the writer and reader have to tacitly recognize the limitations of this (or any other) language. Words only ever convey meaning, meaning that is rooted in the creation of the language over millennia and prone to independent inter-pretation by the user. It is my language, it is the language of this book, and yet it is not really the language of dogs. Yes, my dog, like all other dogs in English-speaking households can understand and may even obey various commands that are given to it in English; but it is not really the language of my dog or of all those other dogs. These dogs are never just listening to the words but also to the body language and the tone of voice (as are humans when they talk to one an-other, though the extent to which each cue is 'listened' to differs across the spe-cies). Yet even this understanding is not the same as a human one. The meaning behind a word can be very different for a dog compared with a human. When we move on to look at subjective words the meanings become yet fuzzier. I, and other authors, may talk of dogs feeling fear, love, affection or other emo-tions; yet these are human words with human meanings attached. Yet as Bekoff (2007, 2004) suggests they are the only words we have. We cannot write in 'dog' (supposing they even have a single language); rather, we must write in a human language especially when writing for a human audience. When doing so, it is necessary to recognize these words are human ones filled with human meanings; but it is not a problem to use them as long as we continue to re-member that we cannot simply transpose all of the meanings associated with words onto dogs. To do so would be one of the worst examples of anthropo-morphism that ignores the rights and abilities of dogs. So for example, when we say a dog demonstrates 'love' we do not mean love in the strictly human way but rather in a more doggy manner. In this case both dogs and humans know about love; there is a common root but a lot of differentiation as well that can all too easily be missed if both parties are not fully listening. In this way I am suggesting a need to go back to the positive roots of anthropomorphism and see it as the process of listening to animals and interpreting them from a human perspective while at the same time avoiding the negative side of anthropo-morphism where the voice of the human completely subjugates that of the dog. If we believe in the rights and welfare of the dog and that it exists within a social setting in which the human is the dominant power, then following an anthropomorphic route is the only way to really ensure those rights and wel-fare. In this way, as Knoll (1997: 21) noted: 'Our best solution, then, may be to take our anthropomorphic descriptions, not as final and established truths, but as inescapable and possibly useful preliminary hypotheses and heuristics.'

The argument I would make then is that we can and should be listening to dogs if we are to truly understand their leisure experiences and their posi-tioning in the leisure environment. Anthropomorphism, in a positive sense, seems to be a valid vehicle for doing so if used carefully. Indeed, if it is taken as an approach to understanding the sentient 'other' then it becomes inevitable as it is impossible to see through any eyes other than our own or interpret from any other standpoint than our own (Moynihan, 1997; Quiatt, 1997). That said, it is vital that we fully listen to the dog as 'other' with all our senses in an open manner that prevents the easy slippage into negative anthropomorphism that sees the dog as object as its natural conclusion.

It is always difficult to come to the end of a piece of writing and to know how to finish it. Will a simple full stop do, or is some final insight the way to go?

A flippant comment may be fitting in this instance, something about it being time to stop writing and take myself and Gypsy for a walk in the sun. Yet while happy with this notion I think a little more is needed. I fully encourage dog owners and non-dog owners to spend time thinking about the issues I have tried to raise in this book, but I also encourage them not to spend so much time thinking about them that they forget to simply enjoy the sharing of time with dogs. Dogs do not seek to over-analyse everything and that is certainly something I need to remember; sometimes walking with the dog, throwing a stick for her at the beach or simply stroking her fur is just pure and simple pleasure for both participants – her and me. There is no need to examine it and to try and dissect what we mean by pleasure; Gypsy and I know and sometimes that is all that matters.

Appendix 1

Breweries and beers utilizing dogs in marketing and branding

Brewery	Location	Beers with explicit link to dogs
III Dachshunds Beer Co.	USA	Ankle Biter Ale, Earth Dog India Pale Ale, Howling Hounds Honey Wheat, Show Dog Vanilla Stout
Basil T's Brewery	USA	Rosie's Tale Waggin' Pale Ale, Ms. Lucy's Weimaraner Wheat
Beer Hound Brewery	USA	Scrappy Doo, Fang, Old Yella
Big Dog's Brewing Co.	USA	Tailwagger Wheat, Red Hydrant, Dirty Dog, Double Dirty Dog, Pinscher Imperial, War Dog Imperial IPA, Leglifter Light, Black Lab Stout, Alpha Dog Double Red, Bad Dog Brown, Chocolate Lab Porter, Dog Gone Saisson, Dog Pound Pilsner, Dog's Bollocks, Doghouse Dunkelweizen, Fire Dog Smoked Wheat, Hop Dog 500, K9 Kolsch, Kilt Sniffer Strong Scotch Ale, Moon Dog Barley Wine, Moon Dog Small IPA, Pit Bull Porter, Rail Dog California Lager, Sled Dog Imperial Stout, Wonderdog Dbl IPA
Big Sky Brewing Co.	USA	Powder Hound Winter Ale
Bike Dog Brewery	USA	None
Black Dog Brew Co.	New Zealand	Chomp, Golden Lab, Kiwi Unleashed, White Fang, Bite, Hair of the Dog, Big Black Dog, Unleashed Simcoe, Unleashed Citra, Tail Chaser, Rich Bitch, Hot Dog
Black Husky Brewery	USA	Twelve Dog
BrewDog Plc	UK	None
Buffy's Brewery	UK	Norwich Terrier

Continued

Brewery	Location	Beers with explicit link to dogs
Bull Dog Brewery	USA	Horndog Honey Rye, Rotty's Red Ale, Weiner Dog Wheat, Boxer (Nut) Brown Ale, Shih-tzu Saison, Beagle Blond, Weimaraner Weizen Bock
Diving Dog Brewhouse	USA	None
Flying Dog Brewery	USA	Raging Bitch, Snake Dog, Under Dog, Doggie Style, In-Heat Wheat, Old Scratch, Double Dog
Growler Brewery	UK	None
Gun Dog Ales	UK	Jack's Spaniels, Booze Hound, Bad To The Bone, Lord Barker, Hot Dog, Chilly Dog
Gundog Brewery	UK	Gundog, Golden Cocker, Gundog Pale, Golden Hunter
Hair of the Dog Brewing Co.	USA	Little Dog, 2013 Doggie Claws, 'Little Dog' Doggie Claws, 'Little Dog' Fred, 'Little Dog' Matt
Hop Dog Beer Works	Australia	None
Hoppy Collie Brewery	UK	None
Laughing Dog Brewing	USA	The Dogfather, Devil Dog, Purebred, Alpha Dog, Rocket Dog, Dogzilla Black, Cold Nose
Lucky Labrador Brewing Co.	USA	Belgian Canine Style Tripel, Black Lab Stout, Blue Dog Pale Ale, Dog Day IPA, Doppel Hound Doppelbock, Hellesaurus Rex, Mild Bite, The Mutt, Super Dog, Super Duper Dog, Winter Wonder Dog
MillerCoors	USA	Red Dog
Minhas Craft Brewery	USA	Lazy Mutt Farmhouse Ale
Moon Dog Brewing	Australia	None
Mud Hound Brewing Co.	USA	None
Parrot Dog Brewery	New Zealand	Pit Bull, Bloody Dingo, Blood Hound, Bitter Bitch, Dogg, Sleuthhound
Pig's Eye Brewing Co.	USA	Pit Bull High Gravity Ice Malt Liquor
Raindogs Brewing Co.	New Zealand	Eagle vs Dog
River Dog Brewing Co.	USA	None
Roger's Beer	USA	The Bulldog IPA, The Hound Dog Scotch Ale, The Mutt Double IPA
Sea Dog Brewing Co.	USA	None
Silvermoon Brewing	USA	Hounds Tooth Amber
Smiling Samoyed Brewery	Australia	12 Paws Pale Ale
Smuttynose Brewing Co.	USA	Old Brown Dog, Really Old Brown Dog
Spanish Peaks Brewing Co.	USA	Black Dog Ale
The Thirsty Dog Brewing Co. Ltd	New Zealand	Black Dog
Thirsty Dog Brewing Co.	USA	12 Dogs of Christmas, 12 Dogs of Christmas Barrel Aged, Barktoberfest, Citra Dog, Irish Setter Red, Kennel Collection, Labrador Lager, Old Leghumper, Rail Dog, Whippet Wheat, Cerasus Dog Flanders Style Red Ale, Old Druid Bloodhound Saison French and Belgian Style Farmhouse Ale, Orthus Belgian Dubbel, Stud Service Stout, Terrier Pale Ale

Brewery	Location	Beers with explicit link to dogs
Tring Brewery Co.	UK	Colley's Dog
White Dog Brewery	Italy	White Dog
White Dog Brewery	UK	Golden Retriever, Scooby Brew, Growler
Windermere Brewing Co.	UK	Golden Retriever, A Bit'er Ruff, W'ruff Night, Isle of Dogs, Dog-th Vader, Ruff Justice, A Winters Tail, Collie Wobbles
York Brewery	UK	Yorkshire Terrier

Appendix 2

Dog cuisine books available via Amazon UK in October 2013

Dog-Gone Good Cuisine: More Healthy, Fast, and Easy Recipes for You and Your Pooch	2014
Dog Treats: The BARKtender's Guide to Easy Homemade Dogtails and Muttinis	2013
My Dog Says I'm a Great Cook!	2013
Canine Cooking: Cooking Made Easy for Your Furry Family Member	2013
Making Pet Food at Home	2013
The Corgi Club 'Corgi Treats' 2013 Cookbook	2013
Elliot's Favorite Treats: Have Your Person Make these 30 Tail-Wagging Treats For You Today!	2013
Canine Kitchen Foods: Natural Food Recipes for Dogs	2013
Wilder by the Dozen: Bone Appetit!	2013
Home-Made Sick Diet For Your Pet Animals	2013
Bones, Biscuits, Cookies, & Other Delights For Your Pooch	2013
AmsterDog's: Tasty Treats for YOUR Top Dog!	2013
Molly Wanna Biscuit: Healthy Allergen-free Dog Treat Recipes	2013
Je Cuisine des Biscuits Pour Mon Chien	2013
The Healthy Homemade Dog Food Cookbook	2013
Recipes for Dogs: Healthy Broths	2013
Fresh Food & Ancient Wisdom: Preparing Healthy & Balanced Meals For Your Dogs	2013
Home Cooking for Your Dog: 75 Holistic Recipes for a Healthier Dog	2013
The Healthy Homemade Pet Food Cookbook: 75 Whole-Food Recipes and Tasty Treats for Dogs and Cats of All Ages	2013
99 Organic Dog Treat Recipes	2013
How To Make Dog Food – Healthy Home Made Dog Food Recipes	2013
Paleo Dog: 7 Paleo Recipes for Man's Best Friend	2013
Better Food for Dogs: A Complete Cookbook and Nutrition Guide	2013
All Natural Raw Dog Food	2013

Continued

You Bake'em Dog Biscuits (Mini Kits)	2003
From Bones to Biscuits: A Healthy, Nutritional Cookbook for Your Dog	2003
Tasty Treats for Demanding Dogs	2002
Cooking for Your Dog	2002
Gourmet Dog Biscuits: For Your Bread Machine	2001
Homemade Treats for Happy, Healthy Dogs	2000
Three Dog Bakery Cookbook: Over 50 Recipes for All-Natural Treats for Your Dog	1998
Natural Food Recipes for Healthy Dogs	1997
Canine Care and Cuisine: The Healthy Dog Book	1997
Howl-iday Dog Biscuits: A Cookbook of Dog Treats for Every Season	1997
Doggie Delights & Kitty Cuisine	1997
Gourmet Dog Biscuits: A Cookbook of Tasty Treats for Your Favorite Fido	1997
Bones Appetit' Gourmet Dog Biscuit Recipes & More	1997
No Barking at the Table: More Recipes Your Dog Will Beg for	1996
The Best Fed Dog in America: Canine Cuisine, Dog Culture, Facts & Merriment	1995
Dog Bites!: Canine Cuisine/Dogs You'll Love and the Homemade Treats They Crave	1993
Bone Appetite: Gourmet Cooking for Your Dog	1989
The Dog Lover's Cookbook: Dr. Tonken's Book of Practical Canine Cuisine	1987
Feeding Fido: All About Good Nutrition and Cooking for Your Dog, Including Recipes, Special Diets and Tail Wagger Treats	1982
Good Dog's Cook Book	1979
The Secret of Cooking for DOGS	1964
Les Secrets de la Nutrition de Mon Chien	undated
VetDepot's Favorite Dog & Cat Treat Recipes	undated

References

Adamson, M.W. (2002) The Greco-Roman world. In: Adamson, M.W. (ed.) *Regional Cuisines of Medieval Europe: A Book of Essays*. Routledge, New York, pp. 1–18.

AFP (2013) China dog meat festival targeted by activists. *The Telegraph*. www.telegraph.co.uk/news/worldnews/asia/china/10130085/China-dog-meat-festival-targeted-by-activists.html, accessed 11 February 2014.

Alington, C. (1929) *Field Trials and Judging*. The Kennel Gazette, London.

Almirall, L. (undated) *Coyote Coursing*. No publisher details presented.

American Kennel Club (undated, a) The economic benefits of AKC dog shows. American Kennel Club, Raleigh, North Carolina.

American Kennel Club (undated, b) Cost of dog ownership. American Kennel Club, Raleigh, North Carolina.

American Kennel Club (2005a) A canine Frankenstein? AKC survey finds dog owners keen on canine costumes for a howling good Halloween. *AKC News*, 14 October. www.akc.org/press_center/article.cfm?article_id=2646, accessed 9 May 2014.

American Kennel Club (2005b) AKC responsible dog ownership day survey reveals rift between dog and non-dog owners. *AKC News*, 7 September. www.akc.org/press_center/article.cfm?article_id=2607, accessed 9 May 2014.

American Kennel Club (2010) 2010 AKC Annual Statistics. *AKC Gazette*. http://viewer.zmags.com/publication/12f7c86c#/12f7c86c/1, accessed 23 May 2014.

American Kennel Club (2012a) Facts and stats: What is agility? classic.akc.org/press_center/facts_stats.cfm?page=9, accessed 4 March 2012.

American Kennel Club (2012b) Facts and stats: What is tracking? classic.akc.org/press_center/facts_stats.cfm?page=12, accessed 4 March 2012.

American Rescue Dog Association (1991) *Search and Rescue Dogs Training Methods*. Howell Bookhouse, New York.

American Veterinary Medical Association (2012) *U.S. Pet Ownership & Demographics Sourcebook*. American Veterinary Medical Association, Schaumburg, Illinois.

Anonymous (2005) *Scottish Outdoor Access Code*. Scottish Natural Heritage, Perth, Scotland.

Anonymous (2009) RSPCA urges dog fight law change. news.bbc.co.uk/2/hi/uk_news/8288182.stm, accessed 15 January 2012.

Anonymous (2012a) RSPCA unit marks 35 years of fighting organised cruelty. Royal Society for the Prevention of Cruelty to Animals. www.rspca.org.uk:80/media/news/story/-/article/35_years_of_SOU_Dec12?, accessed 11 January 2013.

Anonymous (2012b) Pet dogs may be banned on hills. *The Times of India*. articles.timesofindia. indiatimes.com/2012-10-26/pune/34749066_1_pet-dogs-pet-owners-parvati-pachgaon-hill, accessed 30 October 2012.

Anonymous (2012c) TV channel goes to the dogs. Stuff.co.nz. www.stuff.co.nz/entertainment/tv-radio/6766435/TV-channel-goes-to-the-dogs, accessed 21 April 2012.

Anonymous (2013a) Home. The Lake District Sheepdog Experience. www.lakedistrictsheepdogexperience.co.uk, accessed 26 September 2013.

Anonymous (2013b) Dog dazed. Canadian Broadcasting Corporation. www.cbc.ca/doczone/episodes/dog-dazed, accessed 21 September 2013.

Anonymous (2014) Ruth's pet hotel. www.ruthspethotel.ca, accessed 4 February 2014.

Anson, S. (1989) *Bone Appetit!: Gourmet Cooking for Your Dog*. New Chapter Press, Chicago, Illinois.

Arnold, B. (2013) *Fake service dogs are becoming a real problem*. The Dogington Post. dogingtonpost.com/fake-service-dogs-are-becoming-a-real-problem, accessed 4 November 2013.

Ash, E. (1934) *This Doggie Business*. Hutchinson & Co, London.

Ash, E. (1935) *The Greyhound: Coursing, Racing and Showing*. Cassell, London.

Associated Press (2012) Have pet, will travel: Research and planning can ease headache of holiday travel with animals. *The Washington Post*. www.washingtonpost.com/lifestyle/travel/have-pet-will-travel-research-and-planning-can-ease-headache-of-holiday-travel-with-animals/2012/11/06/a8dc50d0-27f3-11e2-aaa5-ac786110c486_story.html, accessed 12 November 2012.

Associated Press (2013) For $349 your pet dog can learn to fly well on a plane thanks to Hollywood special effects sound stage. *Mail* Online. www.dailymail.co.uk/news/article-2417672/For-349-pet-dog-learn-fly-plane-thanks-Hollywood-special-effects-sound-stage.html, accessed 14 September 2013.

Astier, H. (2012) How long will France hunt with hounds? BBC News. www.bbc.co.uk/news/world-europe-20704312, accessed 7 January 2013.

Atkinson, M. and Young, K. (2005) Reservoir dogs: Greyhound racing, mimesis and sports-related violence. *International Review for the Sociology of Sport* 40 (3), 335–356.

Australian Companion Animal Council (2010) *Contribution of the Pet Care Industry to the Australian Economy*. 7th edn. Rockwell Communications, East Kew, Victoria, Australia.

Bachelor, L. (2010) Pub chain puts free dogs' dinners on the menu. *The Guardian*. www.theguardian.com/lifeandstyle/2010/jul/24/dogs-pubs-food, accessed 12 September 2010.

Backer, E. (2012) Investigating the 'family life cycle' model in tourism. In: Schanzel, H., Yeoman, I. and Backer, E. (eds) *Family Tourism: Multidisciplinary Perspectives*. Channel View Publications, Bristol, UK, pp. 156–170.

Baldwin, C. and Norris, P. (1999) Exploring the dimensions of serious leisure: 'Love me - love my dog!' *Journal of Leisure Research* 31 (1), 1–17.

Barrett, B. (2013) Dogs up for adoption after Whistler Sled Dog Company folds. Question. www.whistlerquestion.com/article/20130717/WHISTLER01/307179962/-1/whistler/dogs-up-for-adoption-after-whistler-sled-dog-company-folds, accessed 19 July 2013.

Bateson, P. (2010) Independent inquiry into dog breeding. breedinginquiry.files.wordpress.com/2010/01/final-dog-inquiry-120110.pdf, accessed 17 February 2014.

Bath, A. (2012) Well-heeled pets now getting tattoos. *USA Today*. usatoday30.usatoday.com/news/nation/story/2012-05-03/pet-tattoos-creative-grooming-mohawks/54737844/1, accessed 4 May 2012.

Beetz, A. (2005a) Preface. In: Beetz, A. and Podberscek, A. (eds) *Bestiality and Zoophilia: Sexual Relations with Animals*. Purdue University Press, West Lafayette, Indiana, pp. vii–viii.

Beetz, A. (2005b) Bestiality and zoophilia: Associations with violence and sex offending. In: Beetz, A. and Podberscek, A. (eds) *Bestiality and Zoophilia: Sexual Relations with Animals*. Purdue University Press, West Lafayette, Indiana, pp. 46–70.

Beetz, A. (2005c) New insights into bestiality and zoophilia. In: Beetz, A. and Podberscek, A. (eds) *Bestiality and Zoophilia: Sexual Relations with Animals*. Purdue University Press, West Lafayette, Indiana, pp. 98–119.

Bekoff, M. (2004) Wild justice and fair play: Cooperation, forgiveness, and morality in animals. *Biology and Philosophy* 19, 489–520.

Bekoff, M. (2007) *Animals Matter*. Shambhala. Boston, Massachusetts.

Beirne, P. (1997) Rethinking bestiality: Towards a concept of interspecies sexual assault. *Theoretical Criminology* 1 (3), 317–340.

Beirne, P. (2001) Peter Singer's 'heavy petting' and the politics of animal sexual assault. *Critical Criminology* 10, 43–55.

Beirne, P. (2002) On the sexual assault of animals: A sociological view. In: Creager, A. and Jordan, W. (eds) T*he Animal/Human Boundary: Historical Perspectives*. University of Rochester Press, New York, pp. 193–227.

Belton, B. (2002) *When West Ham Went to the Dogs*. Tempus, Stroud, UK.

Bensky, M., Gosling, S. and Sinn, D. (2013) The world from a dog's point of view: A review and synthesis of dog cognition research. *Advances in the Study of Behavior* 45, 209–406.

Birch, E. and Leśniak, K. (2013) Effect of fence height on joint angles of agility dogs. *The Veterinary Journal* 198, e99–e102.

Blane, W. (1788) *Cynegetica; or, Essays on Sporting: Consisting of Observations on Hare Hunting*. John Stockdale, London.

Bly, L. (2012) Beyond the Westminster dog show, pet travel isn't always easy. *USA Today*. travel.usatoday.com/destinations/dispatches/post/2012/02/beyond-the-westminster-dog-show-pet-travel-isnt-always-easy/628089/1, accessed 20 February 2012.

Bolliger, G. and Goetschel, A. (2005) Sexual relations with animals (zoophilia): An unrecognized problem in animal welfare legislation. In: Beetz, A. and Podberscek, A. (eds) *Bestiality and Zoophilia: Sexual Relations with Animals*. Purdue University Press. West Lafayette, Indiana, pp. 23–45.

Bostock, S. (1993) *Zoos and Animal Rights: The Ethics of Keeping Animals*. Routledge, London.

Borsay, P. (2006) *A History of Leisure: The British Experience Since 1500*. Palgrave Macmillan, Basingstoke, UK.

Boxer, S. (2001) Think tank; Yes, but did anyone ask the animals' opinion? *The New York Times*. www.nytimes.com/2001/06/09/books/think-tank-yes-but-did-anyone-ask-the-animals-opinion.html, accessed 1 August 2012.

Bradshaw, J. (2011) *In Defence of Dogs: Why Dogs Need our Understanding*. Allen Lane, London.

Breyer, M. (2011) Dog dies on flight: safe pet travel tips. www.care2.com/greenliving/dog-dies-on-flight-safe-pet-travel-tips.html, accessed 21 November 2011.

British Columbia Ministry of Agriculture (2012) *Sled Dog Code of Practice*. British Columbia Ministry of Agriculture.

Brown, K. (2013) Fat cats, and dogs – pets hit the gym. SFGate. www.sfgate.com/pets/article/Fat-cats-and-dogs-pets-hit-the-gym-4914730.php, accessed 25 October 2013.

Brown, P. (2003) *Man Walks into a Pub: A Sociable History of Beer*. Macmillan, London.

Brown, S. and Rhodes, R. (2006) Relationships among dog ownership and leisure-time walking in Western Canadian adults. *American Journal of Preventive Medicine* 30 (2), 131–136.

Brown, W. (1934) *The Field Trial Primer*. American Field Publishing Company, Chicago, Illinois.

Budiansky, S. (2000) *The Truth about Dogs*. Viking, New York.

Cameron, L.C.R. (1908) *Otters and Otter-hunting*. L. Upcott Gill, London.

Cameron-Kennedy, D.F. (1991) *A Guide to Foxhunting in Australia*. D.F. Cameron-Kennedy, Melbourne.

CANDi (2013) About us. www.candiinternational.org/about-candi, accessed 10 October 2013.

Carding, A. (1975) The growth of pet population in Western Europe and the implications for dog control in Great Britain. In: Anderson, R. (ed.) *Pet Animals & Society*. Bailliere Tindall, London, pp. 66–88.

Carr, N. (forthcoming a) In search of 'dog': Literary and movie worlds' constructions of dogs in the leisure environment. In: Carr. N. (ed.) *Domestic Animals and Leisure*. Palgrave Macmillan, Basingstoke, UK.

Carr, N. (forthcoming b). The greyhound: A story of fashion, finances, and animal rights. In Carr. N. (ed.) *Domestic Animals and Leisure*. Palgrave Macmillan, Basingstoke, UK.

Carr, N. (2006). Researching the holiday experience from a dog's perspective: Anthropomorphing or Understanding? *Royal Geographical Society/Institute of British Geographers Annual International Conference*. London, UK.

Carr, N. (2011) *Children's and Families' Holiday Experiences*. Routledge, London.

Carr, N. and Cohen, S. (2009) Holidaying with the family pet: No dogs allowed! *Tourism and Hospitality Research* 9 (4), 290–304.

Chang, E. (2010) Inside the cat and dog meat market in China. CNN World. edition.cnn.com/2010/WORLD/asiapcf/03/09/china.animals, accessed 9 March 2010.

Coghlan, A. and Prideaux, B. (2008) Encounters with wildlife in Cairns, Australia: Where, what, who…? *Journal of Ecotourism* 7 (1), 68–76.

Collier, W.F. (1899) *Country Matters in Short*. Duckworth & Co, London.

Cooper, C. (2012) *Canine Cuisine: 101 Natural Dog Food & Treat Recipes to Make your Dog Healthy and Happy*. Atlantic Publishing Group, Ocala, Florida.

Copping, J. (2012) Ban on 'degrading' dances for dogs. *The Telegraph*. www.telegraph.co.uk/lifestyle/pets/9484859/Ban-on-degrading-dances-for-dogs.html, accessed 19 August 2012.

Coppinger, L. (1977) *The World of Sled Dogs: From Siberia to Sport Racing*. Howell Book House, New York.

Coppinger, R. and Coppinger, L. (2001) *Dogs: A startling New Understanding of Canine Origin, Behavior & Evolution*. Scribner, New York.

Coren, S. (2004) *How Dogs Think: Understanding the Canine Mind*. The Free Press, New York.

Council for Science and Society (1988) *Companion Animals in Society*. Oxford University Press, Oxford.

Cox, N. (1697) *The Gentleman's Recreation: Or a Treatise giving the Best Directions for Hunting and Killing all Manner of Chases used in England; with the terms of Art Belonging Thereunto*. 4th edn. J. Dawks, London.

Crispin, S. (2011) The Advisory Council on the welfare issues of dog breeding. *The Veterinary Journal* 189, 129–131.

Croxton Smith, A. (1927) *Greyhound Racing and Breeding*. Gay & Hancock Ltd, London.

Crufts (undated) *About the Kennel Club*. The Kennel Club, London.

Csanyi, V. (2005) *If Dogs Could Talk: Exploring the Canine Mind*. North Point Press, New York.

Cutt, H., Giles-Corti, B., Knuiman, M. and Pikora, T. (2008) Physical activity behavior of dog owners: Development and reliability of the dogs and physical activity (DAPA) tool. *Journal of Physical Activity & Health* 5, S73–S89.

Daly, M. (2001) *Back to Basics with Badgers. Proceedings of the 2000 National Police Wildlife Liaison Officers' Conference*. Department of the Environment, Transport and the Regions, London, pp. 69–72.

Daniels, M., Drogin Rodgers, E. and Wiggins, B. (2005) 'Travel Tales': An interpretive analysis of constraints and negotiations to pleasure travel as experienced by persons with physical disabilities. *Tourism Management* 25, 919–930.

Darcy, S. (2003) The politics of disability and access: The Sydney 2000 Games experience. *Disability & Society* 18 (6), 737–757.

Daruwalla, P. and Darcy, S. (2005) Personal and societal attitudes to disability. *Annals of Tourism Research* 32 (3), 549–570.

Demetriou, D. (2013) Endangered whale meat sold as luxury dog snacks in Japan. *The Telegraph.* www.telegraph.co.uk/news/worldnews/asia/japan/10086027/Endangered-whale-meat-sold-as-luxury-dog-snacks-in-Japan.html, accessed 4 November 2013.

Dennis, S. (2000) *Holidaying with Dogs.* 6th edn. 'Life. Be in it' Special Projects Unit, Melbourne, Australia.

Department of Conservation and Land Management (2002) Pets in parks. www.calm.wa.gov.au/national_parks/pets_in_parks.html, accessed 16 August 2002.

Dogs Trust (undated) *From our home to yours...* Dogs Trust, London.

Donnan, H. and Magowan, F. (2010) *The Anthropology of Sex.* Berg, Oxford, UK.

Drabble, P. (1989) *One Man and His Dog.* Pelham Books, London.

Duffy, R. (2014) Interactive elephants: Nature, tourism and neoliberalism. *Annals of Leisure Research* 44, 88–101.

Duncan, I. (2006) The changing concept of animal sentience. *Applied Animal Behaviour Science* 100, 11–19.

Dunlop, F. (2008) *Shark's Fin and Sichuan Pepper: A Sweet-sour Memoir of Eating in China.* Ebury Press, London.

Durrell, G. (1976) *The Stationary Ark.* Collins, London.

Eckhardt, L.W., Bradley, B. and Kern, J. (2006) *The Dog Ate it: Cooking for Yourself and Your Four-Legged Friends.* Gotham Books, New York.

Edwards Benning, L. (1976) *The Pet Profiteers: The Exploitation of Pet Owners – and Pets – in America.* Quadrangle/The New York Times Book Co., New York.

Elias, N. and Dunning, E. (2008) *Quest for Excitement: Sport and Leisure in the Civilising Process.* University College Dublin Press, Dublin.

Endenburg, N. and van Lith, H. (2011) The influence of animals on the development of children. *The Veterinary Journal* 190, 208–214.

Evans, P. (2008) *Mad Dogs and an Englishwoman.* Bantam Books, London.

Evans, R., Gauthier, D. and Forsyth, C. (1998) Dogfighting: Symbolic expression and validation of masculinity. *Sex Roles* 39 (11/12), 825–838.

Everest, E. (2010) *Canine Cuisine: How to Cook Tasty Meals and Treats that your Dog will Enjoy.* How to Books Ltd, Oxford, UK.

Fennell, D. and Sheppard, V. (2011) Another legacy for Canada's 2010 Olympic and Paralympic Winter Games: Applying an ethical lens to the post-games' sled dog cull. *Journal of Ecotourism* 10 (3), 197–213.

Firth, J. (1998) *Yukon Quest: The 1000-mile Dog Sled Race Through the Yukon and Alaska.* Lost Moose, Whitehorse, Yukon, Canada.

Fitz-Barnard, L. (1975) *Fighting Sports.* The Spur Publications Company, Hill Brow, Liss, UK.

Flanders, N. (1989) *The Joy of Running Sled Dogs.* Alpine Publications Inc., Loveland, Colorado.

Fogle, B. (1983) *Pets and Their People.* Collins Harvill, London.

Ford, L. (1999) *A History of X: 100 Years of Sex in Film.* Prometheus Books, New York.

Fortunato, L. (2007) *The 'Everything' Cooking for Dogs Book: 150 Quick and Healthy Recipes your Dog will Love!* Adams Media, Avon, Massachusetts.

Fox, M. (2009) In defence of dog eating. Stuff.co.nz. www.stuff.co.nz/national/2768167/In-defence-of-dog-eating, accessed 19 August 2009.

Fox, R. (1888) *The Dog Pit.* Richard K. Fox, New York.

Fox, R. (2012) Warning about dogs and wildlife. *Otago Daily Times.* www.odt.co.nz/news/dunedin/199731/warning-about-dogs-and-wildlife, accessed 2 March 2012.

Fox, S. (2013) Animal attraction: Track your dog's fitness with activity tracker. www.khou.com/story/news/local/animals/2014/07/23/12058184/, accessed 19 August 2014.

Francione, G.L. (2004) Animals – property or persons? In: Sunstein, C. and Nussbaum, M. (eds) *Animal Rights: Current Debates and New Directions.* Oxford University Press, Oxford, UK, pp. 108–142.

Frost, J., Wortham, S. and Reifel, S. (2008) *Play and Child Development.* 3rd edn. Pearson, Upper Saddle River, New Jersey.

Garst, S. (1948) *Scotty Allan: King of the Dog-team Drivers*. Wells Gardner, Darton & Co. Ltd, Redhill, UK.

Gillespie, D., Leffler, A. and Lerner, E. (1996) Safe in unsafe places: Leisure, passionate avocations, and the problematizing of everyday public life. *Society and Animals* 4 (2), 169–188.

Gillespie, D., Leffler, A. and Lerner, E. (2002) If it weren't for my hobby, I'd have a life: Dog sports, serious leisure, and boundary negotiations. *Leisure Studies* 21, 285–304.

Gniadek, I. (1993) *The History of the Barbaric Sport of Dog Baiting*. I.R. Gniadek Publications, Wigan, UK.

Godwin, R. (1975) Trends in the ownership of domestic pets in Great Britain. In: Anderson, R. (ed.) *Pet Animals & Society*. Bailliere Tindall, London, pp. 96–102.

Goodall, J. (2007) Foreword. In: Bekoff, M. (ed.) *The Emotional Lives of Animals*. New World Library, Novato, California, pp. xi–xv.

Grebowicz, M. (2010) When species meat: Confronting bestiality pornography. *Humanimalia* 1 (2), 1–17.

Greenebaum, J. (2004) It's a dog's life: Elevating status from pet to 'fur baby' at yappy hour. *Society & Animals* 12 (2), 117–135.

Greyhound Board of Great Britain (2010) Annual Report 2010. Greyhound Board of Great Britain, London.

Griffin, D. (2001) *Animal Minds: Beyond Cognition to Consciousness*. University of Chicago Press, Chicago, Illinois.

Griffin, E. (2005) *England's Revelry: A History of Popular Sports and Pastimes 1660–1830*. Oxford University Press, Oxford, UK.

Griffin, E. (2007) *Blood Sport: Hunting in Britain since 1066*. Yale University Press, New Haven, Connecticut.

Gullotta, T.P, Adams, G.R and Markstrom, C.A. (2000) *The Adolescent Experience*. 4th edn. Academic Press, London.

Guthrie, S. (1997) Anthropomorphism: A definition and a theory. In: Mitchell, R., Thompson, N. and Miles, H. (eds) *Anthropomorphism, Anecdotes, and Animals*. State University of New York Press, Albany, New York, pp. 50–58.

Haden, R. (2009) *Food Culture in the Pacific Islands*. Greenwood Press, Santa Barbara, California.

Hall, C. (2013) Pet dog is groomed to look like YODA from Star Wars. *Mirror*. www.mirror.co.uk/news/weird-news/pet-dog-groomed-look-like-1960420, accessed 22 June 2013.

Halsall, E. (1982) *Sheepdog Trials*. Patrick Stephens, Cambridge, UK.

Hare, B. and Woods, N. (2013) *The Genius of Dogs: How Dogs are Smarter than you Think*. Dutton, New York.

Held, S. and Spinka, M. (2011) Animal play and animal welfare. *Animal Behaviour* 81, 891–899.

Henderson, K. (1984) Volunteerism as leisure. *Nonprofit and Voluntary Sector Quarterly* 13, 155–163.

Herzog, H. (2010) *Some We Love, Some We Hate, Some We Eat*. Harper, New York.

Hess, M. (2012) The airport canine ambassador. www.miami-airport.com/pdfdoc/clips_cool-crazy-jobs-casey.pdf, accessed 14 February 2014.

Hill, C. and Bowling, M. (2007) *Statistics for the Travel & Tourism Industry, 2006*. Blizzard Internet Marketing, Inc., Glenwood Springs, Colorado.

Holmberg, T. (2013) Trans-species urban politics: Stories from a beach. *Space and Culture* 16 (1), 28–42.

Honore, C. (2004) *In Praise of Slowness: How a Worldwide Movement is Challenging the Cult of Speed*. HarperSanFrancisco, New York.

Hood, M. (1996) *A Fan's Guide to the Iditarod*. Alpine Blue Ribbon Books, Loveland, Colorado.

Hopkins, J. (2005) *Extreme Cuisine*. Bloomsbury Publishing Plc, London.

Horowitz, A. (2009a) *Inside of a Dog: What Dogs See, Smell, and Know*. Scribner, New York.

Horowitz, A. (2009b) Attention to attention in domestic dog (*Canis familiaris*) dyadic play. *Animal Cognition* 12, 107–118.

Hultsman, W. (2013) Environmental challenges and championship events: Perspectives from the serious dog sport enthusiast. *Event Management* 17, 1–12.

Humane Research Council (2010) *Companion Animals.* Vol. 1. HRC Research Primer. Humane Research Council, Olympia, Washington.

Huston, L. (2011) Pet lovers react to new Android dog fighting app. Examiner.com. www.examiner.com/article/pet-lovers-react-to-new-android-dog-fighting-app., accessed 30 July 2014.

Ibbotson, L. (2012) Team all smiles for the miles. *Otago Daily Times.* www.odt.co.nz/news/queenstown-lakes/223808/team-all-smiles-miles, accessed 30 August 2012.

Jack, A. (2009) *The Old Dog and Duck: The Secret Meanings of Pub Names.* Penguin Books, London.

Jackson, F. (1990) *Crufts: The Official History.* Pelham Books, London.

Jenkins, P. (1999) Now Fido can make his own holiday claims. *Financial Times* 7 August, 18.

Jennings, P. (2007) *The Local: A History of the English Pub.* Tempus Publishing Limited, Stroud, UK.

Jesse, G. (1866a) *Researches into the History of the British Dog: Volume I.* Robert Hardwicke, London.

Jesse, G. (1866b) *Researches into the History of the British Dog: Volume II.* Robert Hardwicke, London.

Jobson-Scott, D. (1933) *Beagling for Beginners.* Hutchinson & Co. Ltd, London.

Johns, E. (2002) Marketing. In: Hobbs, J. (ed.) *Greyhound Annual 2003.* Raceform, Newbury, UK, pp. 29–31.

Johns, R. (1939) *Smash Dog-fighting & Badgering.* The National Canine Defence League, London.

Jones, E.W.H. (1892) *Sheep-dog Trials and the Sheep-dog. Or Sheep-dog Trials: Their Standard of Adjudication, Origin, and Progress.* Edwin Poole, Brecon, UK.

Jones, M. (2011) *Healthy Wagger's Natural Dog Treat Cook Book.* Amazon. Kindle edition.

Jones, S. (2008) BBC will not screen Crufts after row over ailing dogs. *The Guardian.* www.theguardian.com/media/2008/dec/13/bbc-crufts-animal-welfare, accessed 13 December 2008.

Joseph, C. (2010) Exploring the animal-human bond through a sociological lens. In: Demello, M. (ed.) *Teaching the Animal: Human–Animal Studies Across the Disciplines.* Lantern Books, New York, pp. 299–337.

Jukes, A. (2003) Introduction. In: Herron, J. (ed.) *Trials and Dogs of the South: A History of Sheep Dog Trialing in Southland.* Southland Dog Trial Association, Gore, New Zealand, pp. 9–10.

K9Obedience.co.uk. (2009) Dog fighting continues. www.k9obedience.co.uk/dogcare/rescue/fightingdogs.html, accessed 15 January 2012.

Kalof, L. (2007) *Looking at Animals in Human History.* Reaktion Books, London.

Kalof, L. and Taylor, C. (2007) The discourse of dog fighting. *Humanity & Society* 31, 319–333.

Katz, J. (2003) *The New Work of Dogs: Tending to Life, Love, and Family.* Villard, New York.

Kean, H. (1998) *Animal Rights: Political and Social Change in Britain since 1800.* Reaktion Books, London.

Kelly, J. (1996) *Leisure.* Allyn and Bacon, Boston, Massachusetts.

Kemp, S. (1999) Sled dog racing: The celebration of co-operation in a competitive sport. *Ethnology* 38 (1), 81–95.

Kennel Club (undated) *Open for Dogs: Campaign Briefing.* The Kennel Club, London.

Kennel Club (2012) *Crufts Facts at your Fingertips.* The Kennel Club, London.

Kiley-Worthington, M. (1990) *Animals in Circuses and Zoos: Chiron's World?* Little Eco-Farms Publishing, Basildon, UK.

King, T., Marston, L. and Bennett, P. (2009) Describing the ideal Australian companion dog. *Applied Animal Behaviour Science* 120, 84–93.

Kleven, A. (2013) Dogs wear 'pet me' vests at airport hoping to relieve your stress. MyNorthwest.com. http://mynorthwest.com/920/2286191/Dogs-wear-pet-me-vests-at-airport-hoping-to-relieve-your-stress, accessed 10 June 2013.

Knight, S.and Herzog, H. (2009) All creatures great and small: New perspectives on psychology and human–animal interactions. *Journal of Social Issues* 65 (3), 451–461.

Knoll, E. (1997) Dogs, Darwinism, and English sensibilities. In: Mitchell, R., Thompson, N. and Miles, H. (eds) *Anthropomorphism, Anecdotes, and Animals.* State University of New York Press, New York, pp. 12–21.

Kuhl, G. (2011) Human–sled dog relations: What can we learn from the stories and experiences of mushers? *Society & Animals* 19, 22–37.

LaBelle, C. (1993) *A Guide to Backpacking with your Dog.* Alpine Publications, Loveland, Colorado.

Lammi, M. (2013) Bedtime stories and 'tuck-ins'? Pets get deluxe treatment at facility. *Livingston Daily.* www.livingstondaily.com/article/20130626/LIFESTYLE/306260018/Bedtime-stories-tuck-ins-Pets-get-deluxe-treatment-facility, accessed 29 June 2013.

Landers, J. (2013) Dog eat dog: Pet food not just beef and chicken. *Valley News.* www.vnews.com/lifetimes/5833274-95/dog-eat-dog-pet-food-not-just-beef-and-chicken, accessed 29 April 2013.

Lee, S., Gibbons, J. and Short, S. (2010) Sympathetic reactions to the bait dog in a film of dog fighting: The influence of personality and gender. *Society and Animals* 18, 107–125.

Lehman, H. (1997) Anthropomorphism and scientific evidence for animal mental states. In: Mitchell, R., Thompson, N. and Miles, H. (eds) *Anthropomorphism, Anecdotes, and Animals.* State University of New York Press, Albany, New York, pp. 104–115.

Leslie, P. (2004) *The Wholesome Dog Biscuit: A Barker's Dozen.* Regent Press, Oakland, California.

Lloyd, J.I. (1971) *Beaglers: Harehunting with Harriers, Beagles, and Bassets.* Adam & Charles Black, London.

Locke, A. (1987) *Search Dog.* Souvenir Press, London.

Longman, G. (1896) Beagling. In: Watson, A. (ed.) *Fur and Feather Series: The Hare.* Longmans, Green, and Co., London, pp. 179–190.

Low, P. (2012) The Cambridge declaration on consciousness. fcmconference.org/img/CambridgeDeclarationOnConsciousness.pdf, accessed 18 February 2013.

MacFarland, S. and Hediger, R. (2009) Approaching the agency of other animals: An introduction. In: MacFarland, S. and Hediger, R. (eds) *Animals and Agency: An Interdisciplinary Exploration.* Brill, Boston, Massachusetts, pp. 1–20.

Mackenzie, F. (2008) *How to Start and Run a Petsitting Business.* How to Books Ltd, Oxford, UK.

Mann, P. (1975) Introduction. In: Anderson, R. (ed.) *Pet Animals & Society.* Bailliere Tindall, London, pp. 1–7.

Manning, S. (2012) Dog treadmill sales brisk as pets shape up. www.huffingtonpost.com/2012/08/14/dog-treadmill-_n_1776329.html, accessed 16 December 2013.

Markwell, K. and Cushing, N. (2009) The serpent's stare meets the tourist's gaze: strategies of display at the Australian Reptile Park. *Current Issues in Tourism* 21 (5–6), 475–488.

Martin, J. (2013) Pet projects: How US retailers are going to the dogs. BBC News. www.bbc.co.uk/news/business-24109140, accessed 21 September 2013.

Massey, D. and Jess, P. (1995) Introduction. In: Massey, D. and Jess, P. (eds) *A Place in the World? Places, Cultures and Globalisation.* Oxford University Press, Oxford, UK, pp. 1–4.

Masson, J. (1997) *Dogs Never Lie about Love: Reflections on the Emotional World of Dogs.* Three Rivers Press, New York.

McConnell, P. (2005) *For the Love of a Dog: Understanding Emotion in You and your Best Friend.* Ballantine Books, New York.

McGill, R. (ed.) (2002) *Australian Dogs on Holiday*. 4th edn. K. & L. Gilkes Pty Ltd, Denistone East, Australia.

Meeks, J. (1974) *Memoirs of the Pit*. Pete Sparks, Starke, Florida.

Meens, R. (2002) Eating animals in the Early Middle Ages: Classifying the animal world and building group identities. In: Creager, A. and Jordan, W. (eds) *The Animal/Human Boundary: Historical Perspectives*. University of Rochester Press, New York, pp. 3–28.

Mehanna, S. (2007) *Mutt Munchies: 35 Easy-to-make Dog Bakes*. Hamlyn, London.

Mehus-Roes, K. (2009) *Canine Sports & Games. Great Ways to Get Your Dog Fit and Have Fun Together*. Storey Publishing, North Adams, Massachusetts.

Menn, B., Lorentz, S. and Naucke, T. (2010) Imported and travelling dogs as carriers of canine vector-borne pathogens in Germany. *Parasites & Vectors* 3 (34), 1–7.

Messent, P. (1983) Social facilitation of contact with other people by pet dogs. In: Katcher, A.H. and Beck, A. (eds) *New Perspectives on our Lives with Companion Animals*. University of Pennsylvania Press, Philadelphia, pp. 37–46.

Miklósi, Á. (2007) *Dog Behaviour, Evolution, and Cognition*. Oxford University Press, Oxford, UK.

Miletski, H. (2002) *Understanding Bestiality & Zoophilia*. East-West Publishing, LLC, Bethesda, Maryland.

Miletski, H. (2005) A history of bestiality. In: Beetz, A. and Podberscek, A. (eds) *Bestiality and Zoophilia: Sexual Relations with Animals*. Purdue University Press, West Lafayette, Indiana, pp. 1–22.

Mitchell, R. (1997) Anthropomorphic anecdotalism as method. In: Mitchell, R., Thompson, N. and Miles, H. (eds) *Anthropomorphism, Anecdotes, and Animals*. State University of New York Press, Albany, New York, pp. 150–169.

Mitchell, S. (2013) *Wilder by the Dozen: Bone Appetit: Simple Healthy Timeless Home Made Doggy Food Recipes*. Wilder Wellness Cuisine.

Moore, J. (1929) *The Canine King: The Working Sheep Dog*. Standard Newspapers Pty Ltd, Cheltenham, Australia.

Morell, V. (2008) Minds of their own: Animals are smarter than you think. *National Geographic* 213 (3), 36–61.

Morris, D. (2009) *Training and Racing the Greyhound*. The Crowood Press, Ramsbury, UK.

Morrison, H. (2012) *Dinner for Dogs*. Ebury Press, London.

Moss, A.W. (1961) *Valiant Crusade: The History of the Royal Society for the Prevention of Cruelty to Animals*. Cassell, London.

Moynihan, M. (1997) Self-awareness, with specific references to coleoid cephalopods. In: Mitchell, R., Thompson, N. and Miles, H. (eds) *Anthropomorphism, Anecdotes, and Animals*. State University of New York Press, Albany, New York, pp. 213–219.

Mut Hut Pet Emporium Inc. (2011) Welcome to Mut Hut. http://muthut.com, accessed 23 May 2014.

Munro, H.and Thrusfield, M. (2005) 'Battered pets': sexual abuse. In: Beetz, A. and Podberscek, A. (eds) *Bestiality and Zoophilia: Sexual Relations with Animals*. Purdue University Press, West Lafayette, Indiana, pp. 71–81.

Murray, R. (2013) Pet-lover dishes frozen yogurt for dogs from Yappy Treats cart. NYDailyNews.com. www.nydailynews.com/life-style/eats/yapp.y-treats-frozen-yogurt-dogs-article-1.1386999, accessed 6 July 2013.

National Greyhound Racing Club and Genders, R. (1990) *The NGRC Book of Greyhound Racing: A History of the Sport Completely Revised and Updated by the National Greyhound Racing Club*. Pelham Books, London.

Nestle, M. (2008) *Pet Food Politics: The Chihuahua in the Coal Mine*. University of California Press, Berkeley, California.

New Zealand Companion Animal Council (2011) *Companion Animals in New Zealand*. The New Zealand Companion Animal Council Inc., Manukau, New Zealand.

Nicholas, F. (2011) Response to the documentary Pedigree Dogs Exposed: Three reports and their recommendations. *The Veterinary Journal* 189, 126–128.

Norris, P., Shinew, K., Chick, G. and Beck, A. (1999) Retirement, life satisfaction, and leisure services: The pet connection. *Journal of Park and Recreation Administration* 17 (2), 65–83.

O'Brien, J. (2013) Scots pet owners take in dogs stolen for illegal meat trade. BBC Scotland News. www.bbc.co.uk/news/uk-scotland-highlands-islands-23779700, accessed 24 August 2013.

O'Grady, P. (2007) *Woofing it Down: The Quick & Easy Guide to Making Healthy Dog Food at Home*. AuthorHouse, Bloomington, Indiana.

Ogilvie, C. (2006) Powder hounds. *The Province*. 8 January, pp. B8–B9.

Oka, K. and Shibata, A. (2009) Dog ownership and health-related physical activity among Japanese adults. *Journal of Physical Activity and Health* 6, 412–418.

O'Mahony, J. (2012) World's first dog pedometer goes on sale to tackle pet obesity. *The Telegraph*. www.telegraph.co.uk/technology/news/9711201/Worlds-first-dog-pedometer-goes-on-sale-to-tackle-pet-obesity.html, accessed 30 November 2012.

Onion, R. (2009) Sled dogs of the American North: On masculinity, whiteness, and human freedom. In: MacFarland, S. and Hediger, R. (eds) *Animals and Agency: An Interdisciplinary Exploration*. Brill, Boston, Massachusetts, pp. 129–155.

Osborn, A. (2011) Ukraine accused of culling stray dogs ahead of Euro 2012. *The Telegraph*. www.telegraph.co.uk/sport/football/competitions/euro-2012/8931419/Ukraine-accused-of-culling-stray-dogs-ahead-of-Euro-2012.html, accessed 11 November 2013.

Palmer, J. (1983) *Working Dogs*. Patrick Stephens, Cambridge, UK.

Paws Point (undated) The dog beer story. www.dogbeer.com.au, accessed 1 November 2013.

Payne, R. (2013a) The effect of spaying on the racing performance of female greyhounds. *The Veterinary Journal* 198 (2), 372–375.

Payne, R. (2013b) Greyhound sports injuries: Racing careers fractured by anatomical imperfections? *The Veterinary Journal* 196, 280–281.

Pearce, F. (1874) *The Kennel Club Stud Book: A Record of Dog Shows and Field Trials*. Kennel Club, London.

Pet Food Manufacturers Association (2010a) Historical pet ownership 1965–2004. www.pfma.org.uk/_assets/docs/Historical%20pet%20population%20data(1).pdf, accessed 21 December 2013.

Pet Food Manufacturers Association (2010b) Pet population 2008 to 2012. www.pfma.org.uk/pet-population-2008-2012, accessed 21 December 2013.

Pet Food Manufacturers Association (2010c) Pet population 2013. www.pfma.org.uk/pet-population, accessed 21 December 2013.

Pfau, T., Garland de Rivaz, A., Brighton, S. and Weller, R. (2011) Kinetics of jump landing in agility dogs. *The Veterinary Journal* 190, 278–283.

Pieper, J. (1965) *Leisure: The Basis of Culture*. Collins, London.

Podberscek, A. (2009) Good to pet and eat: The keeping and consuming of dogs and cats in South Korea. *Journal of Social Issues* 65 (3), 615–632.

Power, E. (2008) Furry families: making a human-dog family through home. *Social & Cultural Geography* 9 (5), 535–555.

Power, E. (2012) Domestication and the dog: Embodying home. *Area* 44 (3), 371–378.

Power, J. (2013) It's raining cats and dogs. *Brisbane Times*. www.smh.com.au/environment/animals/its-raining-cats-and-dogs-20130921-2u6lo.html, accessed 28 September 2013.

Price, M. (2012) Testing times for dogs and sheep. *Otago Daily Times*. www.odt.co.nz/news/queenstown-lakes/211024/testing-time-dogs-and-sheep, accessed 30 May 2012.

Quiatt, D. (1997) Silent partners? Observations on some systematic relations among observer perspective, theory, and behaviour. In: Mitchell, R., Thompson, N. and Miles, H. (eds)

Anthropomorphism, Anecdotes, and Animals. State University of New York Press, Albany, New York, pp. 220–236.

Racher, J. (2005) Travelling with dogs: Are dog-friendly hotels in Canada meeting the needs of dogs and their owners? BSc thesis, Brock University, Canada.

Reeves, M., Rafferty, A., Miller, C. and Lyon-Callo, S. (2011) The impact of dog walking on leisure-time physical activity: Results from a population-based survey of Michigan adults. *Journal of Physical Activity and Health* 8, 436–444.

Regan, T. (2004) *Empty Cages: Facing the Challenge of Animal Rights.* Rowman & Littlefield Publishers, Inc., Oxford, UK.

Reichmann, J.B. (2000) *Evolution, Animal 'Rights', & the Environment.* The Catholic University of America Press, Washington, DC.

Reid, E. (1980) *Canine Gladiators: Of Old and Modern Times.* Stockquest Ltd, London.

Retired Greyhound Trust (2010) Annual Review 2010. Retired Greyhound Trust, Worcester Park, UK.

Rice, B. (1968) *The Other End of the Leash: The American Way with Pets.* Angus and Robertson, London.

Riley, R. (2012) *The Dog Food Doctrine: The Shocking Truth about Your Canine's Cuisine.* The B24 Group. Amazon. Kindle edition.

Rivera, M. (2009) *Simple Little Vegan Dog Book.* Book Publishing Company, Summertown, Tennessee.

Rogerson, J. (1991) *Understanding Your Dog.* Popular Dogs Publishing Co. Ltd, London.

Romero, S. (2012) Finally, a place in Brazil where dogs can go for discreet sex. *The New York Times.* www.nytimes.com/2012/11/12/world/americas/animalle-mundo-pet-a-motel-for-tail-wagging-romance.html, accessed 20 November 2012.

Rooney, N., Bradshaw, J. and Robinson, I. (2000) A comparison of dog–dog and dog–human play behaviour. *Applied Animal Behaviour Science* 66, 235–248.

Rooney, N., Bradshaw, J. and Robinson, I. (2001) Do dogs respond to play signals given by humans? *Animal Behaviour* 61, 715–722.

Rooney, N., Sargan, D., Pead, M., Westgarth, C., Creighton, E. and Branson, N. (2009) *Pedigree Dog Breeding in the UK: A Major Welfare Concern?* Royal Society for the Prevention of Cruelty to Animals, Horsham, UK.

Rosenberger, J. (1968) *Bestiality.* Medco Books, Los Angeles.

Rothgerber, H. (2013) A meaty matter. Pet diet and the vegetarian's dilemma. *Appetite* 68, 76–82.

Royal Society for the Prevention of Cruelty to Animals (2012) Frequently asked questions. www.rspca.org.uk/utilities/faq/-/question/ENQ_Five_Freedoms/category/Pets, accessed 31 December 2012.

Rudy, K. (2011) *Loving Animals: Toward a New Animal Advocacy.* University of Minnesota Press, Minneapolis.

Salmon, M. (1977) *Gazehounds & Coursing.* North Star Press, Saint Cloud, Minnesota.

Sanders, C. (1999) *Understanding Dogs: Living and Working with Canine Companions.* Temple University Press, Philadelphia.

SARDA England (2014) History. www.sardaengland.org.uk/history.html, accessed 3 February 2014.

SARDA Scotland (2014) About call outs. www.sarda-scotland.org/about-call-outs, accessed 3 February 2014.

Scales, S. (2000) Introduction. In: Alington, C. (ed.) *Field Trials and Judging.* Swan Hill Press, Shrewsbury, UK, pp. 1–2.

Schwabe, C. (1979) *Unmentionable Cuisine.* The University Press of Virginia, Charlottesville, Virginia.

Scott, W.H. (1820) *British Field Sports: Embracing Practical Instructions in Shooting-Hunting-Coursing-Racing-Cocking-Fishing, &c. With Observations on the Breaking and Training of Dogs and Horses; also the Management of Fowling Pieces, and all Other Sporting Implements.* 2nd edn. Sherwood, Neely, and Jones, London.

Semencic, C. (1984) *The World of Fighting Dogs.* T.F.H. Publications, Hong Kong.

Serpell, J. and Paul, E. (1994) Pets and the development of positive attitudes to animals. In: Manning, A. and Serpell, J. (eds) *Animals and Human Society: Changing Perspectives.* Routledge, London, pp. 127–144.

Shaw, G. and Coles, T. (2004) Disability, holiday making and the tourism industry in the UK: A preliminary survey. *Tourism Management* 25, 397–403.

Shepherds Walks (2013) About us. http://shepherdswalks.co.uk/about_us, accessed 27 November 2013.

Siddique, H. (2008) Britain sees dramatic surge in dog fighting. *The Guardian.* www.guardian. co.uk/uk/2008/jun/03/animalwelfare.ukcrime, accessed 15 January 2012.

Siegal, M. (1994) *Understanding the Dog you Love: A Guide to Preventing and Solving Behavior Problems in your Dog.* Berkley Books, New York.

Silverman, P. (1997) A pragmatic approach to the inference of animal mind. In: Mitchell, R., Thompson, N. and Miles, H. (eds) *Anthropomorphism, Anecdotes, and Animals.* State University of New York Press, Albany, New York, pp. 170–188.

Singer, P. (2004) All animals are equal. In: Sterba, J. (ed.) *Morality in Practice.* 7th edn. Thomson Learning, London, pp. 474–483.

Sled Dog Association of Scotland (2007a) About us. www.sdas.org.uk/aboutus.html, accessed 15 February 2012.

Sled Dog Association of Scotland (2007b) Home page. www.sdas.org.uk, accessed 15 February 2012.

Small, J., Darcy, S. and Packer, T. (2012) The embodied tourist experiences of people with vision impairment: Management implications beyond the visual gaze. *Tourism Management* 33, 941–950.

Smith, R. (2011) Investigating financial aspects of dog-fighting in the UK. *Journal of Financial Crime* 4, 336–346.

Sniffing Butt Dog Bone Brewery (undated) Our brews. beergraindogtreats.com/category/our-brews, accessed 1 November 2013.

Stapen, C. (2013a) Guilt trip: Pet travel can be stressful for people, too. *USA Today.* www.usatoday. com/story/dispatches/2013/06/20/pet-travel-survey/2439747, accessed 22 June 2013.

Stapen, C. (2013b) Should pets fly on jets? *USA Today.* www.usatoday.com/story/dis-patches/2013/11/26/tips-airplane-travel-pets-dog-cats-fly-on-planes/3705725, accessed 1 December 2013.

Stebbins, R. (1996) Volunteering: A serious leisure perspective. *Nonprofit and Voluntary Sector Quarterly* 25 (2), 211–224.

Stebbins, R. (2007) *Serious Leisure: A Perspective for Our Time.* Transaction Publishers, New Brunswick, Canada.

Steele, D. (2007) *2007 Sled Dog Sports Participant Survey.* International Sled Dog Racing Association, Merrifield, Minnesota.

Steiner, G. (2005) *Anthropocentrism and its Discontents.* University of Pittsburgh Press, Pittsburgh.

Stonehenge (Walsh, J.H.) (1875) *British Rural Sports: Comprising Shooting, Hunting, Coursing, Fishing, Hawking, Racing, Boating and Pedestrianism, with all Rural Games and Amusements.* Frederick Warne and Co., London.

Strutt, J. (1875) *The Sports and Pastimes of the People of England.* William Tegg & Co., London.

Szasz, K. (1968) *Petishism: Pet Cults of the Western World.* Hutchinson & Co., London.

Tantara, (1893) *Hare Hunting.* Horace Co., London.

Thio, A. (1983) *Deviant Behavior.* 2nd edn. Houghton Mifflin Company, Boston, Massachusetts.

Thomas, E.M. (2000) *The Social Lives of Dogs: The Grace of Canine Company.* Simon & Schuster, New York.

Tuan, Y.-F. (1998) *Escapism.* The Johns Hopkins University Press, Baltimore, Maryland.

Twichell Roberts, D. (2004) *The Good Food Cookbook for Dogs: 50 Homemade Recipes for Health and Happiness*. Apple Press, Hove, UK.

Valentine, G.and McKendrick, J. (1997) Children's outdoor play: Exploring parental concerns about children's safety and the changing nature of childhood. *Geoforum* 28 (2), 219–235.

Van Slyck, A. (2006) *A Manufactured Wilderness: Summer Vamps and the Shaping of American Youth, 1890–1960*. University of Minnesota Press, Minneapolis, Minnesota.

Varsava, N. (2013) The problem of anthropomorphous animals: Toward a posthumanist ethics. *Society & Animals* 1–16. http://booksandjournals.brillonline.com/content/journals/10.1163/15685306-12341270, accessed 9 May 2014.

Voith, V., Wright, J. and Danneman, P. (1992) Is there a relationship between canine behavior problems and spoiling activities, anthropomorphism, and obedience training. *Applied Animal Behaviour Science* 34, 263–272.

Wagstaff, J. (1995) *Crufts Obedience Champions*. Pembrokeshire & Canine Press, Fishguard, UK.

Walsh, M. (2007) *Cooking for Dogs*. New Holland Publishers Ltd, London.

Wan, M., Kubinyi, E., Miklosi, A. and Champagne, F. (2009) A cross-cultural comparison of reports by German Shepherd owners in Hungary and the United States of America. *Applied Animal Behaviour Science* 121, 206–213.

Webster, D. (2013) The economic impact of stray cats and dogs at tourist destinations on the tourism industry. CANDi International. www.humaneadvisor.com/wp-content/uploads/2013/06/The-Economic-Impact-of-Stray-Cats-and-Dogs-at-Tourist-Destinations-on-the-Tourism-Industry-2013.pdf, accessed 1 February 2014.

Wedde, I. (2007) Walking the dog. In: Simmons, L. and Armstrong, P. (eds) *Knowing Animals*. Brill, Leiden, pp. 266–288.

Wedderburn, P. (2012) Pet subjects: What is the law on allowing dogs in bars, restaurants and shops? *The Telegraph*. www.telegraph.co.uk/health/petshealth/9583690/Pet-subjects-What-is-the-law-on-allowing-dogs-in-bars-restaurants-and-shops.html, accessed 5 October 2012.

Westgarth, C., Christley, R., Pinchbeck, G., Gaskell, R., Dawson, S. and Bradshaw, J. (2010) Dog behaviour on walks and the effect of use of the leash. *Applied Animal Behaviour Science* 125, 38–46.

Whyte, W. (1927) *The Sheep-dog: Judging and Conduct of Trials and the Art of Breaking-in*. Whitcombe & Tombs Limited, Auckland.

Wise, S. (2002) *Drawing the Line: Science and the Case for Animal Rights*. Perseus Books, Cambridge, Massachusetts.

Wong, E. (2011) After online campaign, Chinese dog meat festival is canceled. *The New York Times*. www.nytimes.com/2011/09/30/world/asia/dog-meat-festival-is-canceled-in-china.html?_r=0, accessed 3 October 2011).

Wood, L., Giles-Corti, B., Bulsara, M. and Bosch, D. (2007) More than a furry companion: The ripple effect of companion animals on neighborhood interactions and sense of community. *Society and Animals* 15, 43–56.

World Society for the Protection of Animals (2011) Bear baiting. www.wspa-international.org/wspaswork/bears/bearbaiting/savagebloodsport.aspx, accessed 11 July 2011.

World Travel Market (2007) *WTM Global Trends Report 2007*. World Travel Market, London.

Wyndham, S. (2003) Real dogs always die. In: Adelaide, D. (ed.) *Acts of Dog*. Vintage, Sydney, pp. 47–73.

Yabroff, K.R., Troiano, R. and Berrigan, D. and (2008) Walking the dog: Is pet ownership associated with physical activity in California? *Journal of Physical Activity and Health* 5, 216–228.

Yau, M., McKercher, B. and Packer, T. (2004) Traveling with a disability: More than an access issue. *Annals of Tourism Research* 31 (4), 946–960.

Zilcha-Mano, S., Mikulincer, M. and Shaver, P. (2012) Pets as safe havens and secure bases: The moderating role of pet attachment orientations. *Journal of Research in Personality* 46, 571–580.

Index